ISLAMISM

ISLAMISM

What It Means for the Middle East and the World

TAREK OSMAN

YALE UNIVERSITY PRESS
NEW HAVEN AND LONDON

For information about this and other Yale University Press publications, please contact:
U.S. Office: sales.press@yale.edu   www.yalebooks.com
Europe Office: sales@yaleup.co.uk   www.yalebooks.co.uk

Set in Minion Pro by IDSUK (DataConnection) Ltd
Printed in Great Britain by TJ International Ltd, Padstow, Cornwall

Library of Congress Cataloging-in-Publication Data

Osman, Tarek.
   Islamism : what it means for the Middle East and the world / Tarek Osman.
      pages cm
   Includes bibliographical references and index.
   ISBN 978-0-300-19772-3 (alk. paper)
1. Islamic fundamentalism. I. Title.
   BP166.14.F85O86 2016
   320.55′7—dc23

                                                                                    2015030479

A catalogue record for this book is available from the British Library.

10 9 8 7 6 5 4 3 2 1

Contents

Introduction

In its fourteen centuries of history, Islam has been much more than just a faith. It has spawned elaborate legal systems to govern and guide a wide range of aspects of, and behaviour in, the lives of Muslims. Islam has been the basis for legitimizing political rule in various communities, countries and empires. It has inspired scores of philosophies that have sought to discern the essence and wisdom of the God of Islam, the meaning of being 'Muslim', and the purpose of the message that Muslims believe was sent in the seventh century by God, through the Archangel Gabriel, to a merchant in the Arabian Peninsula, the Prophet Mohammed, and which they believe is God's last dispensation to humanity. In its earliest days, Islam was a 'reformation of a world sickened by ignorance and injustice'.[1] Over time, and as it entrenched its power, Islam became the overarching umbrella of a civilization that brought together different peoples – Muslims and non-Muslims – and that produced a rich artistic oeuvre and major advances in science.[2] And it has been the 'cause' that various militant groups, in different ages, have invoked as they have wreaked havoc in different parts of the world.

As Islam expanded, in the seventh and eighth centuries, from the Arabian Peninsula to Persia, Iraq, the eastern Mediterranean, North Africa and southern Europe, it gradually infused its rules into the lives of those societies. The newcomers (not just rulers, fighters and jurists, but also large communities that had left the Arabian Peninsula to settle in the new 'Islamic lands') absorbed many of the norms and customs of their new homes. Over time, these exchanges gave rise to new cultures in each of these 'lands'.

The different political, economic and social experiences that these societies underwent in subsequent centuries sharpened the differences between their cultures. For example, the communities of the south of Egypt, an inward-looking agrarian region, developed a culture that was vastly different from that which evolved in the maritime-oriented societies of the eastern Mediterranean, a region that had witnessed varied interactions with many peoples and civilizations.

Different cultures developed different understandings of Islam. The Islam of tenth-century Islamic Iberia (Andalusia) or seventeenth-century Ottoman Turkey was the frame of reference for plural societies with relatively high levels of openness and tolerance. The Islam of twelfth-century Morocco[3] or eighteenth-century Najd, in the central part of the Arabian Peninsula,[4] was a strict legal and value system governing austere societies.

Not a single political authority managed to bring these cultures together. And yet, from the twelfth or thirteenth century, when Islam was entrenched as the primary constituent in the cultures of the wider Middle East (the Arabian Peninsula, the eastern Mediterranean, North Africa, Persia and Turkey), it became possible to speak of an 'Islamic world'. Despite the different cultures and diverse understandings of Islam, what brought that 'world' together was the fact that, for the largest segments of people in the vast majority of those societies, Islam was the basis for legitimizing power, organizing society, passing laws, and identifying and classifying the state (any state) as Islamic.

This changed in the first half of the nineteenth century. The exposure of the Arab and Islamic worlds to Western, and particularly European, modernity gradually eroded the quasi-ubiquitous acceptance of these parameters. Elites of politicians, social leaders, cultural luminaries and influential figures in different parts of the wider Middle East advocated and led gradual changes in how political legitimacy, legislation, state order and national identities were defined and understood.

The work of those leaders aimed to reduce the influence and limit the role that Islam had had in politics and society. For them, Islam was (or should be perceived as) just a religion: its political, legal and social manifestations were various forms of 'Islamism' that modern (or modernizing) societies should move beyond.

This alarmed the Islamists – those groups that continued to believe that Islam transcends the framework of a religion, with its specific tenets of the faith, rituals and prohibitions that all Muslims must follow. For them, it was (and continues to be) a political, economic and social system.

The word *system* is intentional. For the vast majority of Islamists, the principles of the faith entail submitting to those rules that – as a Muslim – one believes were laid down by God in a divine revelation to the Prophet Mohammed. The vast majority of the most widely accepted interpretations of Islamic theology, law and jurisprudence over the past ten centuries apply these rules to politics, economics and many aspects of social life. These interpretations view the Islamic *Ummah* (the global community of Muslims) as an entity that shares more than just common theological beliefs and historical experiences. The *Ummah* here is a political entity: a Muslim's belonging to it is at least equal to his/her national affiliation. These interpretations do not acknowledge man-made legal systems. Some of these interpretations divide the world into the abode of peace (the land of Islam) and the abode of war (the rest of the world).[5] Others are less assertive and do not invoke such a view. But within the most widely accepted views of Islamic theology, from the tenth century until now, Islam is understood to be a quasi-comprehensive structure that covers Muslims' spiritual and material lives. All of this means that, for those widely accepted interpretations, being (or becoming) a Muslim is a holistic framework. Here, a Muslim is not expected to embrace a modular form of belonging, accepting some parameters and rejecting others. One is expected to be 'all in'.

The immense social development that the Arab and Islamic worlds experienced from the early decades of the nineteenth century led certain Islamists to define the system differently. From the late nineteenth century, some Islamists, especially those who had had extended exposure to Europe, put forward ideas that distinguished 'the pillars of the religion' (the fundamental tenets of the faith) from its application in life; they separated *al-deen* (the faith) from *al-dunia* (life). This meant that, from within some of the most distinguished Islamic institutions, venerable voices limited the scope of Islamism. Almost always, this was done without using the term 'Islamism', which has hardly ever appeared in serious Arabic Islamic literature, either before or after the nineteenth century. In the first few decades of the twentieth century – a period of impressive cultural effervescence in the Middle East – some Islamic scholars went even further, and almost totally severed Islam from the factors that form Islamism.

This divided the Islamists. In the last two centuries, schools of theology have adhered to different versions of the old, widely accepted interpretations of Islam. Some have sought to reinterpret the interpretations. Others have put forward new ideas that have reshaped the parameters concerning the role of Islam in society. The result has been a spectrum of 'Islamisms': some views that strongly invoke certain interpretations of Islam in political and social life; others that have adopted a light-touch approach. Several schools of thought have looked back to earlier episodes in Islamic history, to the *salaf* (the predecessors), trying to draw inspiration from times when Islam was the frame of reference for successful states, prosperous economies, victorious armies and inspiring cultures. Others have innovated, trying to redefine the parameters for applying Islam to their societies, delicately admitting that all the widely accepted interpretations of Islam (those that had dominated Muslims' thinking over the previous few centuries) were failing to guide, let alone regulate, modern societies. A few thinkers went further and subtly tried to redefine Islam itself.[6]

Secularists and Islamists engaged in successive ideological wars (which at times descended into waves of violence) that exercised some of the best minds of the Arab and Islamic worlds. There were periods when secular and Islamist thinkers worked together to shape forms of secularism that respected the decisive influence that Islam had had on the different cultures of the wider Middle East, as well as forms of Islamism that limited the religion's presence in the public space. Often the Islamists disagreed totally with one another: this repeatedly led to recriminations and, in some cases, to inquisition-like confrontations and legal trials.[7]

Amidst all of this, modernity was changing Middle Eastern politics, economies and societies. Modern states appeared. Traditional nomadic and wheat-based agrarian societies were increasingly moving towards industrialization and reliance on commodity trading, primarily in cotton and oil. Educational systems were gradually being secularized. Gender barriers were crumbling. And urban centres were getting larger and, in almost the whole of the Middle East outside the Arabian Peninsula, more cosmopolitan. Ordinary Muslims (the majority of the region's colossal middle and lower-middle classes and the poor) were slowly but surely embracing new ways of life.

Modernity did not necessarily challenge traditional understandings of Islam. It did not always (or even in most cases across the wider Middle East) erode Islamism. To some extent, that was because the economic and social development of most Arab and Islamic societies was slow and had varying degrees of success. But politics did provide a challenge: the elites of politicians and cultural luminaries who promoted secularism effected a top-down separation between Islam and Islamism. Mustafa Kemal Ataturk's de-Islamization programme in Turkey in the first half of the twentieth century was the most prominent of these attempts. Other leaders followed suit. The results they sought were legion: some wanted a complete separation of Islam and Islamism; others wanted to crush certain elements of Islamism (e.g. the practice of basing political legitimacy on Islam, and thereby on the approval of the most prominent scholars), but to tolerate, and often utilize, others (e.g. belonging to the *Ummah*). All of these secularization attempts, however, were envisioned and imposed from the top.

The Islamists' responses varied. Some coalesced into groups that started out as social and educational organizations, and later evolved into political ones. The Muslim Brotherhood, which was founded in Egypt in 1928, is the most prominent example. Those political Islamist groups, whether in North Africa or the eastern Mediterranean, sought to advance their views, expand their membership, build up their financial resources, and strengthen their brand. Over time, they lost many of their educational and religious roots, but they gained influence within large social segments.

Others ignored politics, detached themselves from their surroundings, established enclaves within society and sought to practise what they felt – what they were convinced – was true Islam. The social lives of these groups were heavily influenced by conservative and traditional interpretations of the earliest episodes of Islamic history: the period in the seventh century when the Prophet Mohammed ruled over an expanding community in the western Arabian Peninsula, and the two centuries that followed. Those groups wanted to imitate the *salaf* (the predecessors), shunning many of the features of modernization, especially modern ideas, that their societies were increasingly embracing.

A few of those groups crossed the line between detachment from society and demonization of society. As a result, parts of the Arab and Islamic worlds were to endure repeated, and often lengthy, episodes of violence and terror.

These divisions – in ideology and thinking; in defining, embracing or rejecting Islamism; in entering into or shunning politics; and in espousing or condemning the use of violence – did more than merely split the Islamists. It raised the question of who (if anyone) can define what true Islam is, what it entails, its core and essence, and crucially whether anyone can claim to represent it.[8] The intellectual wars intensified.

With the exception of what happened in Iran after the 1979 Islamic Revolution swept away the secular Pahlavi royal family and ushered in the Iranian Islamic Republic, these intense intellectual interactions, these various interpretations of Islam and these different manifestations of Islamism all remained distinct from the most important waves that had shaped the Middle East over the past 150 years. The Arab world's opening up to and active interaction with Western ideas in the century from the 1850s to the 1950s that came to be known as the Arab liberal age,[9] the revolutionary wave of socialist Arab nationalism (following the withdrawal of colonialism from the Arab world after the Second World War), the wars between the Arabs and Israel, the transformative economic changes from the late 1970s onwards (from central command socialism to various forms of market-driven economics), and the dramatic changes in Arab art and culture over the past century – all these major trends unfolded in almost complete detachment from Islamism. Often these transformative currents defined themselves in opposition to Islamism, but they hardly ever borrowed from it, embraced its framework, or even acknowledged the major social presence that it had (and has).

Some Middle Eastern monarchical regimes used Islamist claims to anchor their legitimacy or to widen their support among the (typically large) conservative segments of their societies. (We explore that in detail in chapter 7 on the Gulf's view of Islamism.) Other regimes co-opted certain Islamists, especially the apolitical ones, to use their social presence in confrontations with domestic enemies, often the political Islamists. In some cases, secular nationalist regimes worked with political Islamists. In one case – Sudan in the early and mid-1990s – a nationalist regime integrated leading Islamists into its fabric, and for a while called itself an 'Islamic Republic'. The experience proved short-lived and ended in a classic Islamist-secularist confrontation. Never, however, did any powerful Arab regime adopt – let along espouse and support – the forms of Islamism that the large Islamist groups have advocated. In many cases, the Islamists were socially marginalized, economically ignored, politically persecuted and publicly demonized.

This meant that the Islamists, and especially the political Islamist groups, spent many decades operating underground, usually secretly and often illegally. This engendered suspicion – both of the state's institutions among the Islamists, and of the Islamists among large sections of Arab and Middle Eastern societies.

For most observers of the Middle East, throughout the twentieth and the first decade of the twenty-first century Islamism was a phenomenon lurking beneath the surface. The vast majority of the region's countries were under the control of authoritarian, militaristic regimes and sheikhdoms dependent on oil and gas revenues. Islamism was always seen as a potent social force with huge constituencies. But it was removed from the upper echelons of political and economic decision-making, and from the most influential powers in media, business and finance in those societies. It was regarded as a (if not *the*) force of opposition to the ruling regimes.

Throughout the 2000s, almost no prominent observer expected the Arab Islamists to ascend to power any time soon. The regimes that controlled the largest and most strategically important parts of the Arab world seemed solidly entrenched in their positions. The leaders of some of these republican regimes – such as in Egypt, Libya, Tunisia and Yemen – wanted, expected and planned to pass on their rule (some would say their entire countries) to members of their own families. Thus in Syria in 2000, following the death of President Hafez Assad who had ruled the country since 1970, his son Bashar inherited the presidency.

The Arab uprisings that began at the end of 2010 and gained immense momentum in early 2011 changed that. Some of those long-serving Arab presidents fell – rather quickly and rather easily. Entrenched regimes were shaken, and a vacuum appeared in many Arab power structures. The intensity and rapidity of the changes plunged some countries into a cycle of chaos and violence. Others progressed on fragile political paths. In almost all these countries, however, the Islamists seemed to be acquiring power. The uprisings appeared to lead to a dramatic ascendancy of the Islamists in several of the most strategically important regions of the wider Middle East.

But this ascendancy did not last long. Two years on and the Islamists were already beginning to lose power – by way of popular demonstrations, interventions by entrenched power centres in their countries, and as a result of pressure applied by rich Middle Eastern countries that have a major influence over pan-regional media and key economic resources. By the end of 2014, many large Arab Islamist groups had returned to their pre-2011 positions: marginalized, and often persecuted.

For many international observers, the Islamists' rapid rise and subsequent fall was perplexing. For almost all of the Arab societies that underwent these changes, the experiences were agonizing. The changes have given rise to the sort of acute social polarization not witnessed the region by for at least seven decades, since the end of colonialism in the aftermath of the Second World War.

This polarization stems from divisions and conflicts between nationalism and liberalism; between different forms of nationalism; between Arabness and other ethnicities in the region; and, crucially, between secularism and Islamism. It also accentuates old divisions between the Islamists themselves. The conflicts reflect the vastly different ways the various segments of Arabs see their societies, their future, and their countries' and their own identities. Islamism lies at the core of most of these conflicts. In the last five years (since the beginning of the uprisings that came to be known as the Arab Spring), nothing has wrenched Arab societies more forcefully than the old and recurring struggle between modernization and Islamism, between Islamism and the effects of the colossal changes that these societies are undergoing, and between the forces that represent Islamism and those that see Islamism as a great danger – to their countries, the region and themselves – which ought to be crushed.

As it has been for decades, Islamism remains a feature (and often a tool) of geopolitical struggle. In the last five years, Islam's two largest sects (Sunnism and Shiism) have formed the backdrop for a grand confrontation. Sunni Saudi Arabia, supported by a coterie of other

Sunni countries in the Middle East, and Shii Iran, supported by several Shii non-state actors in the region, have engaged in a multifaceted cold and hot war that has been unfolding in different theatres in North Africa, the eastern Mediterranean and the Arabian Peninsula. This sectarianism has exacerbated and muddled the Islamism–secularism conflict.

The vacuums created by the Arab uprisings have allowed militant Islamism, a centuries-old phenomenon, to reappear. Large groups of militant Islamists leveraged on the unfolding divisions, transformations and wars, and have come to hold sway over large parts of the Middle East, asserting their authority over hundreds of thousands of people, controlling significant economic resources and establishing themselves as a force to be reckoned with.

The intensity of the havoc wreaked by these groups has made the world sit up and pay attention. Most international observers have found it shocking in the second decade of the twenty-first century to see groups attempting to create a seventh-century type of state at the heart of the Middle East.

For many who watch this region from afar, Islam itself has become suspect: a religion that promotes, if not embodies, violence. Within the Arab and Islamic worlds, the spread of militant Islamist groups has caused panic and chaos, and has exacerbated the loss of central authority in several countries (Libya, Iraq and Syria, for example). It has also triggered a moral crisis within the Islamic world. What impacts are felt by this attempt to resuscitate the earliest form of an Islamic state, yet one stripped of all the religious, historical, cultural and moral features that made the original a fertile seedbed for a rich civilization? A struggle for the soul of Islam has begun.[10]

Neither the struggle for, against and over Islamism, nor the nascent struggle within Islam itself, explains the changes, transformations and myriad conflicts currently unfolding in the wider Middle East. But these struggles lie at the core of many of them. Dissecting Islamism helps observers make sense of the Middle East's recent history, appreciate the excruciating social experiences of many of its societies during the past five years, and envisage potential scenarios for its foreseeable future.

Some observers regard Islamism as an ideology, and analyze it as such. Their focus is on the thinking of the largest political Islamist groups, especially the Egyptian Muslim Brotherhood, the Tunisian Annahda, the Turkish Justice and Development Party, and the Moroccan party of the same name (known by its French acronym, PJD). Observers trace the origins of these groups, the ways in which their thinking has developed over the last century, and the foundational basis of that thinking in political science and sociology; and they identify the transformative episodes and figures in these groups' histories. Rigorous observers delve into Islamic theology and history, trying to relate these groups' views to different theological interpretations and to threads that ran through long periods of Islamic history. Those who adopt this approach typically eschew the militant Islamist groups, seeing them as unrepresentative of the most influential and popular forces of Islamism. They also usually focus on political thinking and how it has been applied in practice – for example, in electoral manifestos, campaigning, and in the short period in recent years when the political Islamists ascended to power. These are salient issues, without which no understanding of Islamism is complete. But this approach pays limited attention to the way in which these groups' Islamism is supposed to provide frames of reference for different societies with vastly differing experiences and cultures. And so it does not fully appreciate – and therefore does not properly investigate and present – the social tensions that Islamism (and especially its recent rise) has generated.

Other observers focus on the militant Islamists as the most potent force in Islamism. Some adopt alarmist narratives, depicting the political Islamists as marginal actors and emphasizing that the violent groups that use force (often shockingly) in the name of Islam represent the will and desire of major sections of Muslims, especially in the wider Middle East. The focus here is not on the thinking, development and modus vivendi of Islamism; rather, it is on the impact of its most perilous component's work. This approach assumes that the militant Islamists create struggles, exacerbate social tensions and trigger major responses by powerful states in and outside the Middle East. And that, by having the ability to bring about such major results, these groups entrench themselves as the players with the most significant influence on the wider Middle East. Thus, they 'deserve' to be studied in detail. And indeed they do deserve this – but not because they have shaped (or will shape) Islamism. That they will not do. No, they should be included in any serious analysis of Islamism because of the conflicts they give rise to within Islamism, and because of the danger they pose to Islam itself.

Some observers look at Islamism as a key feature in the 'transitions' embarked on by the Arab world since the eruption of the uprisings five years ago. According to this view, the Arab countries are on paths leading from autocratic, oppressive and closed political systems to forms of democratization (defined as democracy as it is understood in the West), and the focus is on political processes, building institutions and entrenching values and norms. In this approach, the Islamists are mere players and Islamism is but one factor in these processes. And, irrespective of how observers who hold this view see Islamism (as contributing to the evolution towards democracy or as a barrier on the way to it), the approach borrows heavily from the experiences of Europe after the Second World War, and especially from the experience of central and eastern Europe after the fall of the Berlin Wall in 1989 and the end of the Cold War in the early 1990s. These are valuable and illuminating experiences, but they share very few features with what has been taking place in the wider Middle East.

Observers who take this approach also typically conflate the West's experiences of Christianity in the most recent three centuries with Middle Eastern countries' experiences of Islam. Some expect the Middle East to arrive at a relationship with Islam that is similar to the accommodation that the West (and especially Europe) has reached with Christianity. This is problematic, because whereas the notion of

Christendom has been heavily diluted in the West by waves of modernity and by the intellectual and scientific advances of the last two centuries, Islamism remains strong in the Middle East. And crucially, it is far from certain that the majority of Arabs and Middle Easterners aspire to liberal democracy as it is practised in the West – especially given that many in the Islamic world have grave apprehensions regarding aspects of that form of democracy (e.g. the extent of free speech).

Another approach gives little weight to the role of Islam and Islamism, and analyzes the Middle East's current conflicts through the lens of geopolitics. Here, the rise and fall of the political Islamists in the last few years is but one part (or consequence) of larger confrontations between wealthy countries with varying and often opposing interests, such as Qatar and Saudi Arabia; or is the result of interventions by Western powers, primarily the US. An extension of that thinking sees the wars taking place in the eastern Mediterranean, the spread of militant Islamist groups, and the tension between large communities of Sunnis and Shiis as episodes in the strategic struggle between Sunni Saudi Arabia and Shii Iran. Geopolitics has always stoked conflict in the Middle East. Several Western countries, and especially the US, have at different times used Islamist forces for their own purposes, most notably when the US helped to arm thousands of Muslim fighters from all over the world to confront the (atheist) Soviet Union after it invaded (Islamic) Afghanistan in 1979. But reducing the immense social changes currently taking place in the wider Middle East to geopolitics fails to capture many dimensions of this huge transformation.

This book will use different elements from each of these approaches. Its central thesis, however, is that Islamism is a multifaceted and complicated social movement, which has had different worldviews, references, leaders and advocates, and whose constituencies have varied hugely over the past two centuries. But it has always reflected social phenomena with deep historical and cultural foundations. This means that any serious attempt to understand Islamism needs to trace the origins and development of the largest political Islamist groups; look at their economic bases and networks; investigate how they vary not only in terms of ideology and thinking, but also in how they have adapted to political and cultural circumstances; analyze the international case studies and experiences that have inspired them; look at how militant Islamism has grown, and why; and crucially consider how the Islamists' evolution, accession to power and ways of operating have triggered responses from their ideological enemies, the old regimes they replaced and those who felt threatened by their rise. The most important part of the analysis is to reflect on why wide social segments across the Middle East have rejected Islamism, often vehemently.

This analysis of Islamism looks towards the future. The book reflects on how the Islamists' experiences in the last five years, in different parts of the wider Middle East, are affecting the thinking of some of their most influential groups. It also looks at how the acute social tension engendered by the rise of Islamism is changing the behaviour of traditionally apolitical Islamists, militant groups and influential secular groups. And it looks at how the Western powers that interact heavily with the wider Middle East are evolving their view of Islamism, as well as at how many Islamists are changing their views of the West.

The book limits its discussion of Islamism to the Arab world, Turkey and Iran. It does not cover Islamism in Afghanistan, Bangladesh, India, Indonesia, Pakistan or sub-Saharan Africa. Nor does it address the myriad Islamist movements in the West, some of which are leading innovation in Islamic thinking and some of which are becoming increasingly radicalized. This decision is motivated by two reasons. First, the different versions and manifestations of Islamism in the wider Middle East have various links, pan-regional influences and spill-over effects that connect the disparate parts into a macro story. By contrast, the various types of Islamism outside the Middle East are the products of different histories, cultural influences, and social, political and economic circumstances. These differences make each type a stand-alone phenomenon, sharing little with the Islamism at the heart of the Islamic world. Second, because of Islamism's long history in the wider

Middle East, and because Middle Eastern Islamists have always had a decisive influence on Islamism, it is my belief that they will shape the future of the phenomenon as a whole.

This book is about Islamism, not Islam. Although in the last chapter and in the conclusion I make a few references to key trends that, I believe, will have a significant influence on the future of the religion itself, the book does not confuse Islamism with Islam. These trends are introduced towards the end because they will have a direct impact on Islamism in the Middle East.

This book is intended for general international readers. It does not assume prior knowledge of the Middle East, Islam or Islamism. And yet it is intended as a serious, stand-alone presentation of Middle Eastern Islamism, its future, how it has affected (and will continue to affect) the region, and how that future will impact international powers with interests in the Middle East. In discussing where the phenomenon has come from and where it could go, it is my hope that this book presents new perspectives and ideas; critiques old assumptions and understandings; and speculates on potential future trajectories. In all of this, the intention is to inform those who are new to the subject, as well as to encourage those who have observed it for a long time, to think in different ways – or at least to question established ways of approaching Islamism. This is particularly important now, as the political transformations and social polarizations that the Middle East has been undergoing over the past five years have given rise to acute wars of propaganda for and against Islamism.

CHAPTER ONE

The Islamists' Coming to Power

The fall of the Ottoman Empire in 1922 marked the end of the last Islamic caliphate, which had enjoyed wide recognition in Turkey, North Africa and the eastern Mediterranean. Though countries like Egypt, Tunisia and the regions that constitute today's Syria and central and northern Iraq had effectively been independent of the Ottomans since about the mid-nineteenth century, they continued to be formally regions of the Ottoman Empire, with the official legitimacy of their rulers derived from the sultan's endorsement. The sultan was the most widely recognized 'caliph' (successor to the Prophet Mohammed) in the whole of the Islamic world.[1] The abolition of the caliphate meant that the basis for legitimizing power in the countries that had been part of the Empire crumbled. The leaders of those countries were now free to adopt new governing structures and legitimacies.

Some leaders in the Arab world were tempted to declare themselves caliphs. The Hashemites, who were descendants of the Prophet Mohammed, and who in the nineteenth century ruled the Hijaz (today the western province of Saudi Arabia, and which includes Mecca, Mohammed's birthplace and Islam's holiest town), cooperated with the British Empire in the hope of installing the head of the family as the new caliph.[2] Egypt's ruler at the time toyed with the same idea. Quickly these dreams were dashed. Waves of secularism were transforming the region. The notion of an Islamic caliphate was viewed by the vast majority of the region's political, social and cultural elites as a relic of the past.

The new countries that emerged from the fall of the Ottoman Empire were founded on modern constitutions, inspired by European ones, structured around elected parliaments (even if the percentages of the voting populations were dismally small), and headed by kings who styled themselves according to the Habsburgs', the Savoys' and the Windsors' vestiges of power. Islam continued to be a feature of power. The Egyptian king was effectively the patron of al-Azhar, the thousand-year-old mosque and university and the Sunni Islamic world's most prestigious seat of learning. The Tunisian *bey* (an Ottoman title denoting the head of the country's ruling house) sponsored al-Zaitouna, Tunisia's revered house of Islamic learning. But these were symbolic, and often cosmetic, measures. Power was now detached from Islamic legitimacy.

Scores of social constituencies in the Arab world detested the separation of Islam and the state. Dozens of groups were set up to revive the caliphate under a myriad of claimants. The idea of a secular state was itself anathema to many thinkers, who saw such a thing as a violation of Islamic rule and jurisprudence. As the years passed, the aspiration of resuscitating the caliphate subsided, but the idea of effecting a revival within Islamic societies gained momentum. The rationale was that Islamic societies had been defeated by the West, occupied, and were now compelled to move towards Western modernity, not because Islam or the systems that its scholars had devised were lacking, but because Islamic societies had descended into backwardness and lethargy. An 'Islamic revival' (reviving the religion within the societies, not the religion itself) was expected gradually to strengthen the Muslims and return their societies to their old glory (when Islamic states rivalled the strongest and most advanced in the world, such as was the case from the ninth to the fifteenth centuries). Most of these 'revival' projects were bottom-up: educational systems were supposed to incorporate subjects

2

at which the West had excelled (in this view, primarily science), and yet instil in 'Muslim children and youths' the 'values and principles of Islam'. Societies needed to industrialize, regain the work ethic of 'those who had built the Islamic civilization into a beacon of advancement', and become more competitive. Over time, this education, moral strengthening and drive towards regaining 'Islam's rightful place in the world' were supposed to effect a transformation within the Islamic world.[3]

The Muslim Brotherhood, established in the late 1920s by the charismatic schoolteacher Hassan al-Banna, in the Egyptian city of Ismailiya, became the largest and most prominent of the groups espousing that thinking. Hassan al-Banna launched a *daawa* (call), a word that connotes a grand message (reviving Islam within society) and an invitation to join (his group).

Al-Banna's *daawa* began as a set of vague and simple rules, ranging from emphasizing honesty to praising a good work ethic. He was a gifted public speaker and leader. As his sermons began to attract attention, so he transformed his message into something grander: building an organization whose aim was to represent this 'Islamic revival' in Egypt. Over time, al-Banna started to infuse his sermons with bigger ideas: the fragmentation of the Islamic world after the fall of the Ottoman caliphate, the need for strengthening Islamic identity, and the aspiration of uniting Muslims. Al-Banna wrote scores of *rasail* (messages) and articles, and delivered hundreds of sermons. But he hardly ever presented a coherent and detailed view of how his group was supposed to achieve these vague, grand ideas.

Vagueness helped the organization. People infused their own interpretations and views into al-Banna's words. For some, the Brotherhood was a 'school', in and through which members were educated and improved, where 'they grow into their best potential' and gradually become 'role models for their social circles'. For others, the organization was much more than a school: it was the basis for an 'army of *duaa*' (preachers or callers) who would go on to spread the 'message', return society to 'true Islam' and as such effect that Islamic revival.[4]

In the span of two decades (the 1930s and 1940s), the Brotherhood grew from a small cell around al-Banna into a network of over 3,000 branches across the whole of Egypt, with more than 450,000 active members. Al-Banna himself gained quasi-legendary status. Almost all prominent Egyptian politicians of the 1930s and 1940s approached him; many, including King Farouk, Egypt's ruler at the time, sought to placate him and use his organization. Among the Brotherhood's members, he became an *imam*, a revered religious scholar and a social and political leader, one whose thinking and legacy were to be studied and emulated.

Success brought transformation. The Brotherhood's educational mission, the basic idea upon which it was created, lost momentum. The organization became deeply involved in Egyptian politics. It never formed a political party, but the group and its founder acted as one: building coalitions with political parties, attacking others, supporting parliamentary campaigns and opining on various political issues. The first Arab–Israeli war of 1948, following the creation of the State of Israel, took the Brotherhood to the eastern Mediterranean. Though the Brotherhood was hardly a leading force among the Arab troops that attacked the nascent Jewish state, the 'Brothers' who went to the region proselytized, created cells and spread the 'call'. Some stayed after the end of the war and established their own networks of cells in the eastern Mediterranean. By the end of the 1940s, there were budding Brotherhoods in Jordan, Syria and Iraq.

Hassan al-Banna was murdered in 1949 (almost certainly on orders from the Egyptian royal palace) – a result of Egypt's turbulent politics at the time.[5] The Brotherhood lost much of its political acumen and connections, as well as its most effective preacher and marketeer. Those who succeeded him in the group's 'Guidance Bureau' (the highest governing body of the organization) were far less savvy and charismatic. The group quickly lost its prominent place in Egyptian politics. The country's July 1952 coup abolished the Egyptian monarchy, ended the parliamentary system and, in less than two years, began a campaign to crush the Brotherhood. We discuss in chapter 5 how the Arab nationalists, and especially Egypt's Gamal Abdel-Nasser (leader of the '1952 revolution', as it came to be known in Egypt), defined themselves as secularists, and why that led to confrontation with the Brotherhood.[6] Throughout Arab nationalism's years of ascendancy, from the mid-1950s to the mid-1970s, the Brotherhood endured marginalization and repeated waves of persecution. The group was hardly a helpless victim, though. Since the early 1940s, it had formed a secretive armed faction that mounted several attacks on Egyptian politicians. But the war of wills between the Brotherhood and the regime was not a war of equals. Most of the group's leaders ended up in prison or left Egypt as exiles for the Gulf States or Europe (Switzerland was a particularly popular destination for a number of the group's most prominent strategists). By the end of the 1950s, it seemed that the Brotherhood had lost all the social and political successes it had achieved in Egypt in the previous three decades.

Other Brotherhoods avoided confrontation with the ruling regimes. The Jordanian branch of the Muslim Brotherhood has, for decades, been the most successful in the eastern Mediterranean. Al-Banna's call resonated with the Palestinian refugees who had lost their homes in the 1948 war between Israel and its Arab neighbours and were compelled to rebuild their lives in nearby countries, such as Jordan. The mix of religion and politics, the promise that hard work and piety would together bring about a much better future, inspired thousands of those refugees. The Brotherhood's success in Jordan was also a result of an understanding between the group and the country's King Hussein, who ruled Jordan from 1952 until his death in 1999. Hussein, a descendant of the Hashemites, who trace their ancestry to the Prophet Mohammed, understood and appreciated the legitimacy that Islam can bestow on political leaders. His state was created as (and continues to be called) 'the Hashemite kingdom', directly invoking the link to the Prophet as the basis for establishing and legitimizing the family's rule over that part of the Arab and Islamic worlds. Hussein realized that the Brotherhood's 'call' strongly resonated within the traditionally pious Arab societies. He also wanted to avoid the same kind of confrontation with the Brotherhood that Egypt's Gabal Abdel-Nasser had got into. Though there were often moments of acute tension, generally Hussein and the group tried to avoid political antagonism. That meant that Hussein allowed the Brotherhood to operate in the country and tolerated its strong presence in the educational and charity sectors, especially those that targeted the Palestinian refugees. On the other side, the Brotherhood never seriously challenged the king's rule, legitimacy or major decisions. At times, when the Brotherhood's strong presence within the Palestinian community in Jordan set it at odds with some of the country's indigenous Trans-Jordanian tribes, it even seemed that the Brotherhood enjoyed some royal protection, which diminished any action that might be mounted against it by the security apparatus that was traditionally controlled by Trans-Jordanian elites.[7]

Another type of understanding was found in Morocco. As with Jordan, Morocco was (and continues to be) ruled by a family descended from the Prophet Mohammed. Unlike Hussein, King Hassan II, the Moroccan monarch between the mid-1960s to the end of the 1990s, relished confrontation. Spells of his long reign came to be known as 'the years of the bullets'. The Brotherhood had hardly any success in establishing a branch in Morocco.[8] Some of its ideas, however, resonated with various political groups in the country. Many of the leaders who struggled against the French presence in Morocco (from 1908 to 1956)[9] had used Islamic slogans to build momentum for their groups. This made sense in the pious Moroccan society and in a country that, ever since its foundation and up to the present day, has never been ruled on any basis but Islamic legitimacy. After the French withdrawal from Morocco, these groups coalesced into political parties, some of which (such as al-Istiqlal) went on to become a breeding ground for influential ministers and politicians. Others faded in the country's intricate political landscape. But the mix between nationalism and Islamism endured. Over time, political Islamist groups began to appear. Most were illegal, never recognized by the state. King Hassan II's regime used intimidation, coercion and persecution against many of them. A number went underground. But most of these groups came to realize that to have any chance of operating in Morocco they needed to emphasize their respect for the palace's legitimacy (and convince the palace of that), and their willingness to operate in the country as ordinary political parties within the system that the palace orchestrated. As was the case in Jordan, the largest groups within the Islamists – those that accepted the palace's legitimacy (including its claim to Islamic suzerainty over the country's 'faithful') – were allowed to expand their presence among the disenfranchised. This became clear policy after Hassan's son, King Mohammed VI, ascended the throne in 1999.

Monarchies were generally more amenable to the political Islamists. In Kuwait, the Islamic Constitutional Movement, a group that began life influenced by the Egyptian Muslim Brotherhood, has for decades been extending its reach towards the country's vibrant and pulsating business and commercial community. The Islamists reached an understanding, not only with the royal family, but with the country's immensely influential, and generally liberal, leading merchant families. This meant novel and lenient interpretations of what was permitted in Islamic finance (an area of major importance to these trading dynasties with economic interests near and far). It also meant accepting the country's secular laws and the very conspicuous and influential roles that Kuwaiti women have traditionally played in the economy and in society.

As times changed in Egypt, the Egyptian Brotherhood itself reached its own understanding with the regime. Nasser's successor, Anwar Sadat, wished to bring about rapprochement with the Brotherhood. He allowed the organization to re-establish its presence in Egypt, which (as we will see in chapter 2) provided the impetus for its resuscitation and huge expansion of its social and economic infrastructure in the country. In return, Sadat wanted the Brotherhood's support in his campaign against Nasser's legacy of Arab nationalism and socialism.[10]

Half a century after the fall of the Ottoman Caliphate, by the mid-1970s the largest and most conspicuous of the political Islamist groups in the Arab world seemed to have settled into accepting the political order in their countries. Save for a few confrontations, most notably in the late 1970s and early 1980s between Syria's secular Assad regime and the Syrian branch of the Muslim Brotherhood, the political Islamists shied away from directly challenging either the secular nationalist Arab republicans or the monarchists (in the Gulf, Jordan and Morocco). They were content with building constituencies in universities (especially by controlling student unions), professional syndicates and municipalities. They continued to excel at combining religious rhetoric with the day-to-day concerns of the lower middle classes and the poor. And they typically adhered to Hassan al-Banna's vagueness: avoiding strong positions that could antagonize large sections of society, coming across as amenable, always willing to discuss and engage. In Egypt, Jordan, Kuwait and other places, the political Islamists created their own newspapers and media platforms. The Egyptian Muslim Brotherhood's was, predictably, called *Al-Daawa* (*The Call*). The macro objective was to widen its message and assert its presence as a significant political actor. But it was hardly ever to challenge the regime. The grand aspirations of ending the Islamic world's fragmentation and uniting the Muslims seemed to have been forgotten.

These 'understandings' were forms of co-optation. By the 1980s and 1990s, almost all Arab regimes, and especially the republics, had moved far away from populist fiery Arab nationalism. The ideas from the 1950s and 1960s of uniting the Arab world, bringing about a 'historic developmental leap', 'liberating Palestine',[11] standing up to the West, and installing 'justice and dignity from the Atlantic Ocean to the Gulf' (denoting the area from Morocco at the westernmost end of the Arab world, to Bahrain, the easternmost) proved empty, bankrupt and, for many, intellectually vacuous. The consent previously given by wide segments of the Arab middle and lower-middle classes and poor to leaders such as Egypt's Gamal Abdel-Nasser and Tunisia's Habib Bourghuiba had been diluted. By the 1990s the Arab republics had descended into dysfunctional, corrupt and often sad personal or familial fiefdoms. As the years moved on, rulers such as Egypt's Hosni Mubarak, Libya's Muammar Gaddafi, Tunisia's Zeinalabideen Ben-Ali and Syria's Hafez Assad became obsessed with remaining in power. Interior ministries and security apparatuses became hugely influential. And so the regimes' relationships with the political Islamists became functions of rewarding and coercing, with the sole objective of taming these groups into continuing their acceptance of the status quo.

Most of them did continue to accept it. The experience of the Egyptian Muslim Brotherhood in the 1980s and 1990s offers a good example. The group's years of persecution and exile in the 1950s and 1960s had instilled a bitter and important lesson in its leaders' memories and psyches. They were keen to avoid any serious confrontation with the regime, and so the only way they could envisage again entrenching the Brotherhood in society without antagonizing the country's leaders was to build a solid economic infrastructure that could offer services to Egypt's vast swathes of poor and lower-middle classes. The Brotherhood remained a political group: it contested several parliamentary elections in the period from the late 1970s to the mid-2000s. But in none of these did it try to secure large parliamentary representation. In Egypt's 1984 parliamentary election, the Brotherhood partnered with a staunchly secular party (al-Wafd) to emphasize – to the regime far more than to any other political actor in the country – that its Islamism was neither a threat nor a barrier to its engagement in domestic politics, just like any other player.

The Brotherhood was also keen to placate the country's secular elite. Though its services network had given it immense reach and influence, it realized that wide sections of the country's upper classes, and especially the intelligentsia that controlled the public and private media, viewed it with suspicion and often disdain. Several strategists inside the Brotherhood claimed that the group was 'mistakenly' considered an enemy of the heritage of Egypt's 'liberal age'. Indeed, scores of Egypt's (and the Arab world's) liberal intellectuals saw the Brotherhood as their cultural nemesis, whose project was the antithesis of Egypt's and the

Arab world's 'liberalism' in the first half of the twentieth century (a period in which the region witnessed major advances in translation, education, art, culture, religious discourse and the mechanisms of political representation, in addition to the beginnings of constitutional ruling systems). The group's 'call' was seen as a threat to 'progress', to Egypt's and the Arab world's 'modernization path'. That was hardly a creation of the intelligentsia's imagination. For over three decades, from the 1940s onwards, the Brotherhood's social stances (for instance with regards to the role of women in society, mixed gender education, and freedom of speech on religious issues) gave the impression of being strongly opposed to the values that Egypt's and the Arab world's liberal age represented. The Mubarak regime not only greatly exacerbated that impression, but also intentionally associated the Brotherhood with expediency and malice. One example among many was the Egyptian TV series *al-Gamaa* (*The Group*), which was broadcast in Egypt and the Arab world in 2010, in which Hassan al-Banna was depicted as a ruthless and cunning operative, motivated by nothing but personal ambition and hunger for power. The Brotherhood sought to transform its public image. It repeatedly reached out to secular writers, journalists and film-makers, began to pay tribute to the heritage of Egypt's liberal age, and interestingly borrowed from the lexicon of the secularists. Throughout the 1990s, many of its leaders paid homage to the traditional supremacy of Egyptian art in the region, and repeatedly emphasized Egypt's 'soft power' in the Arab and Islamic worlds.[12] On several public occasions, the group's leaders put forward young female members to represent the organization.

Morocco's leading (legal) Islamist group, the PJD, offers another example of an Islamist group that accepted the status quo and was willing to work within the parameters set by the ruling regime. After almost four decades under the rule of the highly assertive King Hassan II, Morocco entered the twenty-first century seeking to come to terms with its recent past. Huge sections of Moroccan society, and especially within the country's middle class, looked to the young king,

Hassan's son Mohammed VI, as the harbinger of an open and tolerant political system, particularly when compared to his father. The Moroccan Islamist movement, which was persecuted during Hassan II's reign, found reprieve after Mohammed VI's accession to the throne. The PJD was allowed to operate in national politics and to widen its presence across the country. Its leaders became prominent voices in promoting the Moroccan royal family as the 'crucial balancer' in the country's multi-ethnic society. The PJD's leaders also kept a close eye on how the palace might interpret their actions. In the country's 2002 parliamentary elections, the PJD limited its campaigning to less than half the districts in order to avoid winning the elections and appearing as if it wanted to aggrandize power. A few months later, in the country's municipal elections, the party decided to contest less than 20 per cent of the districts, despite having the human and financial resources for a significantly larger campaign. The party's leaders publicly and repeatedly asserted that any change in Morocco should take place through an evolution, sanctioned by the king, and not through revolution.

Some political Islamist groups, however, did not accept the status quo in their countries – Tunisia's Annahda being the most conspicuous example. From the 1950s on, the Muslim Brotherhood had no chance of either establishing a branch in Tunisia or building a large constituency there. Unlike all other countries in the Arab Maghreb (Algeria, Libya and Morocco), Tunisia's experience with Western occupation was relatively peaceful. It did not involve waves of violence, serious armed struggle or prolonged periods of persecution of the leaders of the liberation movement. The most prominent leaders of that movement, most notably Habib Bourghuiba, were assertively secular, seeing a very limited role for Islam in public affairs. Bourghuiba coined the term 'the bigger jihad':[13] the Muslims' striving to catch up with the world and escape lethargy, as opposed to strictly following rituals. Through this concept, Bourghuiba argued that Muslims need to relinquish many of the established rules of Islamic jurisprudence that – as he saw it – inhibit their progress. In his view, these rules ranged from the acceptance of polygamy to fasting during Ramadan (Islam's holy month) if that results in a decline in one's productivity. In the decades from the 1940s to the 1980s Tunisia witnessed a major development of its civil society. Its secular labour unions became actively involved in the movement to liberate the country from France and in drafting the country's post-independence constitution of 1956. The country adopted by far the most progressive social laws in the Arab world, especially in guaranteeing equal social and economic rights for men and women. All of this resonated with Tunisia's traditional maritime and trading culture, and gave rise to wide acceptance of secularism. From the mid-1970s to the late 2000s, it was the only Arab country to prohibit polygamy in law and to sanction different Friday prayer times; and where the percentage of women wearing the Islamic veil (or *hijab*) was less than a quarter of all adult females.

Annahda appeared in the late 1970s as an amalgamation of various Islamist groups that saw Bourghuiba's policies as a deviation from the established – and in the eyes of its leaders, correct – rules of Islamic jurisprudence. Annahda's arguments were both religious and political. It emphasized that neither Bourghuiba (who became president in 1957) nor the political elite that had coalesced around him, including Zeinalabideen Ben-Ali (who succeeded him as president in 1987), had established a democratic system that respected the wishes of the majority of Tunisians. In this view, Tunisia's secularism was a top-down imposition on its citizens who, Annahda's leaders believed, did not want such a complete separation of religion and state. Supposedly, Annahda's Islamism was not an imposition of a specific ideology, but rather a representation of the repressed aspirations of a wide segment of Tunisians.

Argumentation was Annahda's forte. The writings of the leaders of the movement, and especially of Rached Ghannouchi,[14] were much more sophisticated than those of the leaders of any other Arab political Islamist group between the 1970s and the 1990s. Ghannouchi was concerned with presenting a succession of arguments that would show how Islam could be a frame of reference for a modern political entity in which citizens are not segmented on the basis of religion, and for a modern society that was increasingly adopting political, social and human freedoms as they came to be defined in the West in the second half of the twentieth century. He contended that, from its very early days, Islam was a religion and a state. 'Prophet Mohammed was God's messenger and the founder of al-Medina' (literally 'the town'), the oasis he named and to which he emigrated ten years after commencing his call to Islam in Mecca, and which was to become the theological and political capital of the new religion. Al-Medina was a political entity that comprised the community of Muslims, a few groups that did not embrace Islam, and Jewish tribes that had lived in the oasis for decades. At its foundation was the 'prophetic constitution' that Mohammed had imparted to all al-Medina's residents upon his arrival, and which, in Ghannouchi's view, guaranteed equal rights and freedoms to all residents, irrespective of religion. Ghannouchi's central point was that, from its very beginnings, Islam had drawn a distinction between the religious community (the Islamic *Ummah*, or community of believers) and the state (in this case, al-Medina); and so, by extension, the Islamic obligations were to fall on the *Ummah* and not on the political state, which comprised non-Muslims with equal rights and responsibilities.

Ghannouchi's prominence and popularity gave these ideas (and others that appeared in his many books and essays) a wide reach and guaranteed broad dissemination. Other Islamist thinkers in different parts of the Arab world – many with direct links to political Islamist groups – followed the same line. This line clearly demarcated religion (with all its tenets, pillars and obligations) from the state (with its man-made concepts, constitutions and laws). It also differentiated between, on one side, the *Ummah* and the community (any community) of Muslims, and on the other, the society of the nation state. And crucially, the Islamists were slowly putting forward arguments that explicitly accepted the legitimacy of the nation state, not just as a political entity but as the main milieu within which Muslims belong. Here, belonging entails allegiance. According to this line of thinking Muslims are thus required to have allegiance to *both* the Islamic *Ummah* and their nation states. The Islamists never departed from proclaiming their countries 'Islamic', although the definitions of that became increasingly vague (as we will see in chapter 4). But by accepting that these states were different from any Islamic community, it followed that they would have rules, obligations and identities that were different from those of any Islamic community. This distinction was the first step towards accepting that the citizens of these countries, irrespective of their faith, had equal rights. This was a significant development for and within Arab political Islamism.

Few Tunisians or Arabs paid attention to such ideas, especially when they came from marginalized Islamists, who in the 1980s and 1990s were in exile. But Annahda was trying to present itself and its thinking as compatible with the secularism to which Tunisians had grown accustomed in the previous half century. Annahda was also presenting an intellectual argument for its rejection of the Tunisian political system. Unlike the other large Arab political Islamist groups, Annahda was neither willing to accept the status quo, nor to be co-opted by the ruling regime.

The strategies of the different political Islamist groups did not matter much. No Islamic revival project occurred. The regimes that had ruled the Arab countries for the previous half-century, since the end of European colonialism in the 1950s, remained in firm control of their states; and not a single Arab Islamist group managed to eject a monarchical or republican regime in the region. Though the Islamists had oscillated between confronting the regimes, accepting the status quo and rejecting it with various ideas and intellectual frameworks, by the end of the 1990s and in the early 2000s the regimes remained the decisive forces in the region, setting the political agenda, pulling all the levers of decision-making and – through reward and coercion – orchestrating the Islamists' presence in their countries' politics.

The mid-2000s, however, brought the Islamists unforeseen opportunities. Many Arab regimes were under Western, and especially American, pressure to loosen their grip on society. The neoconservative strategists in US President George W. Bush's administration believed that they could use American influence over their Arab allies to push for measures of democratization in the region. The logic was that a gradual democratization would destroy the roots of Islamic violent fundamentalism, which feeds terrorism (such as the 11 September 2001 attacks on New York and Washington). At the same time, several Arab regimes, such as Mubarak's in Egypt and Ben-Ali's in Tunisia, reckoned that some opening-up of their political systems was needed, in order to smooth the way for passing on the presidencies to their chosen family members. Civil society organizations were also demanding free elections and improvements in the political and human rights conditions in their countries. These factors created an opportunity for organized opposition groups to muster their efforts and achieve some political gains.[15]

All of this allowed the Islamists to come into the limelight. Their reach remained limited: it could hardly compare to the command that the then dominant Arab regimes had over their countries' masses. But, at least within the intellectual classes of their countries, the Islamists were coming to be less of an unknown quantity. Their ideas found new platforms and channels to reach sections of society beyond their classic constituencies and beyond the beneficiaries of their social services networks. They presented themselves as ordinary political groups with a religious frame of reference, rather than as religious fundamentalists bent on changing society. The ideas that Ghannouchi and others had put forward in the 1990s were increasingly propagated in a myriad of pamphlets, essays, articles and lectures. Many people remained unconvinced, but the message was delivered. And as the Islamists came into the limelight, they began to interact with different groups and constituencies inside their countries, including those that viewed them with suspicion and those that utterly despised them. Yet again, even in such interactions, the Islamists were widening their exposure and imposing themselves as players who could not be ignored.

In Egypt's 2005 parliamentary election, the Muslim Brotherhood won roughly 20 per cent of the total contested seats, a number that could have been much higher had it not been for tactical interventions by President Mubarak's interior ministry and his then ruling National Democratic Party (NDP) to limit the Brotherhood's successes. The country was in the midst of an economic reform programme, and there were important social (gender-related) laws that the new parliament had to legislate on. The Muslim Brotherhood's members of parliament (MPs) were hardly influential in that parliament, which was conveniently dominated by members of the NDP who were expected to toe the government line. But as a result of the media frenzy over these issues and the group's strong showing in the elections, the Brotherhood's MPs found themselves in the limelight. They were expected to emphasize the primacy of specific interpretations of Islamic jurisprudence, to cast aside any secular argument and to refuse compromise in the name of protecting 'God's laws'. But they turned out to be much less theologically oriented. Though there were occasions on which they abstained from voting, and though there were instances when they proposed different wording for specific legislation (e.g. on banking regulations), the Islamist MPs behaved by and large like those of most other opposition parties. They were neither passionate advocates of Islamic Sharia (jurisprudence), nor avowed warriors against relatively secular social laws. In 2006, Mohammed Habib, the then Deputy Guide of the Muslim Brotherhood (and the second most senior member of the group), stated that 'should the parliament propose a law that violates Sharia, the legislature should have the ultimate jurisdiction in deciding upon the matter'.

Many observers began to note that the Brotherhood, the largest and traditionally most influential Arab Islamist group, had undergone a sea-change. Throughout the 2000s the group engaged with scores of Egyptian politicians, intellectuals and international scholars in various discussions regarding its 'programme for Egypt'. It published a succession of white papers in which it proclaimed its position on many political issues on which it was supposed to have conservative, and often rejectionist, views. For example, the group acknowledged that it opposed allowing a non-Muslim or a woman to become president of the republic, but it accepted that they could hold any other executive, legislative or judicial position. The group repeatedly stated its acceptance of the concept of national citizenship, and asserted that it saw no dichotomy between, on the one hand, Islamic loyalty and belonging to the *Ummah* and, on the other, national allegiance. Usage of the term *Ummah* became sporadic and infrequent; the word 'Egypt' was repeatedly invoked. The group stressed its adherence to democratic procedures, and especially free and fair elections. Some of its leaders entered into lengthy debates with Egyptian, Arab and Western scholars, arguing passionately for the compatibility between Islam and the tenets of modern democracy.[16]

There were also attempts to engage with the country's civil society more broadly than the professional syndicates in which the Brotherhood had traditionally had a strong presence. For example, professors and students with links to the group were among the loudest voices in the late 2000s demanding the annulment of the Emergency Law that had been in effect in Egypt for almost three decades. Some female Islamists joined the prominent Shayfenkom (We Are Watching You) association that was established to monitor, document and report on sexual harassment and intimidation of women, especially at political demonstrations. A group of highly secular and Islamist judges together formed a formidable front within the Egyptian judiciary to oppose the Mubarak administration, and especially the efforts to pass the presidency on to Mubarak's younger son, Gamal. In May 2006, liberal and Islamist protestors faced anti-riot police together, as they surrounded a Cairene court to support the leaders of the judges' group who were there being questioned by a disciplinary tribunal. By operating at so many different levels, engaging with various constituencies, and pronouncing its positions on many political, economic and social issues, the Brotherhood tried to entrench itself as a key force on the country's political scene. It did not directly challenge the regime but it did expand its room for manoeuvre, and gradually and cautiously altered the rules of the game of co-optation.

The political opening-up that came in the mid- and late 2000s also allowed prominent Islamist thinkers to build large followings, especially through TV appearances, for example on the immensely successful Qatar-based al-Jazeera satellite channel. In hundreds of books, essays, articles, lectures and TV shows, they drew on examples from the life of the Prophet Mohammed, as well as innovative readings of Islamic theology and episodes from Islamic history, to underscore the compatibility of Islam with modern secular life, market economics, modes of good governance and, crucially, with the notion of secular nation states. Their impact lay not in the creativity of their theological readings, nor in their command of history or political philosophy. Rather it lay in the fact that their ideas, appearances and fluency gave the Islamists the impression of being not intransigent ideologues or even detached theologians, but engaged intellectuals, concerned with connecting with their societies and finding common ground with the majority of their people.[17]

The timing was fortuitous. Many Arab regimes were on the brink. By the end of the 2000s, President Mubarak was visibly ill and spending most of his time in the tourist town of Sharm-al-Sheikh, more than 500 kilometres from Cairo. His family, and especially his son and heir apparent Gamal, ruled on almost all social and economic matters. Socioeconomic conditions, mixed with shocking levels of corruption and a blurring of power and wealth, built up a perilous level of anger: towards the president, his family and the economic and financial elite that had surrounded the Mubarak administration.

An even more shocking concentration of power and wealth plagued Ben-Ali's Tunisia. Like Mubarak, Bel-Ali was visibly ill, and had delegated many of his powers to his wife, daughter and her husband. A foreign diplomat had described the ruling family as a 'mafia'.[18] In Morocco, the nationalist Istiqlal party, which had dominated the country's parliamentary life for over four decades, was undergoing a difficult generational transfer, during which two major factions in the party were engaged in a bitter struggle. A score of secular political parties had emerged in the 2000s with creative economic programmes, but all vied to strengthen their relationships with the palace and none managed to build any significant constituency, especially in the country's poor south and north.

In Algeria, president Abdel-Aziz Boutafliqua, who had ruled the country since the effective end of the country's civil war in the late 1990s, was acutely ill. A coterie of generals ruled in his name. In Jordan, the political scene was devoid of any power apart from, on the one side, the Brotherhood and its political party, the Islamic Action Front, and on the other, the palace and its large constituency of advisors and counsellors who continued to dominate the government, the parliament and the security apparatus. In Syria, the transfer of power in the country from Hafez Assad to his son Bashar in 2000 remained a bitter and embarrassing memory for millions of Syrians. And, despite Syria's long tradition of successful entrepreneurship, the young president and two of his cousins were emerging as the richest clan in the country. The brutality of Assad the father was being replaced by the rapacity of Assad the son. In Libya, an increasingly mentally unstable Muammar Gaddafi was dividing the country's resources – from its oil infrastructure to its football clubs – among his sons and daughter. The country, whose oil production and demographics[19] could have made it one of the wealthiest states in the world, seemed a depressing surrealist painting.

The Arab world was waiting for an imminent change. It came in early 2011, in the form of a wave of mass demonstrations that began in Tunisia and quickly spread to several other Arab countries. The protests were hardly organized, they lacked central command, and they were largely led by middle-class (and mostly secular) youths who had raised generic slogans to air their aspirations and frustrations: they wanted 'freedom and liberty, respect for their integrity, and justice'. In many countries, most notably Egypt, Libya and Tunisia, the largest blocs of demonstrators also wanted 'the fall of the regime'. Things seemed to be going their way. By the end of the first quarter of that year, Egypt's President Mubarak had handed power to the Supreme Council of the Armed Forces, Tunisia's Ben-Ali had fled the country into exile in Saudi Arabia (after several European countries refused him entry), and the Gaddafi and Assad regimes in Libya and Syria had begun to lose control over parts of their countries.

Despite the beginnings of violence in several Arab countries in 2011, there was promise and potential in the air across the region. The uprisings ushered in new political processes, anchored on holding free elections.

In March 2011, less than six weeks after the ousting of President Mubarak, Egypt held a referendum to change the constitution. It was a battle between the Islamists, who campaigned for passage of the new bill, and almost all secular groups in the country, which deployed all their means to induce the people to reject it. In the end, 77 per cent of voters accepted the changes supported by the Islamists. In October 2011, over 4 million Tunisians voted to elect the members of the Assembly that was to draft the country's new constitution. Over 1.5 million (circa 35 per cent of the registered electorate) voted for Islamist Annahda. The secular opposition, which comprised leading figures from the country's intelligentsia and which was supported by Tunisia's powerful labour unions, secured less than 10 per cent of the Assembly's seats. Six weeks later, in November 2011, Morocco's Islamist PJD came first in the country's parliamentary election, winning 27 per cent of the seats. It became the first Islamist party to lead a Moroccan government since independence from France in 1956. A month later, roughly 42 per cent of Egypt's registered voters backed the Muslim Brotherhood's Freedom and Justice Party (which was hastily formed immediately after the removal of President Mubarak) in the country's hotly contested parliamentary elections. In early 2012, candidates belonging to Kuwait's Islamic Constitutional Movement and other Islamist groups won thirty-five of the parliament's fifty seats. In December 2012, a referendum on another Egyptian constitution, this time drafted by an Islamist Constituent

Assembly and bitterly opposed by all secular groupings in the country, saw 63 per cent vote in favour. Six months later, Libya held its first ever free parliamentary elections. The Muslim Brotherhood failed to win on the party lists, but its supporters dominated the independent seats, which in turn constituted the majority of the new Libyan parliament.

The most dramatic success for the Arab political Islamists was the Muslim Brotherhood's candidate, Mohammed Morsi, winning Egypt's first ever free presidential election in June 2012. Standing on a hastily built podium in Cairo's iconic Tahrir Square – which had witnessed the beginning of the 2011 uprising – Morsi addressed around half a million Egyptians who had been gathering since that morning of 29 June 2012. The atmosphere was jubilant: songs, shouts and Koranic verses emanated from loudspeakers and mobile phones. Banners celebrating the success of the '2011 revolution' that had 'toppled' President Mubarak filled the square. On that hot Cairene afternoon, Mohammed Morsi pushed back his bodyguards, walked towards the people, opened his blazer and shouted: 'I am not wearing a bullet-proof vest; I am not afraid of you, for I am one of you; you put me here; I represent you.' His dramatic act was received with cheers and applause. This was not about Morsi or a mere presidential election: the significance of the moment lay in the unexpected rise of the Muslim Brotherhood to the highest political office in Egypt: the largest and arguably the most strategically important country in the entire Middle East.

By the end of 2012, two years after the eruption of the Arab uprisings (which were triggered by secular youths), it seemed that the transformative change that the revolts had sparked had catapulted the Islamists to the apex of their countries' political power. Many were bewildered by the speed of change in the Arab world. For the Islamists, however, their accession to power seemed like a long-awaited arrival at a destination. It was the end of a long and exacting journey. Many conveniently ignored the times they had been co-opted by the regimes they were now succeeding. The narrative that came to dominate told of years of proselytizing, campaigning, playing hide-and-seek with the region's regimes, suffering persecution and exile, soul-searching in the convoluted world of Islamic theology, attempting to integrate into society, reaching out to the 'other' in their countries, changing their rhetoric, and confirming their democratic credentials – after which, finally, they had reached the end of their roaming in the political wilderness. 'After decades of struggle', they believed that they had triumphed. Some within their ranks saw it thus: 'Islam has won.'

CHAPTER TWO

Halal Money, Halal Regimes

El-Menya is a poor governorate in Egypt. It is not a part of the country's agricultural hinterland in the Nile Delta and nor is it in the lush south of the country, al-Saeed. Apart from a large and increasingly ageing steel smelting complex, it has no industries of mass employment. And unlike several parts of the country's south, it has no significant tourist attractions. Nile shipping could have offered the region some economic potential as a logistical hub for internal trade between the country's north and south, but after decades of neglect Nile shipping remains in its infancy. The limited economic opportunities have incentivized a significant percentage of the governorate's men to emigrate. In the 1970s and 1980s most of the immigrants headed towards Libya and Iraq, at a time when these countries, flush with petrodollars, were open to low-skilled, low-cost workers in construction, transport and agriculture. Others in the 1990s and 2000s were drawn to the real-estate boom in the Gulf, as well as to the large urban hubs in Egypt. As for others in the country, many of el-Menya's families became dependent on the remittances that those men sent back home.

This was a regional phenomenon. The Arab world's poor countries (Egypt, Morocco, Tunisia, Yemen, Sudan, the Palestinian territories, and to some extent Jordan) sent successive waves of immigrants to the

Gulf. Remittances thereby became a crucial driver of these countries' economies, and in several cases the largest source of hard foreign currency. However, in all these labour-exporting countries, the banking systems through which remittances ought to have been channelled were still relatively basic. At the time, less than 20 per cent of Egypt's population had a bank account – and that figure was much lower again in places such as el-Menya. Across the region there was a conspicuous need for a reliable, easy-to-use and cheap money transfer system. Gradually *hiwala* (an informal system of money transfer through a series of intermediaries) emerged to fill the vacuum and meet the need. Usage of *hiwala* mushroomed. By way of some creative alterations in its nature it became a substitute for many banking products. In some cases the *hiwala* system was used to secure against a person's salary in a Gulf country a loan taken out by his family back home. In others, the system was used to guarantee an investment, whether purchasing a piece of land or an animal, such as a cow or a horse. For millions of low-income migrant Arab breadwinners from towns in regions such as el-Menya, *hiwala* became the sole connection with the families they had left behind.

The successive waves of immigration to the Gulf – from Egypt, Tunisia, Algeria, Sudan, Morocco, Syria and Palestine – hardly brought any meaningful development (let alone serious poverty reduction) to el-Menya or the hundreds of similar regions across North Africa and the eastern Mediterranean. But the steady incomes, in US dollars or Gulf dinars and riyals, gradually created new demands and tastes: reliable transportation services (from Egypt's south to such cosmopolitan centres as Cairo and Alexandria, for instance); small private hospitals (with limited services, but which were still better equipped than public ones); video recorders, chest freezers and other relatively luxurious durables; Western sweets and candies. The *hiwala* system that served most el-Menya villages was operated by a business group in Saudi Arabia, Kuwait and Egypt that had several links to the Egyptian Muslim Brotherhood. The new hospital that was established in the largest town in the governorate in the early 1990s was funded by businessmen and philanthropists belonging to the Brotherhood. And the business of importing and distributing low-end sugary sweets – a small luxury in an otherwise deprived place – was run by someone with known sympathies for the group.

The Egyptian Muslim Brotherhood's diaspora years – initially in the period from the 1950s to the 1970s in the Gulf, and from the 1980s onwards in the US and Europe – enabled many entrepreneurial 'brothers' to build thriving businesses. Thrown out of Egypt after Nasser's purge, they had limited chance of returning. They needed to build new lives abroad. Their experience in Egypt had taught them to be financially secure, independent of the state, and to hedge against unforeseen calamities. Many went into business and trading. In Atlanta, Georgia, for example, several engineers and architects developed successful medium-sized construction and engineering services businesses; in the beginning they catered to Arab communities in Georgia and the surrounding states, and expanded as those communities grew larger. In the Gulf, many families established import businesses that focused on fast-moving consumer goods such as food and cleaning products. Gradually, many of these businesses grew into large operations spanning several countries. Almost all of the businesses remained in the private hands of the entrepreneurs and families that had set them up. But the sense of belonging to the Brotherhood, the loyalty to the mother group and the feeling of compassion for the 'brothers' who had suffered persecution connected these businesses to the larger whole. For some, that connection entailed regular, and often fixed, contributions to the group. For others it meant irregular donations when the need arose. Some 'brothers' became 'anchors': those who had achieved significant financial success in the countries to which they had migrated, and who became the people that other 'brothers' arriving in that country went to. In a few cases, notably in the Gulf, the Brotherhood put pressure on some of its members to make financial contributions. But generally, contributions were readily and willingly made, often in quantities larger than the group's leadership had expected. Over time, these contributions evolved into significant streams of cash flow.

Throughout the years of exile, the Brotherhood tried to support some of its members in Egypt through charities, family connections and earlier versions of the *hiwala* systems. But it was outside Egypt that the group put its financial resources to work: funding mosques, establishing businesses that provided job opportunities for members, and setting up charities, primarily for Islamic causes. By the early 1990s the Muslim Brotherhood was arguably the richest Islamist group in the world. And in addition to having reliable revenues and cash flows, the group was able to source and deploy cash in various countries, in effect creating a wide and sophisticated financial network.

As discussed in chapter 1, President Anwar Sadat (who ruled Egypt after President Nasser's death in 1970 until his assassination in 1981) allowed the Brotherhood to return to Egypt. It set up offices there, created media outlets, and fielded candidates in elections to universities' student unions and the administrative councils of the country's professional syndicates. Sadat also gave the group the green light to grow its domestic businesses. After years of socialist central planning, Sadat opened the Egyptian economy to free-market economics. The country witnessed an exponential growth in different sectors. Restrictions on trading were rapidly and haphazardly removed. Speculation in land and various assets ballooned. Tens of thousands of Egyptian business people who had left the country during Nasser's reign returned to capitalize on the bonanza.[1] And there were 'brothers' among the returnees. In the span of a few years, from the mid-1970s to the end of the decade, businesses with various links to the Brotherhood became significant actors in different sectors. In Alexandria, business families closely associated with the Brotherhood quickly acquired significant market share in the (at the time) burgeoning real estate market. President Sadat was relaxed about, and seemed contented with, the Islamists' expansion across society and the economy. Nasserite secular socialism was rapidly marginalized by the rising capitalists, including the Islamists. One of

Sadat's closest friends, and probably the country's most successful businessman in the 1970s, had known sympathies for the Brotherhood. After two decades of ostracism, the Brotherhood was back, and was making serious money.

President Mubarak was less accommodating towards the Brotherhood and the Islamist movement in general, but he was no Nasserite in his approach towards them. Though his administration never favoured the Islamists in economic dealings (e.g. privatizations, real-estate megadeals or major concessions), he allowed the group to continue its business operations with relatively little hassle. Brotherhood members continued to grow their businesses in different sectors.

The group never became a sizeable force in the Egyptian economy, but it had reach. Members owned hundreds of small and medium-sized businesses that employed tens of thousands of people, and around which numerous philanthropic networks were built. In one example among many, two entrepreneurial families with close ties to the Brotherhood started two primary schools in al-Moqatam, a middle-class Cairene suburb, to serve the local community. It was a classic Brotherhood business. From the late 1970s, scores of middle-class Egyptian families sent their children to private schools which were of much higher quality than those the state ran, but they became increasingly expensive. These two schools offered decent education at relatively affordable prices. Notably they were marketed as schools 'where there is an emphasis on religion and instilling values in our children'. This was smart positioning in a conservative, pious society such as Egypt's. The Brotherhood's schools also benefited from the general increase in religiosity within Egyptian society as a result of its exposure to its Gulf neighbours since the mid-1970s. The families of economic migrants in the Gulf were increasingly able to afford private education for their sons and daughters, but they wanted 'conservative' schools – and certainly not the 'foreign' (Catholic, Jesuit and other Christian) schools that, for decades, had dominated private education in Egypt (and other Arab countries). In less than a decade, the two schools had expanded into a chain serving different neighbour-hoods in Cairo, with hundreds of students on the rolls. Dozens of Brotherhood-linked businesses, in different sectors, grew in the same way.

Some Brotherhood-related businesses expanded horizontally: businesses that started in Cairo and Alexandria grew across the country. Others grew vertically: a small construction company that began in the mid-1980s added a steel factory in the early 1990s, later sought to enter the cement market, and by the 2000s was a thriving contracting business.

Almost all other Arab Islamist movements attempted to clone the Egyptian Muslim Brotherhood's economic and financial success. But circumstances were different, with less resources and fewer members. In some cases the utter collapse of order and central command allowed some Islamist groups to develop economic and services infrastructures that were not only large and wide-ranging, but which paralleled and often eclipsed those of the state. This was (and is) the case for the Lebanese Shii Islamic group Hezbollah. Lebanon's civil war, from 1975 to 1990, devastated state institutions and entrenched political and identity sectarianism in the country. In less than two decades, Hezbollah – which was created by a coterie of Shii scholars in southern Lebanon as a services organization focused on the traditionally less-than-affluent Shii minority in the country – grew into an economic and financial empire, extending to almost all sectors in the country. By the mid-1990s, Hezbollah's substantial presence in health, education, transportation, security and social services dwarfed those of the Lebanese state in at least a third of the country. Hezbollah also infiltrated the Lebanese state's official institutions, especially the services ministries. This allowed it to exert significant influence over decisions concerning the expansion of the electricity grid, new water and waste projects and various community services, as well as to expedite services such as the issuance of passports and various state documents to its members and affiliates.[2]

Algeria's civil war throughout the 1990s resulted in relatively similar circumstances. The war, which erupted after the armed forces annulled the parliamentary elections that the Islamists had won, led to a gradual division in society between communities that supported the armed forces (and the state institutions) and those that supported the Islamists. The leaders of the largest Algerian Islamist group at the time, the Islamic Salvation Front (FIS), felt compelled to build their own economic networks that would serve their large constituencies. As the war raged on, the group created skeletal and loosely managed services networks that operated in the shadows of the official economy. Though these scattered services hardly constituted an economic base, they gave the group presence in some of the neediest places in the country. Other Arab Islamist groups neither had the support that Anwar Sadat lent to the Muslim Brotherhood, nor were compelled by civil war to create parallel support services for their members and their families, nor could they rely, as Hezbollah did, on sectarian division and the acute weakening of the central state.

And yet, many Islamists sought to make the best of the prevailing circumstances in their countries. Exile proved to be particularly helpful. Throughout the period from the 1980s to the 2000s, the Tunisian Annahda was unable to operate any significant business inside the country. But in its years in exile, and especially in the 2000s, the group actively provided support to lower-income Tunisians in Europe, and especially in France, Italy and the UK. The Paris-based youth section of the movement advised recently-arrived Tunisians on how to find housing, schools for their children, and even where to buy halal food. It had a thriving cultural programme that offered cultural orientation and tips on how to live in Western societies, as well as the expected religious sermons and Arabic-language courses. These services were extremely valuable to the thousands who had risked all to migrate to Europe and yet who found it difficult to get a job, let alone assimilate in their new country. By providing support and care, Annahda became a guide and a community for these immigrant families; in a way, Annahda's circles became homes away from home.

The same story was repeated in other places. Over 10 per cent of Amsterdam's population was of North African descent, especially Moroccan. The vast majority came from conservative lower middle-class and poor backgrounds. Over several decades, most of them became Dutch citizens, but many of the families wanted their sons and daughters to retain their Islamic identity and some link to their country of origin. Religious schools were set up, especially in the eastern suburbs of the city, where substantial Moroccan migrant groups had settled. Local preachers emerged from within the community, but in most cases those preachers had no local resources to draw upon, no curricula, books, references or sermons, and no cultural links to enrich their religious thinking. And so, many forged links to Islamist groups back in Morocco – either the PJD (see chapter 1) or some other Islamist group, including organizations that were (and continue to be) illegal in the country, such as the Adl w'Ihsane (which challenges the Moroccan monarchy's claim to religious suzerainty). Over time, these connections expanded from the religious to the social and economic. Some Adl w'Ihsane members opened businesses in Amsterdam and other Dutch cities, through which the group generated revenue streams to support members abroad. Success there helped the Adl w'Ihsane – and, indirectly, other Islamists back in Morocco. Funds generated in Europe were used to build local mosques, small hospitals, Koranic schools and other services in the relatively poor el-Reef region and the underprivileged neighbourhoods of Casablanca and other Moroccan cities.

It would be a mistake to assume that the growth and expansion of the Islamists' services networks and their general social presence were the result of centralized, meticulous planning by the leaders of these groups. The expansion was haphazard: entrepreneurs and philanthropists pursued different opportunities and tackled various challenges. In the process, the groups they belonged to or sympathized with extended their presence. In many cases, philanthropic work blurred with commercial opportunities. Creative and active individuals and groups tried to help their communities, as well as make money.

Yet, the success that materialized enticed some groups to put it to political use. The Egyptian Muslim Brotherhood, especially in the 1990s, mapped the coverage of its social services onto electoral districts. Annahda was keen to grow its presence from the relatively underdeveloped and poor interior regions of Tunisia towards the coastal towns. The PJD meticulously extended its religious and social footprint into various Moroccan towns which they reckoned were not strongholds of other political parties. The Kuwaiti Islamic Constitutional Movement actively campaigned within several marginalized communities where it had done philanthropic work.

Money bought influence. In Egypt, Lebanon, Jordan and Morocco, the Islamists made the argument that their 'ability to serve their societies' would be enhanced by representing them. The Islamists' marginalization and their solid standing in less-developed regions helped them. Throughout the Arab world, power has always been concentrated in the capitals, at the administrative centres of the state. For a transport project to be undertaken or a big new hospital to be built, the political structures in the capital needed to be mobilized. Concentration of power was exacerbated by the endemic corruption that, for decades, had characterized these bureaucracies. Ordinary citizens in most rural areas had long-held grievances against the central state. And so the Islamists positioned themselves as the opponents of these central states – those who were able to work against, and inside, the structures of the state to deliver to their people. And in many cases, they did deliver. In el-Reef and in several marginalized districts of Casablanca, PJD members of parliament initiated, led and completed projects that improved the areas' infrastructure after decades of neglect. In Jordan, groups associated with the Muslim Brotherhood's party, the Islamic Action Front, led the campaigning to improve services in several areas populated by Jordanians of Palestinian origin. In Lebanon, Shii MPs, usually but not always within Hezbollah's parliamentary blocs, were instrumental in improving the habitually poor conditions of the Shii neighbourhoods of Beirut.

There were also blatant examples of patronage politics. Prospective MPs representing an Islamist group, or local dignitaries – typically business people with many philanthropic interests in the region – would tour deprived constituencies in areas like the remote regions of southern Egypt, usually at well-timed moments, such as before parliamentary or council elections. They would offer basic food staples (sugar, oil and rice) or cash to needy families, often with Koranic recitations going on in the background. The Islamists also played religious festivals to perfection. Prominent sheikhs would be invited to a town to give a lecture, while at the same time a village chieftain would sponsor a 'medical convoy' of doctors visiting from the capital who would offer free health check-ups for local children or destitute families who had come from nearby villages to participate in the festival. Often this would all take place in a small football courtyard, 'a gift' from a certain 'brother'.

The religious blurred with the social, the philanthropic with the commercial. Islamist philanthropists became almost father figures in their areas of influence: the people to go to if someone wanted to find a job for his son or prepare for his daughter's wedding. Influence was an extension of financial largesse. Such patronage constituted the spinal cord of these groups' ways of operations across hundreds of towns and villages throughout the Arab world.

The Islamists' ability to 'deliver' set them apart from their opponents. They repeatedly and consistently sought to tarnish the largest secular forces of their countries both as distant urbanites with only tenuous connections to the 'real people' (the vast majority of the poor and lower-middle classes of their societies) and as 'desk types', with nothing to offer but rhetoric. Islamist media platforms relished the image of the 'solution providers', those who serve their communities: 'God's people who fear Him, and so exert their best for their constituencies.'

As the 2000s allowed the Islamists more freedom, they developed their message. Groups such as the Egyptian Muslim Brotherhood (and to a lesser extent the Moroccan PJD and the Jordanian Islamic

Action Front) began to argue that they could not only 'deliver to their constituencies' but also 'deliver to their country'. In the 2000s, their programmes, white papers, manifestos and (increasingly) electoral campaigns elaborated on what they would do for their countries if they were 'empowered'. The Egyptian Muslim Brotherhood put forward blueprints for what later came to be known as the Renaissance Project. It outlined the group's plans for developing more than ten economic sectors in Egypt, including detailed action points and case studies drawn from emerging countries such as Brazil, Indonesia and Turkey. In explaining their project, the group's members cited developmental experiences in Asia and Latin America, drew lessons from various financial crises and combined sociopolitical thinking with macro-economics. The Islamists were not the only opposition group to come up with detailed economic plans. But unlike almost all opposition forces they had expertise in managing services on the ground; they had access throughout their countries, which enabled them to hear griev-ances and to gather data; and they had the financial resources to promote their plans across their lands, not just in 'cultural salons', the traditional preserve of most Arab secular parties. Also, unlike most of their secular competitors, the Islamists had the credibility gained from decades of supervising sophisticated networks that covered numerous sectors. Some Islamists directly challenged their state's economic thinking. In Kuwait in the mid-2000s, MPs close to the Islamic Constitutional Movement published a series of white papers in which they presented their view of a new social contract between the state and the citizens. They detailed how the proceeds of the country's immense oil wealth ought to be used, how the state budget needed to be improved, and how the country's social policies were in dire need of a complete overhaul. They engaged experts, drawn from the larger Islamist current. Quickly, their ideas stirred debate in the country's vibrant media. Other Islamists in Jordan and Morocco took similar steps.

This was a strategic development. The Islamists were beginning subtly to look beyond widening their influence in rural or underprivileged areas, winning elections in professional syndicates or student unions and gaining some representation in parliament. Without directly challenging their countries' ruling regimes, the Islamists were positioning themselves as groups that had the capacity to rule.

They were helped by the increasing withdrawal of the state. In the 2000s, many Arab countries, such as Egypt, Tunisia, Syria and Morocco, witnessed respectable economic growth rates of over 5 per cent, an improvement in the competitiveness of several industries, and notable advances in infrastructure. However, the distribution of the benefits of this economic progress was highly skewed in favour of the top echelons in society. The vast majority of Egyptians, Tunisians, Syrians and others lived in very difficult socioeconomic circumstances. The late 1990s and the 2000s also witnessed a rapid increase in the pace of privatization, currency devaluations, and significant liberalization of prices in many Arab countries. This resulted in runaway inflation on basic goods; the evaporation of thousands of jobs, including in the public sector; a deterioration in the availability of housing; and a conspicuous increase in poverty levels, not just in distant rural areas, but also in those countries' urban centres.[3] At the same time the economic policies pursued by the regimes also catapulted some into dramatic fortunes. Business groups close to the Mubarak, Ben-Ali, Assad and other such families across the region had quasi-monopolies over licences to produce and sell building materials, telecom services and often food staples such as wheat and sugar. This and other abuses of position, alongside the blurring of power and wealth, gave the sense that the economic liberalization of the time was designed to benefit the rulers, their families and acolytes, and the establishments that surrounded them. Amidst all this, the Islamists' work on the ground, especially among the massive poor and lower-middle-class segments of their societies, gained deeper significance. The Islamists became leaders of, and providers for, communities that were strongly antagonistic to the central, yet increasingly detached and corrupt, state.

These oligopolies and the entanglement of power and wealth meant that the Islamist forces were unable to operate in any of the large economic sectors that were dominated by the regimes' acolytes. Major industries, large-scale real-estate transactions that entailed large land banks, any industry that needed major energy feedstock or governmental off-take, or any business that would involve huge banking credit – all were off limits to the Islamist groups and their leading business people. This exclusion denied the Islamists major economic opportunities. Not a single member of the Egyptian Muslim Brotherhood, the Islamic Action Front, the PJD or the Adl w'Ihsane featured in their respective country's list of the richest, best connected or most influential business people. Compared to the top established businesses in their countries, the Islamists' economic networks generally had to rely on self- or external financing. And yet the Islamists' reach and their ability to make money were not curtailed. The markets were large enough. And, learning from experience, the Islamists successfully strengthened their presence in the sectors that benefited from their particular country's demographics, and therefore met with colossal demand.

In one interesting example in Egypt, businessmen linked to the Muslim Brotherhood created a clothing retail chain that targeted the lower segments of the country's middle classes. The outlets were designed as mini shopping centres that, in addition to clothing, had areas for walking, cafés, children's playgrounds and places where men and women could meet and socialize separately. They were intentionally located in highly condensed neighbourhoods in several large Egyptian cities. With the hot weather, crowded streets and polluted air, these clean, air-conditioned and well-run malls became shopping, leisure and relaxation destinations for conservative families that wanted to meet in places where the genders were separated, where veiled women (or women who covered their faces entirely) were welcome, and where the Koran was recited in the background. The chain's expansion in the early 2000s, and the level of investment in its premises, indicated that it was generating huge cash inflows. In another example, a Jordanian merchant group close to the Islamic Action Front set up a food importing and distribution business that focused on rice and spices used in traditional Jordanian and Palestinian dishes, but packaged and priced to cater for demand in the highly condensed Palestinian refugee camps that surround Amman. Here the investments were light, the money cycle short, the margins small but stable, and the cash flows steady.

The Islamists' businesses also covered economic sectors that had high profit margins and significant growth potential, especially information technology, informatics and digital content. An Egyptian software company helped Saudi, Qatari and Emirati companies to Arabize international accounting and production-management software, a highly lucrative business in which the work of a small set of software engineers was sold and resold to various companies across the Gulf. It also required frequent maintenance, itself a very attractive financial revenue stream. The company grew from four engineers in the late 1990s to over forty by the end of 2010. Its multiple accounts in the Gulf generated millions of dollars in revenue and enabled its managers to build strong relationships with senior business people in the region. Over time, these relations helped those engineers, and friends and acquaintances, to develop other businesses. Another company established by Egyptian, Palestinian and Jordanian engineers – two of them from families that had long associations with the Muslim Brotherhood in these countries – set up an Arabic digital content business in Qatar. By employing relatively low-salaried content generators in Egypt and Jordan and selling internationally priced digital solutions in the Gulf, the company generated substantial profits from its second year of operation.

Though many of these businesses were known to the security apparatuses of the Arab regimes in the 1990s and 2000s, they remained relatively small, with limited market shares across most sectors, and did not challenge the major economic empires that the regimes' acolytes owned. In some respects, the security apparatuses viewed these businesses as a safety valve. In Egypt, for example, the emergence of successful and thriving Brotherhood-controlled business reassured many strategists inside the regime that the group now had economic interests to protect. These were not just services or philanthropic activities offered to the poor and the needy, but personal businesses whose owners wanted to grow them and guard them. Leading figures in the Egyptian regime in the 2000s reckoned that the richer some of the Muslim Brotherhood's members (and funders) became, the more they would have 'a stake in the system and would not dare try to rock the boat'.

For a while this seemed a prescient understanding. Throughout the second half of the 2000s, neither the Egyptian Muslim Brotherhood nor the Jordanian Islamic Action Front (nor any other Islamist group with substantial economic resources) tried to deploy its riches to stir up dissent against their ruling regimes. Whereas the Islamists' political messages became more sophisticated, their economic activities remained in the background, funding the expansion into different regions, the enlargement of their services networks and their increasingly active media platforms. The Islamists did not really seek to dominate parliaments; and when they campaigned assertively, it was usually against the secular opposition rather than the regimes. There were not even any attempts to channel some of the wealth into challenging the regimes' members' and acolytes' economic hegemony. From the perspective of many Arab regimes, the Islamists' businesses were restraining factors rather than empowering engines.

From the Islamists' perspective, however, a virtuous circle had been created. The services networks expanded their reach, entrenched their influence and strengthened their brand. The larger their private businesses grew, the richer they became, the more they were able to support their groups and help them expand their services and philanthropic work. Confidence swelled.

The Islamists' economic work was a new application of the old Islamic notion that Islam is *deen wa dawla* (religion and state). Scores of Islamic scholars viewed this notion in vastly different ways. Sayyed Qutb, one of the twentieth-century's most influential Islamist thinkers in Arab Islamism (and discussed in the following chapter), argued that this understanding was fundamental to Islamic faith, to being a Muslim. For him – and the tens of thousands of Islamists who followed his ideas – it meant that Islam transcended a belief system or a set of religious convictions: it was God's framework for how believers should live. Thus, Islamic jurisprudence should be the unquestionable, unrivalled ruling system that was to govern all aspects of state and society, from the basic tenets of politics and rights in the state to economics. In this view, the Islamists' economic and financial activities were not just ways to fund their 'call to the religion': they were integral parts of living as Muslims in Islamic societies that should follow Islamic rules in every aspect of life.

Other Islamists had a much more flexible understanding. Gamal al-Banna, the younger brother of the Muslim Brotherhood's founder, Hassan al-Banna, argued that Islam is *deen wa ummah* (religion and nation), a crucial distinction that implied (and, in al-Banna's writings, explicitly stated) that Islam was a faith – an intellectual system that guided mind and soul and inspired behaviour, but the place of which was not in the intricate details of its adherents' daily lives. This meant that religious scholars should not interfere in matters that modernity (whether science, economics or other disciplines) had advanced to new understandings.[4]

Political Islam's interpretations of *deen wa dawla* (religion and state) did not pay much attention to theological struggles. The Islamists, practical and pragmatic as they had always been, focused on what the merger between religion and power meant on the ground, among their support bases and constituencies; and how that translated into more presence, power, influence and money.

But the notion of *deen wa dawla* had a subtler meaning that many Islamist strategists saw and delicately and shrewdly promoted. By funding and managing vast networks that offered health, education, transportation and even marriage services, the Islamists assumed the role of the provider. They were gaining not just social presence and political influence, but also legitimacy over the people, who were increasingly dependent on them. And as this was taking place under an Islamic umbrella, that legitimacy had unmistakably religious hues and tones. The Islamists never publicly touted the idea of being 'Islamic providers'. Neither the Muslim Brotherhood, the Islamic Action Front, Annahda nor any other Islamist group presented its services as being provided by 'rulers' to 'subjects'. They also never required direct allegiance from those who benefited from their services. And yet these groups realized that a subtle political relationship linking them to their societies was being forged – one that bypassed the central states and legitimized the groups' influence. In this regard, the Islamists neither adopted Sayyed Qutb's comprehensive understanding of *deen wa dawla* nor adhered to Gamal al-Banna's relaxed and detached approach. Their pragmatism and focus on delivering on the ground resulted in a practical implementation of how *al-deen* (religion) could be a *dawla* (state): becoming the framework by means of which ordinary people receive basic services.

Economics changed the Islamist groups more than expansion, repression, exile and political change. The expansion of the services, philanthropy and business networks led to a fundamental shift within the Islamist groups. Whereas most had usually recruited and promoted their cadres on the basis of commitment to their Islamist ideology, in the 2000s they sought out young professionals with a background in, and a modern understanding of, a wide range of fields such as finance, management, engineering, information technology, computing, education and media. The change in these groups' personnel strategy gradually brought about a change in how they 'looked'. The vast majority of Arab Islamist groups' spokespersons had traditionally been old, invariably male scholars, speaking in classical Arabic and focusing on theology, history and preaching. But by the mid-2000s, many Islamist groups had started to promote professionals, entrepreneurs, businessmen (and women), academics and even actors and singers as their public faces. The four most prominent representatives of Tunisia's

Annahda (especially in youth circles) were: Rafeek Abdel-Salam, an Oxford-educated and London-trained media professional (who later became Tunisia's foreign minister in the first Annahda-led government after the 2011 uprising); Mehrezia Lebaidi, a Tunisian woman who had lived in Paris for decades and who spoke three languages fluently; Ossama al-Sagheer, a young professional with extensive knowledge of the media, gained through years of studying and working in Italy; and Yusra Ghannouchi, the young, assertive and eloquent daughter of Annahda's leader Rached Ghannouchi.

In Egypt's Muslim Brotherhood the change was even more profound. Though the position of the 'General Guide' continued to be occupied by a series of elderly men belonging to the organization's 'old guard', the most powerful 'brother' in the 2000s was Khairat al-Shater, the Deputy General Guide and the group's supreme strategist. Al-Shater, who had spent decades building a thriving business empire with interests across many sectors, spearheaded the Brotherhood's Renaissance Project. He surrounded himself with a large group of businessmen, consultants, entrepreneurs and experts in various economic sectors. At dozens of meetings with Egyptian, Arab, European and American counterparts, especially after Egypt's 2011 uprising, al-Shater would invite his guests to join him in a small office where he would assume the central seat at a meeting table surrounded by the 'experts' whose 'areas of specialization' were discussed at those meetings. He was neither pretentious nor intrusive. The 'expert brothers' would take the lead in the discussions, presenting their views, asking questions and debating ideas and details. But amidst the mega-projects and the grand developmental plans sat the man who ran an organization that, just two decades earlier, had been content with setting up a simple hospital or a basic *hiwala* office.

The evolution of the Arab Islamist movements from marginal forces in their countries' economies to financial powerhouses, led by a new breed of managers, did not herald the fall of the old regimes that had controlled the Arab world for decades. But the advent of the Arab uprisings rapidly transformed the situation. The rapid removal of

Ben-Ali, Mubarak and Gaddafi, and the momentum that the 'Arab Spring' built up in 2011 and 2012 shocked many observers, especially in the moneyed (and highly secular) circles that had been close to those regimes. Probably the first person to leave Egypt after the January 2011 uprising had gained momentum was Hussein Salem, one of President Mubarak's closest friends and, arguably, the most successful individual business entrepreneur in Mr Mubarak's thirty-year reign. The billionaire, who came to be known as the 'owner of Sharm-al-Sheikh', flew to Spain amid rumours that he had been carrying bags filled with hundreds of millions of dollars. Salacious details aside, his flight revealed a sentiment that in the course of 2011 and 2012 would become very powerful and conspicuous among many of the most prominent business people in countries such as Egypt, Tunisia and Libya. For them, the wave that had catapulted the Islamists to power across the region seemed to herald at best unfavourable political regimes that viewed them with suspicion; at worst they could be hostile authorities that would actively work to deprive them of their fortunes.

Some Islamists did indeed reveal hostile intentions towards those financial power centres. In post-2011 Egypt, two governments formed and backed by the Muslim Brotherhood took steps to investigate two of the country's most successful business families who had hardly been close to the Mubarak administration. That one of them was Christian and a major supporter of the Egyptian Church did not send out the best message regarding the Islamists' agenda. For some, it all smacked of sectarianism; for others, of glee at economic assets to be acquired. But these measures were sporadic, not systematic, and to a large extent were exclusive to the Egyptian Muslim Brotherhood. What was systematic right across the region was the economic change that the rise of the Islamists had unleashed.

As the economic powers of the times before the uprisings quickly curtailed their businesses, tried to limit their exposure to their countries, and worked on transferring their liquid assets to havens such as London and Dubai, the economic vistas stretching out before the Islamists seemed open and ready for exploitation. The Islamists' businesses began to expand at an exponential rate. One of the Egyptian Muslim Brotherhood's prominent and successful entrepreneurs who had a close personal relationship with President Morsi expanded his business from retail to financial services, building materials, real estate and construction – all in one and a half years. And while less than two years earlier it would have been inconceivable for that man to get the required licences – let alone the necessary funding – to undertake such a dramatic expansion, now all roads were open. The Brotherhood's Renaissance Project grew into a state plan. Technocratic ministers, appointed by the Brotherhood, made regular references to it. It became the framework within which all investments in infrastructure, improvements in the public sector and changes in government would take place. Government ministries and several state agencies witnessed the arrival of 'consultants' (invariably from the Brotherhood's cadres or close sympathizers) who seemed, and in several cases were, more influential than the technocratic ministers. Decision-making regarding any major project in the country found its way to the handful of 'committees' that had appeared within the Brotherhood, and especially those that surrounded Khairat al-Shater. The Deputy General Guide seemed the effective ruler of Egypt. Western diplomats and visiting dignitaries strove to find individuals who knew him, had access to his circles and could secure meetings with him. Many senior professionals in international business and the banking giants that had designs on Egypt's 90-million-strong market dispensed with meeting officials and spent most of their working time in the country with representatives of the Brotherhood. In one case, during a visit to Cairo in late 2012, the head of the project financing practice at one of the largest European investment banks refrained from ordering a cognac, his classic after-dinner drink, for fear that 'someone would see him and word would spread to our new friends'.

New organizations with clear connections to Islamist groups began to appear with pronounced economic planning missions. The Egyptian EBDAA (Start) was the most famous of at least a dozen Islamist economic entities that quickly raised significant funds, set up commit-tees to plan business opportunities in various sectors, and had active media platforms that promoted their ideas. Neither the PJD nor Annahda managed such rapid and conspicuous expansion into their countries' economies. But in different ways – for example, through the creation of new centres and 'foundations' – it seemed clear that they had plans for how their political success was to translate into significant economic presence and influence. In Libya, despite the turmoil into which it had sunk after the removal of Gaddafi, several Islamist groups, including the local Muslim Brotherhood branch, quickly sought to gain influence over the country's largest sovereign wealth funds, which controlled tens of billions of dollars of Libyan investments across the world. The Brotherhood also tried to exert influence over the Central Bank which commanded the flow of proceeds from the country's oil exports. One of the earliest requests put before Libya's Islamist-dominated parliament, elected in 2012, was to Islamize the country's entire banking sector, which meant ending all non-Sharia-compliant operations in the country.

The Islamists also tried to gain control of their countries' media. In Egypt, the Brotherhood quickly overhauled the management structures of the leading state-owned print and visual media groups, removing editors and professionals who had served the previous regime and replacing them with people from within the Islamist camp. The coun-try's venerable state-owned newspaper *al-Ahram*, arguably the strongest media brand in the Arab world, was placed under the control of the Brotherhood. The group also put a lot of lobbying effort and funding into ensuring that it won the elections to the Journalists' Syndicate, which, through various arms, had influence over many of the country's media outlets. From 2011 to 2013 at least fifty new Islamist newspapers and TV stations popped up across the Arab world. Some, such as the al-Hafez channel, secured broadcasting via the Egyptian-owned Nilesat, traditionally close to the state.

For the Islamists, all of these measures were ways of 'delivering' to the people. They regarded the rapid expansion of the Renaissance Project and the placement of 'consultants' who controlled the executive and tried to secure influence across the media as 'taking control'. For them, all of that was part and parcel of what it meant to win elections, form governments and rule a country.

And yet their rapid rise across the economy, particularly at a time when the countries' old economic powers were withdrawing, was shocking to many segments in society. The Islamists seemed to be grabbing power on all fronts. For many in Egypt, the Brotherhood was 'Brotherizing' the state and the economy; in Tunisia, Annahda was 'Islamizing the country'; and even in Morocco, where the PJD ruled in coalition with secular parties with vastly different ideologies and social and political loyalties, the PJD was seen by many as having 'a subtle plan to take over the state institutions'.

After undergoing a transformative change in its politics, economics, rhetoric, look and feel, leadership structures and mind-set, political Islam had arrived at the top. It appeared that the old regimes had been marginalized, and had suffered a devastating blow. The secular elites were shocked. But political Islam found that it faced a new type of competition, from groups that proclaimed themselves to be the true Islamists: the Salafists.

CHAPTER THREE

The Salafists, from Cultural Salons to Jihadists' Battlefields

Sheikh Soleiman al-Aouda, a softly spoken man with piercing eyes and a short, henna-dyed beard, has for over two decades been a pillar of the conservative Salafist Islamic school of theology, Wahhabism. He is a prolific preacher, offering his opinions on topics ranging from Islamic banking to the themes of popular Arabic TV dramas. He delivers his views with the confidence, intellectual certainty and staunch conservatism so characteristic of senior Salafi authorities – those who regard the *Salaf* (the righteous predecessors – especially the early Islamic communities that surrounded the Prophet Mohammed) as role models, uphold the traditions of that early community and oppose innovations as signs of apostasy. Their views are anchored in deeply entrenched convictions and are hardly swayed by changing circumstances. For scores of Salafist scholars, women should not be seen in public and should remain segregated from males; education should be anchored in Islamic theology and memorization of the Koran; and most visual art should be forbidden. Even in politics they put traditions ahead of priorities. In 1992, al-Aouda was among the leading Salafist authorities in the Arabian Peninsula who opposed Saudi King Fahd's decision to allow US forces to be based in the kingdom in the war to eject Saddam Hussein from Kuwait, on the basis that such a presence could not be tolerated on 'the land in which Islam's two holy shrines, in Mecca and Medina, exist'.

In the years since the beginning of the Arab uprisings, al-Aouda has become a leading supporter of the youth movements trying to bring about change. He has spoken about the compatibility of Islam and genuine political representation, the urgent need for a major reform of how Islamic monarchies (including the Saudi kingdom) are ruled, and the right of young people to be angry at the deteriorating conditions across the *Ummah* (the global community of Muslims). Though he has always had a wide base of fans and followers, his unequivocal support for the Arab uprisings earned him a massive following among young Arab Muslims, including many secular groups. He had 4.8 million followers on Twitter at the beginning of 2015. Most of his YouTube videos have been watched over a million times. The comments of his fans, whether on webpages or in Riyadh's scattered cafes, are full of praise for his views, 'courage at speaking his mind', and, as one young Saudi woman from an affluent background put it, his 'ability to connect with us'.

Al-Aouda's intellectual flexibility and openness to new ideas echoes the birth of modern Salafism towards the end of the nineteenth century, specifically in Egypt and the eastern Mediterranean. The region was undergoing immense change: secular schools were replacing religious ones; dozens of newly established presses were printing Arabic translations of English, French, German and Italian scientific treatises, political essays, novels and plays; Western-educated bureaucrats were beginning to create civil services, and in the process sidelining religious scholars from their countries' administrative authorities and from the rulers' courts; new large landowners, industrialists and bankers were eroding religious endowments' market shares in local economies; Western clothing was becoming increasingly popular among most city-dwelling men; gender-mixing in public places was no longer unheard of; Arabic literature was evolving beyond poetry and plays into novels, short stories and Arabized versions of Comédie-Française dramas; and cinema was slowly meeting with burgeoning demand.

The elders of the religious establishment saw this wave of modernization as a deviation not only from heritage and tradition, but also from 'Islamic values' based on Koranic rules and Prophet Mohammed's teachings. Predictably, the establishment's leaders mobilized to stem that wave of change. Reformers of the education system in Egypt, such as Yacoub Artine,[1] faced acute resistance from religious scholars. There was a surge of funding for *kuttabs* (religious schools) in villages. Egypt's al-Azhar, then and now by far the most influential religious institution in Sunni Islamism, substantially increased its annual enrolment of students studying to be preachers. Other religious institutions, such as the office of the Beirut Mufti and the Sheikhdom of the Qairawan mosque in Tunisia, significantly expanded their social support and the distribution of their Islamic alms. Some went on the offensive. The 'father of Arab theatre' George Abbayad was repeatedly forced off his premises by conservative groups that saw his work as a threat to public morality. Religious scholars championed a campaign to preserve the Turko-Arab fez, a symbol of tradition and rejection of Western imports. In the early 1920s, after the fall of the Ottoman caliphate, leading figures in al-Azhar enthusiastically urged Egypt's King Fouad to dispense with the country's nascent constitutional monarchy and to proclaim himself the *Ummah*'s new caliph.

But some Salafists had different views. Throughout the last two decades of the nineteenth century, the Indo-Afghan scholar Gamal al-Din al-Afghani and his Egyptian student (and, later, partner in several journalistic endeavours) Mohammed Abdou put forward a new narrative. They wanted Muslim societies to return to the basic rules set out in the Koran and to the 'meanings that could be extracted' from Prophet Mohammed's life. By that they meant that Islam, at its core, was a 'rational religion' that addressed the mind, with a message based on a 'linguistic miracle' (the Koran) that intellectually challenged Mohammed's contemporaries. The focus here was on the word 'rational'. For al-Afghani and Abdou, the rationality of Islam meant that it was a religion designed to improve the lives of its believers and the conditions of 'its societies'. Its essence lay in addressing the mind through compelling arguments. For al-Afghani and Abdou, this was the fundamental logic and strength of Mohammed's message. In this view, the Koran was open to interpretations that transcended those that had dominated Islamic thinking in the previous centuries. *Ijtihad* (reasoning to develop solutions to questions not clearly covered in the Koran) was not just acceptable in the late nineteenth and early twentieth centuries: it was imperative for the Islamic nation to surmount its ills. And it was an activation of an Islamic 'duty' to think, question and 'apply the mind'. Al-Afghani and Abdou acknowledged that the Islamic civilization's golden age (during the reign of the Abbasid dynasty in the ninth and tenth centuries) was anchored in absorbing the intellectual achievements of the Hellenic philosophers, and in a social and political atmosphere that welcomed innovation, independent thinking, and free and open interactions between the various cultures that comprised and enriched the Islamic *Ummah*. By default, this entailed a willingness to interact with, and learn from, the West. In this perspective, Islam was to look on the West not as a historic enemy, opponent or even 'the other'; but rather as a culture from which it could borrow. Rather than seeing modernity as a threat, they saw it as a scientific and social force that improved societies, and also, crucially, as an opportunity to rejuvenate Islamic thinking and discourse.

By the first decade of the twentieth century, Abdou had become Egypt's mufti (the country's supreme arbiter on Islamic jurisprudence), and as such the country's leading Islamic authority, which lent the duo's ideas immense influence. Al-Afghani and Abdou and, later, scores of their disciples wanted to effect major change in how the Islamic establishment – especially in Egypt (the land of al-Azhar) and in Istanbul (the capital of the Ottoman caliphate) – viewed the transformation that their societies were undergoing at the time. They proposed sweeping changes to al-Azhar's educational curricula, overhauling the entire schooling system that the Ottomans had imposed on wide sections of the Islamic parts of their empire, and reducing the religious authorities' participation in decision-making.

Abdou was not against a decisive social role for Islam. His thinking was anchored in flexible and enlightened interpretations of the religion, but still it revolved around the religion. Indeed, he saw Islam as the fundamental identity of most societies in the Islamic *Ummah*. But he saw it as a 'sea without shores that could absorb the flows of various rivers'. Abdou was particularly animated by the notion that Islam could be the framework through which Islamic societies absorbed modernity. Al-Afghani and Abdou presented the West to their readers as advanced, progressive, egalitarian, just, hardworking and a model to be emulated. But they were not uncritical of it. Both thinkers called on 'Islamic societies to resist European interventions in their countries' lives'. But they distinguished between the political on the one hand, and the social and cultural on the other. They wanted their societies selectively to import from the West ideas, developments and concepts, which would enable genuine advancement and 'an informed awakening'.[2]

The Egyptian Azharite scholar Refaa Rafae al-Tahtawi had done something similar a few decades earlier, in his book *Takhlees al-Ibreez fi Talkhees Pareez* (*Extracting Gold in Summarizing Paris*).[3] In the book, al-Tahtawi sought to document and reflect on what he had observed, experienced and learnt in his four years in Paris in the early nineteenth century. For him, Paris (probably the most vibrant centre of European civilization at the time) was a gold mine, from which Arab and Islamic societies could extract precious lessons – in the relationship between rulers and ruled, in recognizing modern social and individual rights, and in social manners. But in al-Tahtawi's view, Paris's (and Western civilization's) 'gold' was surrounded by less valuable, as well as harmful, materials from which he wanted to shield Islamic societies. He saw his job as 'extracting what is valuable and worthy, the gold', and delivering it to his people.

After returning from Paris, al-Tahtawi started a translation school that would enrich the intellectual and cultural milieu of Egypt and the entire region. Because of his closeness to Egypt's rulers at the time, his school gained significant financing. Within a couple of decades it had become the Arab world's most prestigious languages and literary college. But unlike al-Azhar's Arabic colleges, al-Tahtawi's focused on European, and especially French, literature. He offered critiques to the texts he translated, including a rich commentary on France's 1789 Declaration of Rights. Here was one of the Arab world's most renowned Islamic teachers presenting Western ideas enriched by the developments of the Enlightenment, through an Islamic framework.[4] For al-Tahtawi, this merger of ideas was fundamental to the progress of Islamic societies.

Al-Tahtawi's impact was primarily confined to Egypt, and was felt in the highest echelons of society. Al-Afghani's and Abdou's work, however, achieved a much wider audience across the Islamic world, especially in the first two decades of the twentieth century. Their ideas not only inaugurated a new way of teaching Islamic theology, but effectively gave rise to a new school of thought that defined Salafism as a return to the early foundations of Islam, to the 'rationality of the Mohammed-ian message', 'when the religion was open', and before 'alien influences had seeped into the practice of religion'. The two scholars' thinking differentiated between the 'good Salaf', who were to be emulated, and other 'Salaf' who had presided over periods of deterioration and decline.[5]

Al-Afghani and Abdou propagated their ideas through newspapers that they established in Egypt, the eastern Mediterranean, Turkey and, later, Paris, aiming to reach the then expanding Arab and Islamic middle classes. Often they had state support: for a period in the late nineteenth century, for instance, al-Afghani was one of the closest advisors to Ottoman Sultan Abdelhamid II. In other periods they were ostracized and suffered acute difficulty in raising funds and, crucially, finding distribution channels for their work. At all times, however, their work was highly intellectual: arguments and counter-arguments in essays and articles, peppered with references to Islamic theology and various schools of Western philosophy. What was lacking was any connection to the rapidly changing lives of these Islamic societies' middle and lower-middle classes and poor. Al-Afghani and

Abdou became intellectual superstars within the higher social strata of Cairo, Tunis, Damascus and Istanbul. Over time, their names became household brands in the smart districts of these and other Islamic cities. But, unlike groups such as the Muslim Brotherhood, they – and the many thinkers and scholars who followed in their footsteps – had no presence in the Arab and Islamic worlds' grand mosques, zawyas (small prayer houses) or kuttabs. They also failed to connect with the middle classes to whom they had been so interested in reaching out. Their ideas had hardly penetrated the groupings of farmers, labour associations or the professional syndicates that were beginning to appear in the Arab and Islamic worlds in the early decades of the twentieth century. They were simply too elite and too remote from the everyday concerns of the street.

This progressive form of Islamism also had a mixed (and often confused) relationship with the Islamic world's major royal houses: the Ottomans, the Mohammed Ali dynasty in Egypt and the Hashemites in the eastern Mediterranean. These royal families saw this movement as helpful décor in their attempts to modernize their countries. These dynasties, with their legitimacy based on different forms (and degrees) of Islamic mandate, needed the canonical support that was accorded to figures such as al-Afghani and Abdou, especially at times when the countries' religious establishments were staunchly opposed to some of the modernization drives of the age. Abdou, in particular, became a social luminary and a superstar on the speaking circuits. But with this progressive movement failing to gain ground in society at large, and remaining ensconced in intellectual ivory towers, the two men's efficacy diminished in the eyes of the ruling families. Over time, they came to see Abdou and al-Afghani as a burden: demanding financing for ambitious projects such as new colleges, printing houses and newspapers, with limited ability to influence the masses.

Similarly, though admired by many European politicians and intellectuals, this movement was not considered an important ally by the colonial administrators in North Africa or the eastern Mediterranean.

The lack of powerful connections to the royal families and the colonial powers did give those progressive Salafists a reputation for integrity and incorruptibility. Mustafa Kamel, one of Mohammed Abdou's brightest disciples, came to be known in Egypt as 'the symbol of national integrity'. None of that, however, translated into any influence on the street.

The Second World War and the gradual withdrawal of colonialism created a vacuum that Arab nationalism, the most powerful secular political movement that the region had seen in the twentieth century, managed to fill at the expense of the Islamists. The struggle between the nationalists and the Islamists was not only over power and authority, but fundamentally for the loyalty – and representation – of the middle and lower-middle classes. This decades-long struggle pushed Salafism out of the political sphere. In this sense, not only were progressive Salafists marginalized, but all Islamist forces that did not coalesce into coherent, structured groups – such as the Muslim Brotherhood in North Africa and the eastern Mediterranean, and the Wahhabis in the Gulf – became secondary actors in their countries.

The term 'Salafism' itself was lost. Arab nationalists, and in general Arab secularists (Egypt's Nasser and Tunisia's Bourghuiba, for instance) emphasized 'progress', moving forward, secularization, not looking back at early Islamic history, and certainly not romanticizing any 'Salaf'. The large forces of political Islam were inextricably engaged in their fight with Arab secularists. Splinters from the early Salafist movement that al-Afghani and Abdou and their disciples had led lost any political influence. Such detachment, however, allowed Salafism to grow, albeit in an unstructured and different way. As the progressive Salafist movement lost momentum, so those Islamists who had eschewed politics and refrained from challenging their nationalist, secular regimes became the only Islamists allowed to work in their countries. Under strict observation by the ruling regimes, those Islamists focused on the uncontroversial. They lost a lot of the creativity that had characterized the Islamist movement decades earlier. Gradually, the Islamists returned to the same type of Islamism as had existed in the seventeenth, eighteenth and nineteenth centuries. Exposure to, and interaction with, the West withered away. The largest translation centres became independent, and in time became attached to newspapers and magazines and universities, isolated from religious institutions and colleges. Religious curricula, whether in small schools in rural areas or at leading colleges in al-Azhar, fell under the influence of traditionalists rather than modernists who espoused rationalist thinking like that of al-Afghani and Abdou. To some extent large sections of the Islamists deliberately distanced themselves from creative thinkers who had attempted to build new bridges between Salafism and modernity.

Abbas Mahmoud al-Akkad was known among his supporters as the 'giant of Arab thinking'. In the 1930s and 1940s he had investigated and dissected various strands of Islamic thought and philosophy. But in the 1950s and early 1960s he was rarely invited to lecture at any Islamic university, was never published by any press linked to any Islamic institution, and could not secure a senior teaching position, despite being one of the staunchest defenders of early Islamic thinking and experience. His unconventional (some would say nonconformist) approach to analysing the nature of divinity, the characteristics of the Koranic text and the personalities of towering figures in Islamic history hardly endeared him to the region's religious institutions.[6]

Ahmed Ameen, a scholar who argued that 'the dawn of Islam' was during its 'age of confidence' and at a time when its institutions were willing to engage with the world and not cling to antiquated notions, was also shunned; his books hardly featured in the reading lists of public schools and colleges.[7]

Exposure was also increasingly limited. Almost all large Islamic universities in the Arab world had newspapers, but without exception all had limited circulations, no more than one-tenth of their countries' leading national newspaper; they focused predominantly on religious issues; and, unlike the newspapers and magazines that the early rationalist Salafists had created, had almost no interaction at all with Western media, presses or academic centres.

53

The thinking was also changing and becoming much more insular. Sheikh Mahmoud Shaltout, the most prominent Islamic scholar in the Arab world in the 1950s, moved away from the ideas of al-Afghani and Abdou, despite having had a long experience of working with the latter. Though he led an attempt at rapprochement between Sunni and Shii theologies, Shaltout limited the bulk of his oeuvre to classic interpretations of the Koran. He wrote a lot about how ordinary Muslims ought to live their lives, delving into behaviour and social norms. That made his work accessible to millions of readers. But he hardly questioned leading Islamic schools of thought; and, unlike al-Afghani and Abdou, he never challenged the leading Islamic establishments in the region. Sheikh Abdelhalim Mahmoud, who succeeded Shaltout as the prominent scholar of his age (in the 1970s), was more traditional. Between the late 1970s and the 1990s, Sheikh Mohammed Metwali al-Sharaawi emerged as the first – and by far the most successful – Islamic TV preacher. His followers numbered in the tens of millions across the Arab and Islamic worlds: for over two decades, every Friday, hundreds of thousands of TVs would tune in to the charismatic, jovial scholar interpreting the Koran and illuminating its resplendent language to his audience. But al-Sharaawi neither championed modernization of the religion nor sought ways of situating it in a modern world. When once asked about the West's advances and the Islamic world's relative backwardness in science and technology, his answer implied that God had enslaved the (Western) world to deliver useful products to the Muslims. This was far removed from the nineteenth-century Salafists' anxiousness to catch up with the West and to learn from it. Salafism was consistently retreating into the conventional and the ordinary, and was losing the urgency to reconcile traditional Islamic thinking with modernity.

Economics played a role in the shift that took place within Salafism. In the decades that followed the Second World War, and especially during the heyday of Arab nationalism in the 1950s and 1960s, there were major drives towards providing free education, as well as efforts to modernize manufacturing and increase the share of industry (rather than agriculture) in the national economies. Urbanization flourished, and gradually the Egyptian, Syrian, Moroccan, Iraqi and other Arab societies witnessed substantial demographic moves from the countryside into towns and cities. And yet, most large Arab countries (that lacked substantial oil wealth) continued to suffer high levels of poverty. Jobs were scarce and real incomes hardly moved. National schooling systems fell rapidly behind comparable systems, such as in India, Indonesia or South Korea. Social mobility stagnated. And in many societies, particularly large conservative ones such as Egypt and Morocco, literacy rates continued to hover around 50 per cent (up to the late 1990s). All of this meant that large swathes of these countries' poor and lower-middle classes hardly had any means of seeking diversified sources of education, culture and exposure.

For tens of millions across the Arab world, Islam continued to be the decisive factor around which all aspects of their life revolved. In communities such as those surrounding the grand al-Hussein mosque in Cairo, al-Seyyeda Zainab shrine in Damascus, the venerable al-Zaitouna mosque in Tunis or the old town in Fez in Morocco, the economic livelihood, social circles, daily life and cultural milieu of millions of people centred on these Islamic places of worship. Tens of thousands of families would find work and economic support through philanthropy networks loosely attached to these grand mosques. The social life of communities – from Friday prayers and the subsequent 'weekly lunches' that bring together families and extended families, to the various Ramadan celebrations, weddings and festivals – rotated around the religious calendar. Even language revolved around religion. The classic Islamic greeting of *assalamu aleikom* (peace be upon you) was more acceptable than *sabbah al-kheir* (good morning). This sort of Islamism was different from that of al-Afghani, Abdou, al-Akkad and their like: it was traditionalist and highly conservative, the product of intellectual stagnation and a gradual return to literalism. These communities were on the receiving end of an Islamism that looked to the past – not for inspiration or in a search for the religion's 'rational' beginnings, but as the unquestionable truth that needed no alteration or revision, and certainly no advancement through interaction with 'infidel' cultures.

This form of Islamism, though highly conservative, appeared harmless to the Arab secular regimes. Unlike the political Islamist groups, the communities that surrounded grand mosques or the huge constituents of popular sheikhs were scattered and unstructured. They were primarily apolitical, without groupings that came together for a certain cause, without leaders with a social or economic agenda, and without ambitions to widen their presence in their countries' civil society (e.g. in student unions or professional syndicates). Their financial resources were based on charity, donations, endowments and Islamic alms. All of that made them difficult to monitor; but security forces hardly thought of them as a threat.

These very pious, conservative groups did not see themselves as a discrete social unit. Whereas organizations such as the Muslim Brotherhood, Annahda and the Adl w'Ihsane had a distinct group sense and clear brands, these communities just thought of themselves as 'Muslims'. Their affinity with each other was social: in the varied activities that brought them together, the way they lived their lives, and the places they inhabited. A conservative family in Tunis's old Medina would happily spend a weekend in the inner city of Sfax, but would feel uncomfortable in liberal La Marsa or Gammarth. Economic stratification also played a role. The vast majority of these highly conservative groups were poor or in the lower-middle classes. But even among the well-to-do (such as the families of successful immigrants in the Gulf) there was a clear demarcation in terms of how (and where) the pious groups and the majority in society spent most of their time.

That led them to be misunderstood by, and often invisible to, many other sections of their societies. In Egypt such pious, conservative communities were traditionally referred to as *sunniah* (those who follow Prophet Mohammed's lifestyle) or *ossoleyoun* (those clinging to the 'roots'); in Tunisia and Syria, they were referred to as the *salafeyah*. For decades these terms carried connotations of simple people, clinging to traditional and often antiquated lifestyles, values and appearances (for example, the men would have long beards and would often wear white robes, while the women invariably covered their faces). In all cases they were detached, left alone and hardly ever seen as dangerous.

But some within these communities were becoming increasingly antagonistic. Permissive social attitudes – gender mixing, women wearing Western clothes – were on the rise. Artistic productions, especially 1970s' Arab cinema, were increasingly daring. And the secular Arab nationalist regimes were conspicuously irreverent toward religion. Nasser abolished al-Azhar's independence and effectively transformed its Council of Grand Scholars into glorified appointees of the government. In Tunisia, Salafists were mortified by Bourghuiba's insistence that Tunisians should defy the Islamic obligation to fast during the Islamic month of Ramadan because it reduced their economic productivity and that of the country. In Egypt, Jehan Sadat, President Sadat's wife, sponsored legal amendments that aimed to place restrictions on what Salafist (and many other Islamists) considered to be 'rights' sanctioned by Islamic jurisprudence, such as a man's entitlement to up to four wives.

The persecution to which many Islamist groups were subjected from the 1950s to the 1970s, most notably in Egypt, Syria, Libya and Morocco, induced these Salafist communities' sympathy for groups such as the Muslim Brotherhood and the Adl w'Ihsane. It was hardly a political matter: political Islamist groups did not manage to increase their memberships significantly among the Salafist communities. But sections within them came to see the struggle between secular regimes and the Islamists as wars against Islam. Sheikh Shaarawi shocked millions of Arabs when he stated that he prayed to God in gratitude after the humiliation of Nasser's Arab nationalism in the 1967 Six Day War against Israel. Sheikh Shaarawi and broad sections of his followers were loyal to their countries, and scores of them had acutely negative feelings towards Israel. But more and more they equated the regimes that ruled them with an alien, and often aggressive, form of secularism that, in their view, was bent on marginalizing not just Islamism, but Islam itself.

Many Salafists began to see their societies as misguided. Popular sheikhs, increasingly with significant followings, repeatedly depicted wide sections of Arab and Islamic societies as living 'un-Islamic' lives. Some began to use the term *kafir* (infidel) when referring to prominent Arab politicians, intellectuals and artists. The idea was that, as these persons were 'clearly rejecting Islamic rules', they were also rejecting Islam, and so became non-Muslims.

Some Salafists went the extra mile: if sections of society were obviously unwilling to adopt, implement and live by the rules of Islam, then they – in toto – were rejecting Islam and effectively deserting the religion. Thus, 'true Muslims' needed to avoid these groups and establish for themselves enclaves where they could live 'truly Islamic lives'. In parts of southern Tunisia, northern Morocco, in Syrian Daaraa and in the agricultural plains surrounding Damascus, groups numbering in the hundreds and often thousands began to detach themselves from society and 'emigrate' to social oases that they had established away from the 'apostasy' that was taking over their societies.

The vast majority of Salafists continued to live their pious, conservative and ordinary lives, interacting normally with their societies. But for some, their societies had returned to a new *jahiliya*: the 'ignorance' in which the Arabs – and the whole world – had lived before the Prophet Mohammed began his message.

Sayyed Qutb was the most prominent theorist behind this thinking. Building on the work of various scholars across the Islamic world, Qutb argued that abandoning Islamic rules constituted rejecting *al-hakemiyah al-ilaheya* (divine sovereignty). In this view, Islam, with its jurisprudence and clear teachings, regulations and prohibitions, and its detailed laws on various aspects of political, social and economic life, constituted God's comprehensive plan for humanity. Abandoning Islamic jurisprudence – or corrupting it with man-made alterations and modifications – implied the denial of God's sovereignty over mankind.

Qutb emphasized Islam's literal meaning of 'submission', denoting that 'submission' fails if it is not followed by an acceptance of God's rules. He firmly believed that the Islamic societies were being exploited by the West, abused by local despots and becoming mired in injustice because they had abandoned true Islam and had compromised their faith with apostasies and corrupting innovations. For him, almost all Islamic societies had veered away from God's rule and returned to a 'new ignorance' from which God had saved the world when Islam was revealed to the Prophet Mohammed. He had no time for those who wanted compromise – the merging of ideas or the incorporation of Western concepts – or who appeared, as he saw it, to be equivocal about the role of Islam in society. He regarded such people as edging towards a rejection of Islam, towards becoming infidels. And if wide sections of their societies supported them, then they too – or indeed those entire societies – were mired in the same 'ignorance'.

Qutb, a failed literary critic, did not have the religious and scholarly pedigree that would have positioned him as a religious authority in Egypt, the land of al-Azhar – let alone that which would have qualified him as a potential major force in shaping modern Salafist thinking across the entire Islamic world. But his ideas were simple. This simplicity lent his thinking immense appeal, especially among the swathes of angry Salafists who abhorred their societies' rampant westernization and who strongly sympathized with the persecuted Islamists of the time. Qutb's language was also poetic. This modern rejectionist put forward his thinking in a prose that was heavily inspired by Arabic poetry and was peppered with Koranic verses and sayings of the Prophet Mohammed. His ideas were gloomy: he saw 'ignorance', 'deviation' and 'injustice' in so many features of the way twentieth-century Muslims were living their lives. But his writing style and vocabulary were those of a masterly writer who knew how to reach the hearts of his (already sympathetic) readers. Qutb's style resonated particularly with the enthusiasm of Islamist youths. He repeatedly talked about a 'new Koranic generation', a militant 'vanguard that won't bow', that would

'strive towards victory' and that 'would be willing to descend to ceme-
teries to ascend Islam'.[8]

Qutb was not a new phenomenon in Islamic history. Historically
there had been several influential movements that rejected the
prevailing social and political systems and which sought to effect
major transformations by recruiting large groups of young, impression-
able Muslims to their cause. In the eighth century, the Abbasid
dynasty used precisely that strategy to overthrow the Ummayads.[9]
But Qutb's main intellectual forebear was Sheikh Ibn Taimiyyah, the
thirteenth- and fourteenth-century 'Islamic reference' (an authority in
theology and jurisprudence to whom pious people turn for advice).
This Damascus- and Cairo-based theologian lived at a time when the
core of the Islamic world (Iraq, the eastern Mediterranean, Egypt and
parts of North Africa) was confronting two threats simultaneously:
the attacks of the Mongol (Tatar) tribes that had descended on Persia
and Iraq, sacked Baghdad and effectively finished off the Abbasid
caliphate in the thirteenth century; and the Crusaders who came from
the West. Ibn Taimiyyah believed that the Islamic world was facing an
existential threat. And so, in his decades of preaching and in a rich
corpus of wide-ranging writings, he sought to summon the 'will' of the
Islamic nation to rise up to confront the threats from east and west.
Perceiving immense peril, Ibn Taimiyyah and the various schools to
which his writing gave rise became intolerant of those who advocated
borrowing from the Hellenic, Persian and Indian traditions, or from
the Islamic philosophies that had evolved in the ninth and tenth
centuries at the height of the Islamic civilization's power, when leading
Islamic scholars translated Greek and Roman books and put forward
highly modernizing and innovative ideas that imbued Islamic thinking
with the output of different traditions.[10] For Ibn Taimiyyah, all these
falsafa (philosophical ideas) could have a place in the Islamic lexicon
when Islam was powerful enough to dominate the world. But when
the religion's heartlands were under attack, the *Ummah* could not
afford such intellectual decadence. A return to the 'core of our beliefs'

was a must. In a way, he was the fieriest and arguably first rejectionist Salafist.[11]

Qutb, sometimes explicitly but often subtly, drew on Ibn Taimiyyah's thinking. This gave his ideas historical and theological depth. It also saved him the need to provide major substantiation for many of his ideas, because his rejectionism could be packaged in the same overarching concepts that Ibn Taimiyyah had laboured over. Drawing on Ibn Taimiyyah also further accentuated the comparison that he wanted to highlight. The westernization that the Islamic world had been undergoing since the late nineteenth and the early twentieth century, and the new 'deviations' (westernized, un-Islamic constitutions, political systems, values and social norms) were, to his mind, similar to the attacks that Islam had endured seven centuries earlier. A historical thread was created which strengthened Qutb's ideas, added to the romanticism of his style, and anchored his message to young Muslims in some of the most respected episodes of jihad (struggle and self-exertion) in Islamic history.

Qutb was hanged in Cairo in 1966 after a court convicted him of treason and attempting to overthrow the Nasserite regime. But his ideas had a life of their own. His writings continued to circulate widely in Egypt and across the Arab world. As groups of Salafists felt alienated from their societies, so some wanted to effect change in those societies by force. Qutb's thinking became an intellectual framework for tens of thousands of young Muslims who were bent on fighting not only the regimes ruling their countries, but also their own people, for 'uplifting God's rule'.[12]

Militant jihadism spread at a time when the largest religious institutions in the Islamic world found themselves progressively marginalized. Cairo's al-Azhar University, Damascus's al-Jamae al-Oumawei, Tunis's al-Zaitouna and al-Qairawan, and several other historical institutions had been brought within their regimes' folds. In almost all of these religious institutions the secular regimes all but controlled the curricula, publications and sermons. Throughout the region, those establishments that could have provided credible and balanced platforms for moderate

Islamism had become branches of their countries' regimes, a development that slowly but steadily diluted their prestige and damaged their authority in the eyes of millions of young Muslims. The many disillusioned, conservative young Muslims who rejected their societies' path and their governments' ideology, did not see in these old institutions places in which they could learn, debate and be enlightened. Rather, they saw them as part and parcel of the regimes they abhorred.

Arab societies were also growing more militarized. From the 1940s to the 1970s many were engaged in various wars – fighting colonialism in North Africa, campaigns against Israel, internal struggles in Yemen, Iraq, Syria and Lebanon. Almost all Arab nationalist regimes promoted a strong sense of militarism: from a prominent role for the military establishments of these countries to a culture of confrontation and mobilization. From the late 1950s to the late 1970s at least 15 million young Arabs were under military conscription and in training. The period also witnessed phases of extensive violence, for instance the war that erupted in the early 1970s between the Jordanian monarchy and factions of the Palestinian Liberation Organization (PLO), clashes between Algeria and Morocco, and flare-ups of violence on the Arabian Peninsula. Military coups occurred regularly in North Africa and the eastern Mediterranean. Violence was a normal feature of Arab politics.

It was an international relations development occurring thousands of miles away from the centre of the Islamic world that provided violent Salafism with a major incentive – and with tens of thousands of trained fighters. After the Soviet invasion of Afghanistan in 1979, the US, supported by its leading Arab allies Saudi Arabia and Egypt, decided to turn Moscow's exercise in its then satrap into a war of attrition against its Cold War arch-rival. Encouraged by their governments, dozens of leading Islamic clerics declared it a religious obligation to aid the 'Islamic cause in Afghanistan'. Official Islamic centres, primarily but not solely in Saudi Arabia, sponsored fundraising for the *mujahedeen* (Islamic fighters). In some cases, governments paid for the air tickets to fly thousands of their countries' young men to Pakistan, from where they could cross the border into Afghanistan. In the decade from 1979 until the end of the 1980s, tens of thousands of Saudis, Egyptians, Jordanians, Algerians and others heeded the call to jihad against 'the atheist communists'. These religious fighters, motivated by a severe militant Islamism, sought not only the liberation of Afghanistan, but also the annihilation of 'God's enemies'. For the first time in decades, a holy Islamic war was organized, sponsored and promoted by several Arab countries (and American intelligence agencies), willing to send their citizens to fight and die in the name of Islam.[13]

The young Arab mujahedeen stayed in Sindh, the Punjab regions and with communities spread across Pakistan and Afghanistan. They had a rich experience, their interaction with the peoples of those regions exposing them to a different type of Islam. On the fringes of the Islamic *Ummah*, far from the centre of its successive empires, bordering different (and sometimes 'hostile') cultures such as the Hindus and 'the Muscovites', and not speaking the Koran's language of Arabic, large segments of the Punjabi and Sindhi adhered to a strictly conservative way of life, and embraced a highly assertive Islamic identity. Their geographical and historical conditions necessitated a vigilant and apprehensive way of looking at the world. The immersion in that culture, in the midst of a long war, left its mark not only on the thinking of the mujahedeen, but also on their temperament.

When the mujahedeen objective was achieved with the Soviet withdrawal from Afghanistan a decade later, the fighters returned to their native countries with a belief that they could triumph against these 'infidel' regimes. The thousands of young men who 'fought for Islam' in faraway lands believed that their next mission was to install Islamic rule in their homelands, by using the means in which they were trained and that they had victoriously employed: guerrilla warfare. Several Arab countries were to endure two decades of fighting, during which large groups of young men sought not only to overthrow their countries' regimes, but to inspire socio-religious revolutions that were supposed to overhaul the entire region.

Egypt's experience with its returned mujahedeen and the communities they had created illustrates how bloody and painful that episode was. From the late 1970s to the late 1990s, militant Islamists carried out more than 700 attacks in the country. Perhaps the bloodiest incident was the Luxor attack in 1997, in which the Salafist jihadist group al-Jamaa al-Islamiya killed fifty-eight tourists and four Egyptians outside a pharaonic temple. In the same year, an ambush by the group near the Egyptian museum in downtown Cairo took the lives of nine tourists. In 1995, eighteen Greek tourists were killed close to the pyramids. But the violence was not only directed at the 'infidel Westerners': Egyptians also suffered. Between 1982 and 2000, more than 2,000 Egyptians died in terror attacks, from the speaker of parliament, to a number of secular writers and commentators – Farag Foda, a prominent and controversial writer, was assassinated in 1992, and in 1994 an attempt was made on the life of Egypt's Nobel literature laureate Naguib Mahfouz – to a series of senior police officers, and children caught up in the blasts.[14]

In the 1990s, Algeria was to endure a civil war that claimed the lives of at least 100,000 people. The confrontations started a few months after the country's regime annulled the results of the 1991 parliamentary election, which the Islamic Salvation Front had won. In 1992, after the Front was banned and scores of its leaders arrested, many of its members formed guerrilla fighting groups and began a low-scale campaign against the regime. When scores of young Algerians, including some from the mujahedeen, decided to turn this confrontation into a campaign to 'purge Algeria from the infidels ruling it', the Islamist camp rapidly gained in strength. Militant groups such as al-Takfeer w'al-Hijra and the Organization for an Islamic State launched a succession of extremely violent attacks on state institutions and civilian targets. The regime responded with immense ruthlessness. Algerian society was not only terrorized, but divided. The split was not between those who supported the regime and those who sided with the Islamists: the majority abhorred the violence, and it was clear by the mid-1990s that the most powerful factions in the militant Islamist camp had lost popular support.[15] Rather, the split actually concerned the country's identity. Beneath the fighting and the chaos lay the question of society's cultural orientation: to continue the modernization that the nationalist regime had commenced after independence from France in the 1960s, or to move instead towards a strict form of Islamism. Some of Algeria's notable minds were lost amid a glut of silencing and killing. Taher Djaout, one of Algeria's leading secular voices, was assassinated in 1993 because 'his pugnacious pen had a poisonous effect on Islamic societies'.[16]

The Salafist jihadists' war failed: not a single Arab country fell to the jihadists. On the contrary, by the late 1990s, Arab regimes, especially in the large republics, had managed to infiltrate the largest of the jihadist groups, target their key leaders, drain their financial resources, and crush their operational infrastructures. Leaders such as the Saudi Osama Bin Laden and the Egyptian Ayman al-Zawahiri established themselves initially in countries run by sympathetic regimes, such as Sudan's al-Bashir, and later outside the Arab world altogether, in havens in Afghanistan and Pakistan. Some jihadists, mainly in Egypt and Algeria, put forward apologetic, revisionist treatises in which they argued that their 'jihad in their own countries' was 'a mistake and a sin', and that change should come 'through the call to the religion' and 'persuasive dialogue'.[17] Others fled to Western countries – Britain was a favourite destination because, in the 1980s and early 1990s, it had limited extradition treaties with most Arab countries – where they established religious and media bases to promote their ideas and attack the regimes back home. The failure of the 'jihad within' (inside the Islamic world) gave rise to the 'jihad without' (in non-Islamic lands). This was the beginning of the Salafist jihadists' war against the West, and especially the US.

This emigration was a blessing for the Salafists in the Middle East. Large numbers of pious, conservative Muslims despised how the name of Islam had become associated, in their own societies and globally, with such murderous groups. These communities from across the Arab world feared being associated with the militants. The vast majority in these communities, though they strongly supported an Islamic frame of reference for their societies, had no political ideology and certainly did not agree with the notion of changing their societies by force. But the long and painful experience of jihadism undergone by several Arab societies cast its shadow on these Salafist communities. Men with long beards and women who covered their faces became suspects, not only in the eyes of their regimes' security apparatuses, but in different parts of their own societies. For many, the very concept of 'Islamism' was equated with violence. The impact of the war against these militant groups (or what came to be known as Salafist jihadism) transcended images and social perceptions. The efforts of various Arab security apparatuses to control, infiltrate and quash jihadist groups put significant pressure on other Salafists, even those that Arab regimes knew were in no way implicated in the jihadists' efforts. For example, the *madrasas* (religious schools) that had for decades been operated by Salafist communities in Tunisia, Algeria and Morocco, especially in those countries' agrarian and mountainous regions, were largely closed down. The charitable structures that had existed around some of Egypt's largest mosques were subjected to intense scrutiny by the country's security apparatus. Throughout the 1980s and 1990s, Salafist communities felt they were under suspicion. And so, as the Salafist jihadists gradually started leaving their countries to export their jihad to the West, the Salafist communities in the Arab world felt that a huge burden was being lifted from them.

Just as the start of the 2000s brought the organized groups of political Islam opportunities to emerge from the shadows and enter their countries' national politics, so that decade also proved fruitful for the Salafists. The regimes' suspicions waned and the monitoring relaxed. Like other constituents, the Salafists benefited from the period's economic growth and financial opportunities. The exponential increase in oil prices in the 2000s created immense opportunities in the Gulf. Thousands of Salafists found wealth by trading with Saudi Arabia,

Kuwait and Qatar. Islamic products were particularly lucrative. Tens of millions of dollars were made in importing and selling digital Korans with dozens of interpretations loaded onto their hard drives, electronic gizmos giving the direction of Mecca (to which Muslims should orient themselves for their five daily prayers), and even downloadable mobile ringtones in the form of the Islamic call to prayer. The Salafists never developed the same sort of large economic networks or business groups as the political Islamists, but by the end of the 2000s many Salafist communities were much richer than they had ever been. Neither were the Salafists' financial resources channelled in a systematic and structured way, but there was a noticeable rise in philanthropic services in major communities, such as those surrounding the Arab world's grandest mosques.

Money made the Salafists more conspicuous. A multitude of Salafist mosques sprang up in Cairo, Alexandria, Casablanca, Damascus, and even the Tunisian interior at a time when the intensely secular Ben-Ali regime was still in power. Dozens of websites and even satellite TV stations propagated 'the Islamic way of life', presenting Koranic recitations and interpretations, lessons on jurisprudence and (mediocre) productions enacting episodes of Islamic history. Some focused on the daily concerns of very pious and conservative communities. One particularly popular programme on a pan-Arab Salafist station specialized in mannerisms: was it acceptable to enter a bathroom with the left leg first? Should parents oblige their left-handed children to eat with the right (and not the left) hand? Did Islamic jurisprudence find oral sex acceptable?

Emerging into the limelight, it was clear how little Salafist thinking and rhetoric had changed. As their ideas and ways of life became more conspicuous in their societies, the Salafists seemed extremely conservative, with limited exposure to the modernity that had significantly changed their societies. There was strict gender separation in Salafist communities and in the schools they controlled. Girls as young as ten years of age were forced to wear the Islamic veil. Freedom of expression, particularly when it came to any notion they deemed sacred in Islam, was frowned upon, and often totally unacceptable. For most Salafists, music, theatre and cinema were prohibited (at least in the form that the rest of society knew them). Tourism – through which Westerners would come to 'our land', consume alcohol, wear swimsuits and engage in unholy activities – brought 'God's wrath upon our societies'. All banking transactions entailed usury, and therefore were corrupt. Even pillars of Arab culture were considered symbols of deviation. For a leading Salafist commentator, the twentieth-century Arab world's greatest singer and film actress, Umm Kolthoum, was 'an old woman still moving her body while praising moral depravity, despite her greying hair'.

In contrast to the political Islamists, the Salafists had not progressed beyond the old notion of *deen* (religion) and *dawla* (state). They remained strongly attached to Islam as the sole – and utterly unquestionable – social and legal framework for their societies. There was no spectrum of ideas, ranging from the conservative to the relatively liberal, offering subtle differences as to the meaning of religion and the prerogatives of the state. It was clear and uncompromising. All laws, regulations and rules should follow Islamic jurisprudence – as the largest Salafist groups defined it.

For the Salafist communities, these strict views and positions were givens. And even though they had not fought their regimes or societies in order to bring them to fruition, these ideas (beliefs) remained hopes to which they aspired. They were not alone. Pious Egyptians, Moroccans, Tunisians, Libyans, Syrians, Iraqis and others never thought about these ideas, never paused to reflect on whether their states' and societies' man-made rules and constitutions were valid and proper, or affronts to Islam. But the more they had exposure to these ideas, through Salafist-run TV stations and the plethora of mosques that began to appear in the 2000s, the more they sympathized with them. As a Libyan graduate of an American business school once put it to me: 'Aren't these points clear instructions entailed in the Koran and the Sunna [Prophet Mohammed's behaviours and sayings]?'[18]

The Salafists' lack of 'progress' and their rejection of various notions of modernity, especially in comparison with the political Islamists, made them appear more 'solid', truer Islamists than those whose rhetoric had moved away from classic Islamism. This 'solidity', clarity and consistency won them financial support. Several groups in the Gulf, and especially in Saudi Arabia, were highly sympathetic to the 'purists'. And because the Salafists appeared apolitical, the Gulf's governments, and especially Saudi Arabia, had no qualms about their citizens sending donations to those groups. Charities in relatively poor areas of large Arab countries, such as Egypt, Syria and Morocco, and from the Sunni parts of Iraq, would solicit funding from the Gulf for schools, hospitals and (the particularly encouraged) marriage services. Thousands of Salafist engineers and accountants, as well as blue-collar workers and labourers, found jobs in the Gulf in sympathetic circles.

This purist positioning and the increase in available financial resources helped the Salafists to emerge as serious political actors in the wake of the Arab uprisings of the 2000s. In Egypt's December 2011/January 2012 parliamentary election, two Salafist parties, hurriedly formed in the summer of 2011, won a quarter of the seats. They had no real programme or clear political positions. What they did have were their large Salafist constituencies, their positioning as 'pious people' and a number of TV stations. These assets proved enough to lure a significant percentage of voters to their banners. The speaker of the larger of the two Egyptian Salafist parties at the time, a bright and well-spoken man in his early thirties, with a Master's degree in business administration from an obscure university, was given the relatively easy task of forming a political platform after his party became the second largest in the country's parliament. A few months after Tunisia's 2011 uprising, local communities in Sfax ejected some preachers that the government had appointed, and replaced them with Salafists. In 2012, one of the largest stadiums in the country was filled to capacity when a leading Salafist scholar decided to give a talk there.

What was remarkable was not the Salafists' significant social presence – though this was, indeed, a major (and disturbing) surprise for many Arab countries, especially those with illustrious liberal experiences such as Egypt, Tunisia and Syria. The striking factor was that the Arab uprisings and the political vacuum created by them had lured many Salafists into politics. Suddenly these traditionally apolitical communities had become the constituencies of new, but rapidly growing, political groups. And amidst intense confrontation between the Arab world's political Islamists and secular nationalists, the Salafists seemed to triumph in several electoral contests.

The same vacuum also enticed militant Salafists (or the Salafist jihadists) back into Arab politics. Libya's descent into chaos after the fall of Gaddafi was a huge opportunity for many jihadists. The country, whose oil production before its 2011 uprising was around 4 million barrels a day, had a population of less than 6 million people. Its sovereign wealth funds hoarded tens of billions of dollars in banks across the globe. The central state fell. Two parliaments and two governments held sway in different parts of the country. And the country's oil infrastructure and access to many of its investment arms became a prize for any militant group that could assert its control over them. Suddenly, local tribes were partnering with Islamist militants to form militias, many of which bore Islamist names. From 2013 to mid-2015, Libya witnessed a civil war in which Islamist ideologies merged with tribal loyalties and economic incentives. Across the Sahara, from southern Libya to Niger, various Islamist groups came together, primarily to trade in Gaddafi's arms, which had found their way onto black markets across the region.

Some thought that the fall of central authority in this vast and sparsely populated region offered an opportunity to establish an Islamic emirate there. Foreign intervention – for example, France's campaign in 2013 and 2014 against some of these jihadists – disrupted their operations and forced many of them to retreat from the borders of North African countries deeper into the Sahara. But that intervention did not eradicate their presence. The links between some of these groups and several nomadic tribes in the region, as well as the connection – and economic incentivization – established with jihadist groups operating in

western Africa, especially in Nigeria, gave these jihadists the geographical breadth that allowed them to withstand the attacks by international
forces, and to plan where to direct their future operations.

In the eastern Mediterranean, Syria's 2011 uprising gradually descended into a sectarian confrontation between Sunnis and Shiis of
various stripes, including the Alawites, to whom the Assad family, which
had ruled Syria since the 1970s, belonged. From the prolonged struggle,
the tens of thousands of deaths and the acute sectarian polarization,
jihadist groups emerged as the most active forces fighting the Assad
regime. Some proved successful at securing valuable economic assets
like oil wells and pipelines. In summer 2014, the bands (including
former members of the radical Islamist group al-Qaeda) that came
together to form the Islamic State of Iraq and Syria (ISIS) had an average
daily revenue of more than USD 800,000. Money drew larger numbers
of 'mujahedeen'. By the end of 2014, ISIS fighters numbered at least
20,000.

This type of Salafist jihadism was not directed at a specific
Arab country. In contrast to almost all large Salafist jihadist groups in
the period from the 1970s to the 1990s, observers could not directly
trace the evolution and formation of these new organizations. Relative to
the older groups (of the 1970s and 1980s), they had more rigid structures and were managed in more modern ways. For instance, their
messages were propagated using digital social media: in January 2015,
ISIS's 'cyber-jihadists' managed to hack the Twitter account of a US military command; and that summer the group launched a sleek online
magazine. These groups were also significantly richer than their prede-
cessor Salafist jihadists. They established enclaves, especially in the
eastern Mediterranean, where they managed to offer sanctuary to their
fighters and their families, build schools with primitive yet functioning
educational curricula, establish makeshift hospitals and provide subsidized food to the communities that had come under their command. In
some of the areas that in 2014 were under ISIS control, the group began
to institute quasi-administrative and services structures, such as local

councils. Links began to appear between Salafist jihadists operating in different parts of the Middle East. Al-Qaeda's affiliate in Syria, Jabhat al-Nusra, extended its political, trading and military connections to groups operating in Yemen, especially those that were fighting the Shii Houthis in the country. ISIS sponsored various jihadist groups in eastern Libya.

The Salafist jihadists have managed to carve out a social presence that is unprecedented in modern Arab history (since the early nineteenth century). As a result, in 2014 and 2015 Salafist jihadist thinking, which had been on the decline in the Arab world since the mid-1990s (save for sectarian-plagued Iraq), witnessed a region-wide revival. This was particularly clear among the more than 2 million Syrian refugees in Lebanon and Jordan, who lacked access to education, employment or entertainment. Thousands of youths were increasingly captivated by the piousness and fiery messages of the jihadists. Sayyed Qutb's writings were conspicuously present in large refugee camps such as al-Zaatari in northern Jordan (close to the country's border with Syria). A confidential survey, commissioned by a leading newspaper in the eastern Mediterranean, found that at least one-tenth of all Muslim males under thirty-five in two eastern Mediterranean countries showed clear sympathies with Salafist jihadist groups such as ISIS.

Irrespective of their large geographical footprint and significant financial resources, these new Salafist jihadists shared the same grievances and ambitions as the groups that had terrorized the region two decades earlier. These young Muslims viewed themselves as being in a jihad against infidels and Muslims living in a new *jahiliya*. They were willing to (and did) kill thousands of Muslims, believing themselves to be fighting to establish 'God's rule' on earth. They wanted to overthrow the 'infidel secular' regimes and replace them with Islamic states.

The same cycle that was seen in Egypt and Algeria between the 1970s and 1990s was repeated. The youths that these Salafist jihadist groups attracted to their thinking were initially apolitical, drawn to the groups' piety and their strong sense of community and camaraderie. But, quickly, they acquired political awareness: they were indoctrinated to believe that 'Islam is the path out of the *Ummah*'s lethargy'. Secular nationalists (and Westerners) were demonized as 'enemies of Islam'. Gradually, a strict and puritanical form of Islam began to shape their thinking and lifestyle. They were encouraged to take pride in their 'Islamic identity': grow their beards, shun Western clothing and emulate the look of early Islamic communities. Rapidly they came to regard their societies at best as misled, and at worst as heretical. Radicalization would take hold.

History was repeating itself. The considerable mayhem that Salafist jihadists have caused and the fear they have triggered across the region sullied the general ideology, vilified peaceful Salafist communities, and smeared scores of scholars and religious institutions. The leaders of several Salafist communities in the Arab world repeatedly warned in 2014 that the 'Salafists could endure the same demonization and guilt by association' that they had suffered a decade and a half before. This time, however, the Salafist communities would not find reprieve in any state-sanctioned war against the violent jihadists. Unlike in Egypt and Algeria in the 1980s and 1990s, the spread of the Salafist jihadists during the second decade of the twenty-first century, and the relative sophistication of their operations, has put them beyond retaliatory measures taken by any one country. International alliances against them – for example, the US-led coalition that launched a limited military campaign against ISIS in 2014 – are tenuous and are not willing to engage in long-term and exacting wars. And so Salafist jihadist groups will persist in plaguing the region for years to come.

Large Salafist communities will continue to suffer suspicion and guilt by association. But this will not be their most pressing problem: that would be their lack of experience, structure and discipline. Relative to all other major political actors in the region, and especially the large political Islamist groups, the Salafists come across as disorganized and divided. Less than two years after it was formed, al-Nour, Egypt's largest

Salafist party, was torn in two by internal divisions. Another Salafist party, al-Asala, lost almost a third of its members after two religious scholars left its leadership. Disagreements over which groups to support in Libya's civil war have rent Tunisia's Ansar al-Sharia, which emerged in early 2012 as a potentially serious political group.

And the more the Salafists are drawn to politics, the more their message becomes problematic. Throughout its modern history, Salafism has always been a niche phenomenon. Its communities were relatively isolated and its messages, whether peaceful or violent, have never evolved into major social currents. Since the Arab uprisings that began in 2011, they have been drawn into politics at a time when the region is undergoing arguably its most transformative change since the fall of the Ottoman Empire. This has been complicated by the Arab world's extremely young populations and the rise of a new generation of Muslims who are much better educated and far more exposed to the wider world than any previous generation in Islamic history. Some leading Salafist voices, such as Nader Bakkar in Egypt and Tarek al-Souweidan in the Gulf, have been trying to put forward forms of Salafist thinking that are less steeped in tradition and more open to modernity. These attempts have lacked the intellectual and theological depth of early twentieth-century Salafism, and they do not constitute a movement. They come across as sporadic views from popular figures rather than tightly argued theses from weighty scholars.

The Salafists will not be able to evolve their thinking in the same way that the large political Islamist groups have done. For the Muslim Brotherhood, Annahda, the PJD, the Islamic Constitutional Movement and others, Islam has been a social frame of reference and a political banner. And crucially, since the 1990s, these groups have maintained a distinction between, on the one hand, Islam as a faith and a set of rules, and on the other, their sociopolitical message. In this sense, their Islamism has not entailed strictly conservative social codes and a return to modes of thinking and living that their societies abandoned decades ago. However, the vast majority of Salafists across the region fail to maintain that distinction. Indeed, their organization and sense of identity have been driven by the blur of Islam as a faith and a set of rules, and their daily and social lives. Any serious dilution in the role that Islam is to play in their societies would render their message and identity meaningless.

The Salafists are facing a difficult decision. They could follow the lead of some of their more flexible and accommodating figures and cater to the youth who are increasingly more open to the world, more opinionated and less respectful of old dogmas. This would put them on a developmental path that could lead them to rejuvenating their thinking and rediscovering the late nineteenth- and early twentieth-century interpretations that then enlightened the Islamist movement. But after their long experience in the last century, and with their lack of organization and structure, such a move would likely break their nascent groups and alienate many in their constituencies. The probable scenario is that they will return to relative isolation and marginalization – their status before the 2011 uprisings.

This would be a comfortable position for many Salafists. It is not only Salafist jihadists who see their societies as having strayed from their 'true path': large sections of peaceful Salafists have acute reservations about the modernity that has been transforming their societies. Many regard themselves as 'strangers', fitting Prophet Mohammed's famous dictum: 'Islam was born a stranger, and will return as a stranger, so blessed are the strangers.' As the region continues its slow but irreversible social and economic development, backward-looking Salafists will increasingly feel 'strangers' in their own countries. Gradually, Salafist parties will withdraw from the political limelight and return to their core supporters: pious elderly voters, the communities surrounding grand Islamic mosques, and some of the poorest regions in the Arab world. This will beget passiveness and complacency. Some Salafist leaders will adopt flexible rhetoric, in an attempt to widen their following. Some Salafist politicians will continue to play prominent roles in their parliaments; a few could even emerge as kingmakers in the formation of coalition governments. But, by and large, peaceful Salafism will most likely fall into a gradual, slow decline. It will continue to inform the way in which millions of Muslims see their religion, perceive their identity and lead their daily lives. But, increasingly, it will have limited influence on the battle between the region's political Islamists and the regimes and their secular constituents.

CHAPTER FOUR

The Islamists' Fall from Power

Barely two weeks after his inauguration as president in July 2012, Mohammed Morsi relieved Egypt's defence minister of his position (which he had held for two decades) and overhauled the leadership of several military organizations. In the following two months he appointed a new government and changed the leadership of almost all ministries, major public sector companies and state agencies. Most of the new appointees came from the middle ranks of the Egyptian Muslim Brotherhood or had strong affiliations to its key leaders. Some were sectoral experts with various involvements in the Brotherhood's Renaissance Project. And some just happened to be in the right place at the right time: as he was talking to an up-and-coming young man in the Renaissance Project team, a key aide to the Brotherhood's Deputy Guide Khairat al-Shater received a call asking him to nominate a minister for an important economic dossier: a week later, the young man left his job in the customer service department of a mobile telecoms operator to become a member of the cabinet's economic committee.

The mandarins of Egypt's 6-million-strong civil service found themselves negotiating a situation they had not encountered since Nasser's dramatic expansion of the country's administrative bureaucracy over half a century earlier. The leaders of the country's influential bureaucracy have always thought of themselves as the real managers of the government, the officials entrusted with the functioning of the Egyptian state. Suddenly they had to deal with politicized ministers, drawn from the ranks of an Islamist group that those bureaucrats had long believed (as was the official rhetoric of the Egyptian state for more than six decades) to be illegal, violent and a menace to the state. That almost all of those ministers were relatively minor figures inside the Brotherhood and had to take guidance – and often direct instructions – from the organization's real decision-makers only exacerbated the civil servants' frustration. This was more than just natural friction between an antiquated and privileged bureaucracy and a new group assuming the reins of power. Scores of those senior civil servants felt that the state they had served for decades was being 'taken over' by the Brotherhood.

Mohammed Morsi was exercising his prerogative as the country's elected president to form an administration of his choosing. But the objectives and mandate of that administration were not clear. The government did not include any leading secular figures or youth leaders who had played a prominent role in the 2011 uprising. At the same time, it was notable that none of the Brotherhood's leaders, with the exception of Mohammed Morsi, occupied a key executive position. Morsi neither acquiesced to the idea of having a genuinely technocratic (apolitical) government, nor blatantly formed a Brotherhood government that would put the organization firmly in command. This vagueness bewildered many observers.

In September 2012, a group representing the most eminent secular parties in the country at the time requested a meeting with President Morsi to contest what they saw as 'the failure to deliver on the promises made before his accession to the presidency'. During the meeting, the president spoke for over an hour, emphasizing the 'inclusiveness' that 'his reign' would represent. However, he refrained from making specific promises. When, at the end of the meeting, a participant complained in frustration that he and his colleagues still did not understand the president's plan for including 'the forces of the revolution' in the ruling structure, one of President Morsi's senior aides suggested that they 'could recommend some figures for the presidency to assess their suitability for executive positions'. Many took this as a sign of condescension. No list was ever drawn up.

The rise of the Muslim Brotherhood to the presidency and the overall ascent of the Islamists to become the most powerful political force in Egypt unleashed a new form of nationalism that the country had not witnessed since Nasser's days in the 1950s and 1960s. From 2011 to 2013 almost all leading private TV stations and newspapers, and hundreds of commentators, seemed to be obsessed with defending Egypt's long and rich history against what they considered to be attacks on it. Many sensed a danger that the rise of the Islamists would gradually usher 'Islamic rule' into Egypt. Dozens of articles by leading journalists decried 'the path towards becoming Afghanistan'. Artists and prominent women activists accused the Islamists of a condescending view of women: 'seeing us as mere sexual objects', 'they think with their lower halves'. Some swore to fight for the right of Egyptians not to be led by 'imams', even if those imams had come to power through the ballot box. Irrespective of the change in the Brotherhood's thinking and rhetoric since the mid-century, its dramatic move from being an illegal group to the party ruling Egypt left many Egyptians, especially in the upper-middle classes, disoriented and fearful.

In the second half of 2012, a leading Egyptian Christian entrepreneur was offered the chance to become the governor of Cairo. This was not really surprising: the outspoken businessman had used the various media platforms he owned to argue that the country's public sector and civil service needed to be overhauled through entrepreneurial, private-sector thinking. He felt tempted to accept the post. But when told that he was to work with a team of 'experts' drawn from the Muslim Brotherhood's ranks and would have to 'liaise' with members of the office of the Brotherhood's Deputy Guide, he declined politely. His decision reflected not only the perceived lack of empowerment or his uneasiness with the dual ruling structure that had begun to coalesce in

Egypt (the presidency and the government on the one hand, and the Brotherhood's Guide and Deputy Guide offices on the other); it also reflected a feeling that he – 'a nationalist man whose family comes from a thousand-year-old village in al-Saeed [southern Egypt]' – could not work with a group that 'shuns the idea of Egyptianness'.

A battle in 2012 over the country's new constitution cemented those fears. A Constituent Assembly – drawn primarily from Islamist groups and chiefly the Muslim Brotherhood's Freedom and Justice Party, which had won over 40 per cent of the parliamentary seats in the last election (in which two Salafist parties won a total of around 25 per cent of the vote) – was tasked with writing the new constitution. The draft enshrined Islam as the religion of the Egyptian state. Many Egyptians, especially Christians, questioned what 'the religion of the Egyptian state' meant, and argued that states have no religions. But scrapping that article was a lost cause: it had existed in every Egyptian constitution over the previous half-century and it had the support of the vast majority of the country's Muslims. But there were telling new articles. For the first time in the history of modern Egypt, an Egyptian state document – moreover, the country's constitution – made official reference to groups of Islamic scholars as overseers of the country's laws and regulations. One article defined the 'principles of the Islamic Sharia', which are to guide all laws and regulations, as those principles that are acceptable to Islamic scholars. The constitution gave al-Azhar a vaguely defined moral power over decisions made by parliament: a thousand-year-old religious institution was supposed to review the policies enacted by the representatives of the people. Another article committed the state to 'overseeing . . . the protection of the country's moral values'. For the Brotherhood, the constitution was a compromise between the preferences of the country's secular elite and the demands of the Salafists, who argued and lobbied for a considerably stricter text. But for millions of Egyptians – especially in the middle-class neighbourhoods of Cairo and Alexandria – this constitution not only marked the first step towards a religious state, but more painfully negated what they considered to be the essence of Egyptianness: the seamless flow between religiosity and *joie de vivre*, Islam and Christianity, and a rich national identity that transcended any one religion, let alone a single interpretation of its laws.

Tensions ran high. The secular politicians felt that the Brotherhood, having ascended to the presidency, had gone beyond marginalizing them and was now reshaping the country's political system to its advantage. The groups of youth activists who had played leading roles in triggering the 2011 uprising were now extremely antagonistic towards the 'Brotherization' of Egypt – a term that came to signify what many in Egypt felt were systematic and deliberate attempts by the Muslim Brotherhood to take control of all state institutions in the country.

The Brotherhood and President Morsi entered into successive battles with major state institutions, which they reckoned were intentionally trying to sabotage the group's rule. To gain leverage, President Morsi issued a constitutional declaration in November 2012 by which he granted himself unlimited authority to enact legislation and which provided all his presidential decrees with retroactive immunity from any executive or judicial review. For the Brotherhood and its sympathizers, the president 'was protecting the 2011 revolution from the remnants of the Mubarak era' who wanted to block his (and the group's) every move. For the opponents of the Brotherhood and the majority of the secular forces in the country, Mohammed Morsi had put himself and 'his group' (a reference to the Muslim Brotherhood) above the law, ridiculed the country's institutions, diminished the checks and balances that the 2011 uprising was supposed to lay, and 'become another Mubarak' (as many in the private media came to describe him).

The new constitution, drafted by the Islamists, was ratified in a public referendum. It sent out a strong message that, despite the tension and the intense campaigning by the country's secularists and the major media groups they controlled, the Islamists still had a much stronger presence on the streets, and far more effective means of mobilizing and bringing out their supporters. Alaa al-Aswany, Egypt's and the Arab world's most successful novelist in the 2000s, wrote a series of poignant pieces full of grief about how the Islamists were consistently and persistently using religious slogans to convince many in Egypt's lower-middle classes and the poor that being a 'good Muslim' meant supporting an Islamization programme that denied Egypt's 'long, beautiful, resplendent, and plural identity'.[1]

Most of the senior figures inside the Brotherhood refrained from triumphalism. But many in the group's second rank, and scores of Salafists, hailed the passage of the constitution as a 'victory for Islam'. In al-Mattareya, a relatively poor Cairene neighbourhood, a sheikh spoke on a hastily built platform to celebrate *ghazwat al-dostour* (the Islamic battle of the constitution), an evocative reference that subtly compared the country's secularists to the infidels that the Prophet Mohammed fought in Arabia in the early days of Islam.

Dozens of secular groupings[2] accused the Muslim Brotherhood of 'finally showing its true colours: an ideological organization that did not respect liberalism, the separation between state and religion, and that was bent on grabbing power'. Days after Mohammed Morsi had issued the constitutional declaration, hundreds of thousands of young Egyptians demonstrated in Tahrir Square in Cairo and dozens of public spaces across the country against 'the rule of the Muslim Brotherhood'. The slogan 'No to the rule of the General Guide' (a reference to the leader of the Brotherhood's Guidance Council) became a catchphrase for many protests across the country. Confrontations between protestors and groups loyal to the Brotherhood left dozens dead and hundreds injured. Satellite TV channels broadcast live the clashes taking place across several parts of Cairo and Alexandria. On 4 December 2012, protestors attacked the presidential palace, several groups managed to storm into the compound's inner yard, and President Morsi, at the urging of some senior security professionals, was ushered out of a back door.

Confrontations between youth activists and Brotherhood members or sympathizers took place almost weekly. Many died and thousands were injured. Police routinely shut down key traffic arteries in Cairo and

Alexandria for security reasons or as a result of 'bloody confrontations' – a term that became so widely used that it become the basis of various sour jokes. Clashes between Islamist and secular student groups, and in some cases between professors, became regular scenes in most large Egyptian universities. Work in several professional syndicates stopped as many members refused to interact with 'Brotherized' councils.

The economic situation exacerbated the tensions. Despite the Morsi administration receiving around USD 8 billion of financial assistance from Qatar and USD 2 billion from Turkey, Egypt's strategic reserves of foreign currency had dwindled from over USD 36 billion in the weeks before the 2011 uprising to USD 12 billion by mid-2013, less than was necessary to cover the country's basic imports for four months. Inflation, including of food staples, skyrocketed. Fuel shortages and electricity cuts became an acute problem. The chaos and violence devastated the crucially important tourism industry, which before 2011 had directly employed over 2 million Egyptians and was the key source of income for an estimated 8 million more. Foreign direct investment fell to less than a quarter of its 2010 levels. Gas that Egypt had undertaken to export was diverted to its domestic market to cover the shortages and avert blackouts. The administration came across as confused and often incompetent.

Wide sections of the colossal middle class felt antagonized by what the secular media repeatedly termed 'the Brotherization' of the country, and especially by the perceived threat to the cherished, yet vaguely defined, Egyptian identity. Gradually the Islamist movement in general, and the Muslim Brotherhood in particular, became the 'enemy'. Social polarization reached a level that Egypt had not witnessed in around 150 years – since the beginning of its experience with modernization in the mid-nineteenth century. One of Egypt's and the Arab world's most popular singers released a song about 'us' and 'them' – 'us' represent-ing 'Egyptianness' and 'them' denoting the 'non-Egyptian group', the Brotherhood. The chaos, the social polarization and the economic peril threatening the country gradually became associated in the minds of millions of Egyptians with the '2011 revolution'. It helped that large media organizations with close links to Mubarak-era power groups fanned the flames and deliberately sought to smear the uprising, the 'misguided youths' who triggered it and the 'treacherous groups that stole it'. The balanced voices that repeatedly tried to differentiate between the 'revolution' and 'the problems that were inherited from the mismanagement and corruption of the past thirty years' were lost in the tsunami of fierce rhetoric from both the secularists and the Islamists. It became clear that less than two years after the Brotherhood's emergence as the most powerful political group in the country, and only months after it took control of the presidency, wide sections of Egyptian society, particularly within the urban, educated middle classes, were fiercely antagonistic to the notion of political Islam and especially its lead champion, the Muslim Brotherhood.

Tunisia was calmer, but the same polarizing dynamics were taking hold there too. Many Tunisians, especially from the country's large urbanized middle class along the northern and eastern coasts, were torn between two conflicting feelings: pride and alarm. They were proud of the smooth running of the 2011 election, in which Annahda polled around a third of the votes but confirmed that its rule would be inclusive. Indeed, Annahda formed a government with two staunchly secular parties. It was the first time in over half a century that a free and fair parliamentary election in an Arab country had resulted in an Islamist–secular coalition. The sight of Ali Laarayedh, a member of Annahda who for years had been held and tortured in the interior ministry, entering his former prison as his country's new interior minister, encapsulated the immense change that had taken place in Tunisia. Laarayedh shook hands with some of his previous jailors and promised to 'look to the future'. Annahda's leader, Rached Ghannouchi, refrained from taking any executive position and, despite urgings from several Annahda members, did not put himself forward as a presidential candidate. A surge of nationalism was conspicuous; and unlike in

Egypt, the 'revolution' was embraced and celebrated by all sections of society.

Yet, millions of Tunisians were alarmed. Many Tunisians differentiated between, on the one hand, the Tunisian state, Bourghuiba's legacy and the modernization he had effected in the country, and, on the other, the corruption and blurring of power and money that had afflicted the last decade of the rule of his successor, Ben-Ali. While they abhorred the latter, they felt proud of, and identified with, Bourghuiba. For many of them, the ascendancy of the Islamist Annahda was an affront to his acutely secular legacy, a fundamental pillar of the identity of the largest sections of middle- and upper-middle-class Tunisians.

Annahda seemed different, almost alien, from the Tunisia that those social classes had known in the previous five decades. Not surprisingly, all of Annahda's leaders were practising Muslims; many of them did not speak French (the most widely used foreign language in Tunisia); and some of its younger leaders (those who had grown up in exile in Europe) did not seem to know Tunisia very well. The twenty-something female leader of Annahda's most prominent 'youth foundation' was still discovering 'my country that I never got to know'. The vast majority of Annahda's female leaders and rank and file covered their hair. Even their speaking style was different from that of most Tunisians, and especially its middle classes (one of the most secular in the Arab world): Annahda members began their talks with 'In the name of God, the most merciful and the most compassionate', and there were hardly any instances of *bonjour* or *merci*.

The sudden and conspicuous appearance of Tunisian Salafists aggravated the secularists' alarm. Hundreds of mosques all over the country were taken over by highly conservative young men with long beards and white robes, whose rhetoric seemed to oppose the entire Tunisian experience over the previous half century. In January 2012, in a mosque in Tunis's historic Kasbah district, a young preacher devoted the entire Friday sermon to denouncing Tunisia's 'un-Islamic' gender laws, the prohibition on polygamy, 'the equality between men and women' and 'the consistent straying from the righteous path' – key tenets of Bourghuiba's legacy. He exemplified masses of preachers who emerged after 2011. In May 2012, thousands of young men surrounded al-Kairawan's Grand Mosque, one of the oldest in North Africa, calling for Islamic Sharia to be applied.

Several Salafist parties contested the 2011 election.[3] And while almost all of them had repeatedly underscored their commitment to a 'democratic, inclusive Tunisia', their rhetoric hardly reassured Tunisians. The leading Tunisian Salafist party, Jabhat al-Islah, for example, committed itself to the implementation of Sharia 'in all aspects of life' and emphasized the need to 'remove artificial borders', an allusion to the medieval borderless Islamic caliphates. Tunisians were shocked to learn that a new civil society organization had been formed called 'The Commission for the Promotion of Virtue and the Prevention of Vice' – the name of Saudi Arabia's famous agency, responsible for ensuring the population's adherence to the provisions of Islamic law (as interpreted by that country's strict Wahhabi school of Islamic theology). Some Salafists resorted to violence. In June 2012, a group attacked an exhibition of paintings in Tunis's upmarket suburb of al-Marsa because it displayed 'works that affronted sacred notions in Islam'. During Ramadan that year a group of young Salafists attacked a leading Tunisian Islamic scholar because he based his views on sayings of the Prophet Mohammed that they considered to be 'lacking provenance'.

Official Islamic institutions tried to detach themselves from the state and pander to the rising Islamists. Leading figures in al-Kairawan's Grand Mosque gave a series of sermons, some of which were broadcast on the internet, in which they lamented how 'the state had suffocated Islam' in the previous decades. Other sheikhs – less prominent, but also on the government's payroll – openly called for 'the governance of God'. Prominent sheikhs in the venerable al-Zaitouna mosque aimed to change the decades-old system by which the mosque and its influential Zeitouni Educational Establishment were under the supervision of the justice and the interior ministries. All of this struck many Tunisians as signs of deliberate efforts by Annahda (or at least, efforts blessed by Annahda) to Islamize the country.

Annahda had repeatedly distanced itself from the Salafist movement in Tunisia. While its leader, Rached Ghannouchi, held several meetings with prominent Salafist figures to mollify them over the need for immediate implementation of Sharia and to encourage them to soften their rhetoric, Interior Minister Ali Laarayedh proved himself an assertive enforcer of Tunisia's secular law. Throughout the second half of 2012, he pursued a campaign against groups that had used violence or challenged state institutions. None of this, however, diluted the fears of large sections of the Tunisian middle class: they continued to view Annahda with intense suspicion.

These suspicions projected themselves throughout Tunisia's three-year-long process of writing its first post-uprising constitution. For eighteen months, the Constituent Assembly – elected in October 2011 in what was described as the Arab world's smoothest election of the past half-century – failed to put forward a draft that would gain the support of two-thirds of its members. Numerous debates took place on the 'religion of the state'; on the limits (if any) on freedom of belief, opinion and expression; on safeguarding women's rights; and on the nature of the governing system, which many secularists accused Annahda of manipulating to guarantee its own future supremacy. For months, some of the most prominent MPs charged Annahda with gradually paving the way to the establishment of a theocracy; with engaging in 'double-speak' – one message for the media and the West, and another for its Islamist allies; with manipulating its partners in the governing coalition to advance its 'secret agenda of controlling Tunisia'; and with 'Brotherizing Tunisia', a reference to the Egyptian Muslim Brotherhood. Accusations spread to Annahda's secular allies in the coalition government it formed after the 2011 elections. Mustafa Jaafar, the speaker of parliament and leader of a small liberal party that formed the 'governing troika' led by Annahda, was repeatedly referred to as a

weak politician controlled by the Islamist group. One of the most prominent academics in Tunisia, and the founder of one of its leading think
tanks, could not 'forgive' the secular interim president, Monsef
al-Marzouki (head of another party in the Annahda-led coalition) for
his 'acquiescence in becoming a façade in Annahda's Islamist project'.

Suspicions ran deep. Many secularists invoked writings and speeches
that Ghannouchi had made years ago in exile in London, in order to
substantiate their argument that Annahda's rhetoric of respecting
democracy and inclusiveness was mere talk. Widely watched talk-shows
pored over statements by Annahda leaders, analyzing them in order to
speculate on how they view 'our society'. That many of Annahda's public
figures had limited respect for Habib Bourghuiba aggravated the feelings
of many in the country's middle classes, as well as in the media. Tunisia's
secular and highly influential labour unions mounted their first strike in
over thirty years against the Annahda-led government.

Violence erupted. Throughout 2012, the country that had unleashed
the 'Arab Spring' witnessed repeated confrontations between supporters
and sympathizers of Annahda and various secular groups, ranging from
youth activists to remnants of the Ben-Ali regime. Two outspoken secular
politicians were assassinated by persons unknown (though some indica-
tions pointed to a few Salafist groups). Clashes between secular youths
and factions of the Islamist movement left hundreds injured. Tunisians
watched with dismay the scenes of blood, tear gas and violence at the
centre of their traditionally quiet and quaint cities. And, as in Egypt,
economic conditions deteriorated considerably and conspicuously; and it
was Annahda, the political party leading the governing coalition, that had
to take the heat for that.

As discussed in chapter 1, Morocco's long tradition of mixing Islamism
with politics, the monarchy's religious legitimacy and the existence of
various powerful Islamist movements in the country all served to lessen
the impact of the PJD's ascent to power on the country's secularists. In
contrast to the situations in Egypt and Tunisia, the PJD had been a legal
party for years, had contested parliamentary elections before the wave of

uprisings in 2011, and had voluntarily foregone several opportunities to become the leading player in parliament and local councils. Also unlike in Egypt and Tunisia, the PJD was never perceived to have become the most powerful political actor in the country. The royal palace continued to hold immense influence through its links to several parties, its economic resources and its prestige, and because of the powers that the country's 2011 constitution had reserved for the king. The PJD's coalition partners in the two governments it has formed since winning the 2011 elections have also been powerful parties with significant and large constituencies. Compared with the small parties that worked with the Islamists in Tunisia and Egypt, the PJD's partners have been credible counterweights to the Islamists. And yet, despite all that, the PJD has faced some of the same challenges that the Egyptian Muslim Brotherhood and the Tunisian Annahda encountered.

Unlike its coalition partners, which had had previous stints at leading several governments and had been involved in most of the important economic government portfolios in Morocco, the PJD came to power without any government experience. Some of its leaders, such as Abdel-Illah Bin-Kirane and Saad al-Din-al-Othmani, did have personal constituencies and support bases, primarily because of previous mayoral positions or long experience of activism in unions and universities. But they lacked the know-how of comprehending and navigating the complex structure that was the Moroccan administrative bureaucracy and civil service. A further complication was the influence that the palace continued to wield, directly over all 'sovereign ministries' or indirectly through some of the 'higher councils' that oversaw the government's work. Also, the PJD has been compelled by the political agreement upon which it formed its coalition governments to accept a convoluted decision-making structure in many ministries, in which a minister would belong to one party, his deputy to another and a senior advisor to a third, in addition to the ministry's permanent secretary, who traditionally came from the civil service. Decisions are delayed by knotty processes, personal politics and vague demarcation of responsibilities.

All of this means that the PJD has often come across as unable to assert its executive authority.

The PJD's coming to power threatened Morocco's powerful political and economic power centres. The leading merchant families that had large market shares in most of the country's industries, the most influential army and security officers, a select band of aristocratic families,[4] and various advisors and groupings that rotated within the palace's orbit, had always maintained strict control over the country's political, economic and religious life.[5] Because of its social constituencies and the backgrounds of its leaders, the PJD came to be seen as the opposite of these power centres – as the representative of large segments of the country's lower-middle classes and the poor. The PJD's leaders carefully avoided antagonizing the most influential factions in these power centres. Nevertheless, its rise to power and its significant sway over the executive branch meant that lucrative interests (e.g. monopolies on the sale of certain agricultural commodities, or on services such as transport between some cities) could be disrupted. The PJD generated a wave of alarm among these power centres when, in 2012, it published the list of beneficiaries of some highly profitable fisheries that had been allocated in previous eras using procedures that many local observers politely described as 'marred and uncompetitive'.

The PJD also found itself in the forefront of social and economic struggles that it was hardly prepared for. Throughout the period from mid-2012 to early 2015, it engaged with various unions and syndicates in protracted negotiations over reforms of the commodities and energy subsidies, public sector pensions and the retirement structure of civil servants. The PJD lacked the necessary government experience and rapport with the country's administrative bureaucracy to handle such a difficult reform agenda. And though its social base has always been rooted in the country's poor and lower-middle classes, economic necessity means that it has found itself in the position of having to promote and defend policies that cause pain to its core constituencies in the short term.

The PJD's leaders had no illusions about the limits of their power in the country: none of them wanted to bring about a transformative change in Morocco's society or politics. But the limitations that the unique characteristics of Morocco's political situation imposed on the PJD diminished those ambitions even further. By the end of 2014 and early 2015, the PJD's MPs had much less appetite for action and new legislation than they had when they were elected in late 2011.

Morocco was spared the polarization and violence that Egypt and Tunisia experienced. But the country was also denied the experimentation found in those countries, the eruption of ideas and feelings, and the airing of concerns and dilemmas that had been suppressed for decades. Its Islamists and secularists remained bound by a political system in which the monarchy was the real balancer. And so the victory of Morocco's Islamists in the 2011 election and their rise to power came to be seen as merely a dent in the country's gradual political opening-up that had been going on since Mohammed VI came to power in 1999. To a large extent, the 2011 changes have allowed Morocco's Islamists to enter the country's politics properly and to secure representation that is commensurate with their presence in society. But they do not herald any fundamental change in the country's politics. By early 2015, any hopes of a transformation triggered by the PJD's coming to power had been all but dashed.

The Islamists' experience in Libya also differed from the situation in Egypt and Tunisia. The Libyan branch of the Muslim Brotherhood did not dominate elections in the same way as in Egypt. But as large numbers of members of the 2012 parliament who had run as independents formed 'blocs' calling for the imposition of Islamic Sharia, the restriction of all non-Sharia-compliant banking transactions and similar measures, it became clear that Libya was experiencing its own form of Islamization.

That Islamization could have been smooth. Libya is almost entirely Muslim. For centuries, the tribes of Cyrenaica, Tripolitania and Fezzan (the regions that the Italians united in the 1920s in the state named Libya) followed the Maliki School of Islamic theology, a relatively contemplative discipline. When the Italians were forced out of Libya, a Sufi order called the Senussi, which had grown over decades to command the support and affiliation of the regions' largest tribes, was the sole basis upon which to retain the unity of these different regions. A Senussi became king of the new state, but he was king in name only: he exercised his leadership through religious preaching and advice. When Gaddafi deposed him in 1969, the king found refuge in Alexandria in Egypt, where he remained until his death. After the killing of Gaddafi at the end of 2011, this heritage of contemplative Islamism and the country's homogeneity could gradually have led to the emergence of a plural democracy, inspired rather than shaped by the domestic interpretation of Islam. Some Libyan politicians tried just that. Mohammed Jibreel, a minister under Gaddafi and an early supporter of the rebels against him in 2011, formed a coalition that won the country's first parliamentary election after the uprising. He adamantly refused to be categorized as Islamist or secular. For him, the terms did not apply to Libya. He and his close associates hoped that the Libyan parliament would emerge as an aggregation of various political forces, representatives of different tribes and regions, all coming together to debate, negotiate and rule through a consensual process. Rules, regulations, laws and the form of government that would represent the Libyan people would never contradict Islamic Sharia, but would not be dictated by a single religious understanding, a set of scholars or any organization that saw itself as above the rest of society. It was a stirring vision.

And it seemed tenable. Libya had the potential to produce over 4 million barrels of oil every day; its population in 2013 was around 6 million; and though its economic infrastructure was extremely poor, the country's level of wealth relative to its population made its economic prospects exceedingly bright. Its lack of a strong, old and august liberal tradition seemed an advantage. Whereas countries such as Egypt, Tunisia and Morocco had at least three-quarters of a century of social and cultural secularization, which had seeped into the traditions and identity of their societies, Libya lacked all that. This lessened the prospects of an ideological struggle and the dominance of identity politics.

That stirring vision proved an illusion. By mid-2013, around eighteen months after the death of Gaddafi, Libya was divided between various political factions, tribes and militias. Central authority fell. Several key figures, including a prime minister, were abducted. Supposedly independent institutions, from the constitutional court to the Central Bank, were pulled into the struggle between the different factions. Within the maelstrom, several confrontations unfolded: between northern Arab and southern African tribes, between western and eastern tribes, between factions that had benefited from Gaddafi's largesse and ones that sought to control the country's immense oil wealth, and between several former generals and security chiefs in Gaddafi's army. At various times from mid-2011 to mid-2015, the country's oil industry, which constitutes over 90 per cent of the Libyan economy, ground to a halt. Amidst this multi-dimensional chaos, one struggle emerged as that which would mould the future of Libya: the one between Islamist groups of various affiliations, including the Libyan branch of the Muslim Brotherhood, and nationalist secularists, including former military units that coalesced around several former Gaddafi-era generals. Identity politics merged with economic incentives and tribal loyalties. The promise that the Libyan uprising had unleashed in 2011 descended into another acute polarization between Islamists and secularists.

In January 2014, Tunisia ratified a new constitution, arguably the most progressive in the Arab world. In October 2014 it undertook a relatively peaceful and inclusive parliamentary election. Nidaa-Tunis, a secular party, took 39 per cent of the vote; Annahda took 32 per cent. Two months later, the country chose the 88-year-old Baji al-Sibsi as its first popularly elected president after the 2011 uprising. In January 2015 the winning party selected a former economist with extensive experience in the security sector to form a government. Though parliamentary deliberations took longer than most observers had expected, and though the selected prime minister failed to form a government in the first few weeks of his mandate, the country's political process was progressing: Tunisia was beginning to have a functioning parliamentary democracy with serious respect for the rule of law. These successes made Tunisia a darling of the international community – the sole example of a successful political transition in the Arab world to which international, and Arab, observers could point.

But there was a huge gap between the image gleaned by distant observers and the reality in Tunisia. The acute polarization remained between, on the one side, Annahda and the wider Islamist movement, and on the other, the country's secularists. Many of Annahda's members felt that they were denied their 2011 electoral success. They believed that their party was effectively forced to relinquish its leading role in the executive in favour of a technocratic government controlled by the country's large secular forces. This feeling ran deep through Annahda's strata. Key leaders in the group resigned from the party because of what they considered to be acquiescence on the part of the party's leaders to marginalization, 'despite the mandate that the Tunisian people had given us'. Groups of young members felt that their leadership – and especially Rached Ghannouchi – was 'playing too much politics' when matters of principle were at stake. Ghannouchi was cognizant of the fears that Annahda's ascent to power had triggered; however, his primary concern was to ensure not 'victory', but a sustainable place for Annahda at Tunisia's top political table. For him, sacrificing some gains in the short term was an acceptable price to pay to lessen the antagonism towards the party of large and powerful segments of Tunisian society. That view had limited resonance among the party's younger members. They believed that, despite Annahda's electoral success in 2011, it had been denied the chance to effect any changes. This perception bred anger inside the party and its sizeable constituency.

For the Salafists, the experience of the previous three years was even more depressing. The window of opportunity for them to surface, air their views and attempt to transition into a normal political player in the country proved very narrow. Significant restrictions were placed on them; all Tunisian political parties – including Annahda – failed to culti-vate the peaceful factions in the Salafist movement; and as the Tunisian state engaged in a war of attrition against Salafist jihadists, all Salafists were shunned as 'regressive' or violent.[6] The opportunity to incorporate them into the political milieu of the most open, democratic and tolerant country in the Arab world was lost.

The secularists were also far from content. The inclusiveness that became the defining feature and sign of success of Tunisia's political transition was not without its downside. Almost all the young groups that had triggered Tunisia's 2011 uprising and that animated the coun-try's civil society in the years from 2011 to 2014 failed to have any serious representation in either the 2011 or the 2014 parliament. A few groups, in need of financial resources to organize themselves and to campaign, attached themselves to rich businessmen with extensive economic interests in the country, and often with dubious links to the previous regime. Others joined parties that leading figures of the old regime had established. They calculated that it would be better to operate within a large and powerful party than to be marginaliz-ed without any resources and reach. Opposition to Annahda and its 'Islamist project' was also a key factor in uniting the young activists who had triggered the uprising with interest groups from the old regime. The fear of Annahda's Islamization was more potent than the youths' desire for an overhaul of the country's political and economic system. Resultantly the party that won the 2014 parliamentary and presidential elections, Nidaa-Tunis, was an amalgamation of forces that just three years earlier had been bitter enemies. This was hardly a sign of rapprochement of old foes; rather, it was a union of the secularists against the Islamists. Thus, four years after its 2011 uprising, Tunisia's prospects have shifted from the country's emergence as a vibrant polit-ical milieu containing forces from different ideological backgrounds, to binary polarization between Islamists and secularists.

The same result materialized in Egypt, but with much higher levels of exclusion and violence. Fear that the Muslim Brotherhood could take over the administrative bureaucracy, anger at its condescension towards the country's secular forces (and especially the youth groups that paved the way for its ascent to power), and anxiety about the 'Brotherization' of the state all served to acutely polarize, and nearly paralyze, the country. It became clear that the military would intervene to restore order. And as millions took to the streets, in June 2013, demanding the removal of President Morsi, the military's Supreme Council of the Armed Forces gave him three days to 'comply with the demands of the people'. Minutes after the expiration of the three-day deadline, the military removed Morsi and ushered in a new 'democratic path'.

While Annahda was able to see that its ascent to power had stirred up various fears and apprehensions, and was therefore willing to relinquish some of its electoral gains, the Brotherhood was adamant about fighting for its project. Repeatedly, senior figures inside the Brotherhood invoked a 'conspiracy' against them. But there was little reflection on why millions of Egyptians had, in the span of a year and a half, distanced themselves from the group, or on why it had shifted its stance from regarding itself as a component of the '2011 revolution' to being an exclusive condescending power whose mere name became, in the minds of millions, the antithesis of 'Egyptianness'.

Summer 2013 proved to be extremely violent in Egypt. The security forces' removal of sit-ins by Brotherhood members and sympathizers resulted in hundreds of deaths and injuries. But it was the scene in which that new 'democratic path' was announced that demonstrated the dilemma that the country's secularists found themselves in. The country's then defence minister, Abdel-Fattah al-Sisi, proclaimed the start of a new transition process, while he was surrounded by some of the most recognizable faces of the country's secular movement. Here were the grandees of the movement who, less than three years earlier, had joined millions of Egyptian youths in taking to the streets to express their anger and rejection of authoritarianism, and who had consistently advocated the urgent need for a civic political system, partnering with the armed forces in order to end the Brotherhood's rule and destroy its Islamist project.

Many observers, especially in the West, condemned Arab secularists across the region. The term 'Arab Spring' became a sour joke. Social polarization, the battle between Arab secularism and Islamism, and the spread of violent Salafism dominated large parts of the Arab world. But behind the decisions and actions of Arab secularists lay deep anxieties and profound dilemmas. We explore these in the next chapter.

CHAPTER FIVE

The Secularists' Predicament

As the 'Arab Spring' imploded into social polarizations, chaos and internal conflict, the Islamists fell from power in Egypt and Tunisia, and lost the chance to instigate new political realities in Libya and Morocco. Those countries that had witnessed uprisings but avoided civil wars were back under the control of institutions and power circles from the era before the unrest. Their largest and most prominent secular opposition groups found themselves once again in a position similar to that before the beginning of the uprisings in 2011: marginalized from power, with limited resources and small constituencies scattered across their countries' affluent urban neighbourhoods.

Egypt's largest secular parties[1] aspired to win a few seats in the country's parliamentary election, which, as of mid-2015, was scheduled to take place at the end of 2015 or early 2016. None had any illusions about forming a government, let alone achieving the electoral success that the Islamists enjoyed in 2011 and 2012. Ayman Nour and Mohammed el-Bradei, two of the most famous leaders of the Egyptian secular movement in the 2000s, opted for self-imposed exile in, respectively, Beirut and Vienna. Almost all the youth groups that had played such conspicuous parts in the 2011 uprising were scattered, weakened or divided.

Tunisia's leading secular party, Nidaa-Tunis, won the country's 2014 parliamentary and presidential elections. Its real leadership, however, rested neither with any of the secular youth groups that had triggered the 2011 uprising, nor with Tunisia's large leftist labour movement, which had repeatedly challenged Annahda in 2012 and 2013; rather, it was with elder statesmen from the Bourghuiba era and an aggregation of business interests. Morocco's youth-led '20 February Movement', which had played a prominent role in stirring up large demonstrations in the country in early 2011, was sidelined, leaving a selection of parties with different connections to the country's entrenched power groups as the only checks on the PJD's leadership of the government.

In the various countries, the secularists' partnership with the entrenched powers – a partnership intended to halt the Islamists' march – neither led to the advancement of liberal democracy, nor empowered the secular opposition. In an interview in January 2015 with an Austrian newspaper, Mohammed al-Bradei, who sat next to the then defence minister (and later president) Abdel-Fattah al-Sisi as the latter announced the removal of Mohammed Morsi from power, complained that he 'was used'. It is difficult to believe that al-Bradei and the many secularists who had partnered with the powerful institutions of their states to dislodge the Islamists seriously expected those powers to hand them their countries' thrones: that would have shown a shocking level of naiveté not commensurate with those politicians' decades-long experience. But to denounce the secularists, as many in the West and the Arab world have done, also betrays limited understanding of the immense challenges and dilemmas that they faced.

Almost all the secularists came to the painful conclusion that, without severe restrictions on the Islamists' presence on the streets, on their control of major economic and services infrastructures, on the exercise of power and on the deployment of cash in elections and referendums, the Islamists would continue to win elections. Many secularists believed that they needed time to establish their presence in the different regions of their countries, to build up their financial resources, to recruit candidates and volunteers, and to create media platforms that could penetrate broadly, especially within the poor and lower-middle classes. A prominent young leader from an Egyptian youth group complained: 'It is inconceivable that we were forced to compete with extremely rich groups that had been operating and building their bases for eight decades. We needed time.'

The secularists thought they had triggered 'revolutions' that had removed the ageing presidents and shaken the regimes, only to find the Islamists coming to power and marginalizing them. From their perspective, they had done the 'heavy lifting' of seeing off the old regimes, only to be drawn into a competition of cash and access with the Islamists who had been 'building their bases for decades'. There was a significant level of frustration especially within the youth groups, which felt powerless, lacking as they did any serious financial resources or media platforms. Swathes of secular parties came into being. Some, such as Egypt's Free Egyptians and Tunisia's Free Patriotic Union (UPL), were funded by wealthy businessmen who adamantly opposed political Islam. Others, such as Tunisia's Republican Party, were built on the large followings of their leaders.[2] Those and other parties were not intended to become secular versions of the Muslim Brotherhood, with its massive social presence and financial resources. The founders of these parties wanted to aggregate secular forces into cohesive political groupings that could challenge the large Islamist groups.

It was a monumental task. Over the past six decades, since the abrupt end of the Arab liberal age in the early 1950s, not a single liberal party with independent financing has managed to grow into a major force in its own country, let alone in the region. There have been several attempts. Morocco's National Rally of Independents (RNI), founded in 1977 by a group of liberal-minded lawyers, economists, businessmen and prominent figures in the country's civil society, aimed to position itself as the voice of the middle class, aspiring to economic progress through open-market policies and gradual improvements in the country's political and civic freedoms. Because of the party's close connections to King Hassan II, it was able to utilize many media platforms in the country and to exert influence on the kingdom's powerful bureaucracy. In the 1980s and 1990s, several leaders of the party became senior government officials. But that closeness to the royal palace limited the party's chances of becoming the voice of broad sections of the population, which associated the monarchy with the power nexus that had controlled the country's political economy for decades. That closeness also made the party's financing dependent on the largesse of individuals who were entrenched in that power nexus. The RNI grew into a significant force in Moroccan politics, but it hardly commanded the social presence, brand recognition and nation-wide reach that the country's Islamists enjoyed.

Tunisia's largest labour union (known by its French acronym, UGTT) had a different experience. In the 1950s it played a notable role in the country's struggle for independence from France. Farhat Hashad, one of its key leaders in the period, remains a symbol of Tunisia's nationalism. The UGTT became the most powerful civil society organization in the country; its membership exceeded half a million, scattered across the land. But unlike many unions in Europe and Latin America, the UGTT was not able to build its influence to play a decisive role within any political party in the country. It also continued to adhere to a strictly socialist economic ideology, despite the major opening-up to international markets of Tunisia's economy since the mid-1980s. The UGTT had a tense relationship with the Ben-Ali regime. Throughout his long reign the union kept its distance from his administration; and it subtly resisted some of the economic liberalization (most notably, privatization) that took place under his leadership. But it never openly challenged him. Not once after he took power from Bourghuiba in 1987 did the UGTT organize a strike against the government. And so, though it continued to enlarge its constituency, the UGTT never acquired the political credibility as an opponent of the Ben-Ali regime that groups such as Annahda gained.[3]

Egypt's secular, leftist Al-Tagamoa party managed in the 1980s to achieve a conspicuous presence in the country's largest universities and in some professional syndicates. But despite three decades of active involvement in the country's civil society it has never managed to muster a significant presence in parliament. There have been many other examples of notable and serious Arab secular organizations that have managed to establish themselves as important political voices in their countries, and yet have remained with only limited social constituencies and hardly any ability to rally the masses round their liberal ideas.

Arab secularists have also failed to produce charismatic leaders. This was a major weakness given the Islamists' repeated success at portraying their leaders as heroes. Throughout the 2000s, the Egyptian Muslim Brotherhood cultivated the idea that the leadership of Khairat al-Shater was transformative for the group and for Egypt. This was hardly a new phenomenon: for decades the Brotherhood had deployed immense resources to achieve wide circulation for the writings of its founder, Hassan al-Banna, and for some of its key leaders, such as Mammoun al-Houdaibi. Al-Banna, in particular, was almost sanctified as an 'imam'. Despite having a relatively small oeuvre (of little serious significance in Islamic thought), the Brotherhood consistently sought to present him as a *mujadid* (a scholar bringing about renewal in Islamic thinking), almost on the same footing as Mohammed Abdou and Jamal al-Din al-Afghani. Sayyed Qutb, the 'godfather' of modern Arab Salafist jihadism, needed no organization to promote his work; tens of thousands of Muslim Salafist jihadists continued to circulate his books, speeches and poems. Annahda and the PJD were historically less concentrated around specific figures; yet charismatic leaders such as Rached Ghannouchi, Abdel-Fattah Morou and Saad al-Din al-Othmani enjoyed large personal constituencies and many *mourideen* (followers). The same was true of prominent Salafist thinkers. To this day, the 'lessons' of Sheikh Mohammed Metwali al-Sharaawi continue to number among the best-selling CDs and DVDs across the Arab world. A biographical TV series was even made to celebrate his life. More recently, the followers of the Egyptian Salafist leader Hazem Abu-Ismail named themselves 'Hazemoun', a play on his first name, which also means 'Determined'.

No other leader of any secular Arab party or movement has ever achieved that kind of fame, let alone reverence, in at least seven or eight decades.[4] On the contrary, indeed, Arab secularism has repeatedly engaged in character assassination. Arab nationalists sullied the entire liberal age: leaders such as Saad Zaghloul and Sultan al-Attrach, the icons of Egypt's and Syria's struggle for independence from Britain and France, were marginalized in the wave of hero worship that accompanied the rise of Nasserism in Egypt and across the region. The strongmen of Arab nationalism (Nasser, Assad, Saddam Hussein and others) also diluted the historical role that intellectuals such as the Levantine political theorists Michel Aflaq and George Habash had played in reviving Arab nationalism in the 1940s.[5] In the late 1970s (after the first oil shock, which resulted in an exponential increase in oil prices), as Arab nationalism (the power base of which has always been in North Africa and the eastern Mediterranean) was losing ground to the rising Gulf, the legacies of Nasser and the entire Arab nationalist project became an open target for a wide array of media that aspired to curry favour in the Gulf's palaces. The same trend even took place in culture: leading Arab liberal thinkers such as Taha Hussein and Tawfik al-Hakeem were on the receiving end of smear campaigns. That discrediting of the past has left Arab secularists without any defining figures that could be presented as role models for young Arab generations. It also left Arab secularism without any consensus as to its own recent history.

This lack of a narrative, of pillars around which to anchor its legacy, left Arab liberalism open to exploitation. Throughout the period from the 1950s to the 1980s, the leaders of Arab nationalism – from Nasser in Egypt, to lesser figures such as Assad in Syria, Boumedienne in Algeria, Saddam Hussein in Iraq and Yasser Arafat (for decades, the leader of the Palestine Liberation Organization) – positioned their regimes as extensions of the Arab liberal age from the late nineteenth to the mid-twentieth century. All of them maintained that Arab nationalism was a 'national ideology' that encompassed all religions (whether Islam and Christianity in Egypt, Shiism and Sunnism in Iraq, or the multitude of sects in the eastern Mediterranean); transcended racial differences between citizens (Arabs, Amazighs, Kurds and Berbers); and was detached from the religious authorities of their countries (whether al-Azhar and the Coptic Church in Egypt, the Catholic Maronite Church in Lebanon, the different sects' leaders in the eastern Mediterranean, or the 'Shii references' in Iraq). Some, most notably Nasser, did indeed believe that their strand of Arab nationalism was not only transforming their countries' societies and economies, but also heralding new identities. For Nasser, the notion of 'Arabness' carried powerful connotations of 'a rising nation' after centuries of lethargy, of integrity and of a 'march towards greatness'. The new identity was not supposed to clash with or replace religion: 'Arabness' was the expression of the Arabs' nationality, while religion (Islam as well as Christianity) was the distant civilizational framework in which Arabness resided. It was intentionally vague: such 'Arabness' was never a well-thought-out, well-articulated or well-presented identity. But throughout the 1950s and the best part of the 1960s it intoxicated large swathes of Arabs. That 'Nasserite dream' had crashed, however, by the late 1960s and early 1970s. It had become clear that, as the movement was replicated across the Arab world, it gave rise to corrupt and incompetent systems of rule that were unable to promote genuine development in the region.[6]

The vast majority of Arab 'nationalist leaders' used Arab liberalism as a tool to discredit and oppose the Islamists. They also wanted to exploit the glamour of the Arab liberal age's cultural heritage. They reckoned that by associating themselves with the 'golden years' of 1930s, 1940s and 1950s Arab literature, theatre, music and cinema, they would acquire a certain grandeur, and their iron-fisted regimes would appear softer. Thus the Arab world's strongmen positioned themselves as patrons of the arts; in societies with literacy rates of less than 50 per cent, this also allowed them to set and control their countries' agendas.[7]

Regimes such as those of Mubarak, Ben-Ali, Assad and, to some extent, Gaddafi continued with the same tradition.[8] By associating themselves with 'Arab liberalism', the leaders portrayed themselves as their societies' protectors against 'the peril of Islamization'. This was especially important for the Arab world's hereditary (and predatory) regimes as they confronted the myriad civil society organizations and youth groups that increasingly came together in the 2000s to protest against hereditary rule, political stagnation, corruption, the fusing of power and wealth, and the regimes' disregard for human rights.

As time moved on, the meaning of 'Arab liberalism' changed. In most Arab republics, a vaguely defined 'liberalism' deliberately blurred the lines between liberalism and nationalism, merging the idea of 'being against the Islamization of society' with the notion of 'being patriotic'. The expression of such 'secularism and liberalism' varied. In Egypt, this took the form of rather more daring cultural products (especially in cinema and on TV), a celebration of Egypt's liberal age in the first half of the twentieth century and a revival of interest in pharaonic Egypt. In Tunisia, the Ben-Ali regime adamantly distinguished between the 'Tunisian identity' and 'regressive ideas' (in its view, primarily Islamism), and opposed any expression of Islamic piety – especially Islamic women's headscarves.

These efforts were successful. Despite their immense concentration of political and economic power and their poor civil and human rights records, regimes such as Mubarak's, Ben-Ali's and others became, in the minds of large sections of their own people, associated with secularism – and, for some, liberalism. In my successive visits to Tunisia in the second half of the 2000s, various acquaintances there described the Ben-Ali regime as 'liberal'. Scores of Egyptian and Arab politicians, diplomats and media pundits repeatedly referred to Gamal Mubarak, President Mubarak's son and heir apparent in the second half of the 2000s, as 'a liberal'.[9] The boundaries between being secular, being liberal and opposing the Islamists were very hazy. Throughout it all, the Arab world's magnificent cultural advances in the period from the late nineteenth to the mid-twentieth century became tools and relics used by authoritarian (and often despotic) regimes that revolved around old men. Secular leftist groups, unions, liberal youths and political parties of the centre-left or right had little ownership of the Arab liberalism brand.

Terms matter. Throughout the half-century prior to 2011 there was a deliberate separation between 'liberalism' on the one hand, and 'liberals' and 'secularists' on the other. In their tense confrontation with Western powers in the 1960s and 1970s, many Arab nationalist regimes tried to discredit their liberal opposition as tools of the West, agents 'acting from within' to disrupt the 'Arab people's cohesiveness behind their leaders'. This demonization was not particularly difficult because, for many Arabs, the notion of 'liberalism' carried mixed connotations. It was reminiscent of the cultural advances of the first half of the twentieth century, a heritage that most Arabs (especially the region's middle classes) viewed with nostalgia and pride. Yet, ideas such as the necessity of having multi-party democracies, respecting pluralism, ensuring freedom of expression and opening up to the world (especially the West) aroused suspicion. Throughout the period from the 1950s to the 1970s, the Arab world's central struggles were against Western imperialism and in the Arab–Israel wars. Ensuring pluralism, protecting and respecting political and human rights, and many other democratic features came to be seen by large sections of Arab society as 'Western demands', instructions issued by the condescending West, or innocuous terms that hid 'malicious schemes by the West' to destabilize the Arab world. The Arab regimes, many of which had anchored their legitimacy in the fight against colonialism, differentiated between 'cultural liberalism' (which they favoured and used to augment their prestige) and 'political liberalism' (which they demonized). The distinction went further. While the regimes became the guardians of cultural liberalism, the opponents (in many cases, the 'liberals') became the 'agents' working with the 'enemies' to weaken 'us'.

Economics cemented that distinction. By the 1980s and 1990s, most Arab republics that over the previous three decades had been staunchly socialist and had assumed the role of 'provider' to their societies, were moving towards liberal market economics. Regimes were intentionally changing their basis of legitimacy from Arab nationalism's struggles against colonialism, wars against Israel and the quest for Arab unity, to achieving economic growth. The collapse of the Soviet Union in the early 1990s, the boom years that accompanied Bill Clinton's presidency in the US, and the exponential growth of the communications and computing industries (and especially the internet) bolstered the idea that politics were increasingly obsolescent, almost passé; it was 'the economy, stupid'. For example, throughout the 1990s the Ben-Ali regime was able to perpetuate almost total control over Tunisia's politics – so long as the country's economic growth rate, foreign direct investments, and asset values (especially real estate, where most of the middle class's wealth was invested) kept rising. By establishing a system of patronage and linking economic favour to political acquiescence, the regime maintained its control over all state institutions and large segments of the private sector.

The problem was that in almost all Arab republics, as well as in the non-Gulf monarchies of Jordan and Morocco, the leading faces of Arab liberalism (or those that adhered relatively firmly to the political legacy of the Arab liberal age) were the traditional leftist parties and an array of youth groups – the very voices that in those countries were loudest in their condemnation of privatization, economic liberalization and globalization. It was easy for the regimes to continue with their decades-old smearing of those 'liberals' as senseless, irresponsible and almost foolish forces that could not be trusted with the huge responsibility of steering a country's economy. In 2010, after President Mubarak's party had secured 93 per cent of the vote in a parliamentary election the fairness of which was viewed by most observers with acute suspicion, a collection of secular groups announced that they would form an alternative parliament; President Mubarak dismissed this laughingly by declaring, 'let them amuse themselves'. Condescension and over-confidence aside, he, like many Arab leaders in the 1990s and 2000s, believed that the leftist liberals would not manage to gain the trust of the growing Arab middle classes. The bet here was that these middle classes would see the 'leftists' as voices that belonged to an earlier age – as champions of admirable values, but not as politicians to be handed the reins of the economy. And so, after being demonized as agents of the West, many Arab liberals – at least those that were seen as serious opponents to the regime – were ridiculed as economic novices. Arab liberalism continued to be confined to its cultural components, emptied of its political definition.

Arab secular forces have inherited a succession of failures, despite promising beginnings. Modern Egypt, the state established by the Albanian adventurer Mohammed Ali in the first half of the nineteenth century, after the end of Napoleon's campaign in Egypt in 1802, was a secular project *par excellence*. Mohammed Ali and his successors (most notably his grandson Ismail, who ruled Egypt from 1863 to 1879) were determined to build a modern state, taking their inspiration not from Istanbul and the golden age of the Ottoman Empire, nor from any episode in Islamic history, but from nineteenth-century Paris, Vienna and Rome. The Mohammed Ali dynasty overhauled Egypt's educational and administrative systems, and opened up the country to waves of industrialization and modernization. Tens of thousands of Greeks, Levantines, Jews and Armenians migrated to Cairo and Alexandria, as Egypt emerged as the trading, business and cultural hub of the region. A local private sector in trading and services transformed the economy. The immense economic changes gradually gave rise to a new social stratum of well-educated Egyptians who had been trained in and exposed to Europe, or else Egyptianized immigrants, who slowly altered the country's social structure. Land ownership continued to be the decisive factor in determining wealth; but a new middle class, composed primarily of professionals, administrators and bureaucrats, was taking shape. There was vigorous entrepreneurship, openness to the world, and the beginnings of a cosmopolitan society. From the late nineteenth century to the early decades of the twentieth, Egypt witnessed a sparkling cultural scene: a revolution in Arab literature and music, and the birth of Arab theatre, cinema and journalism. This secular project set the stage for the birth of the Arab liberal age.[10]

This was not an exclusively Egyptian phenomenon. In the second half of the nineteenth century, a number of Tunisian rulers brought about similar economic, social and cultural developments,[11] although, because of Tunisia's smaller size and demographics, on a smaller scale. In roughly the same period, the largest merchant families of Casablanca and Rabat in Morocco established trading relationships with French and Spanish banks, which resulted in major modernizations of their operations and the gradual adoption of French as the main language of business in the country. In the Levant and Iraq, despite the Ottomans' assertive, and often violent, way of ruling the region, different territories began to wriggle free of their strict social code and to adopt Western clothing, systems of governance and, crucially, education.

All these changes weakened authoritarian rule and diluted the concentration of power. In 1881, Tunisia adopted a national charter that spelled out the rights and responsibilities of citizens as opposed to those of the royal family.[12] Egypt's 1923 constitution ensured universal suffrage and the equality of citizens, limited the monarchy's prerogatives and empowered the House of Representatives with major legislative and supervisory rights. New political parties began challenging the region's old ruling families – from the Mohammed Ali dynasty in Egypt to the Hashemites in the eastern Mediterranean. The emergence of an Arab middle class had its counterpart in the development of civil society: welfare associations, community development and professional advocacy agencies, feminist groups and trade unions.

Yet, despite the beginnings of a promising political system, economic progress, cosmopolitanism, and its cultural vivaciousness and glamour, the Arab liberal age failed in the two most important tests it confronted. Not a single Arab country managed to achieve real independence from its colonial masters. And the majority of Arabs remained mired in poverty and class exploitation.[13] Despite the developments in industry and infrastructure, and the major expansion in trading and openness to international markets, the region's middle classes grew at a very slow pace.[14]

What came after – Arab nationalism – also failed. Gamal Abdel-Nasser became the Arab world's hero, the symbol of Arab unity and regeneration. But his project crumbled in the face of military defeat (in the 1967 Arab–Israeli Six Day War),[15] economic stagnation and managerial incompetence. Tunisia's Habib Bourghuiba, Syria's Hafez Assad, Iraq's Saddam Hussein and Libya's Muammar Gaddafi all ended up as autocrats presiding over non-democratic and often severely oppressive regimes. And crucially, after over a century of experimentation with various modes of development, the modern Arab state continued to suffer from weak – and in some cases non-existent – institutions. The regimes attempted to consolidate their power by creating administrative structures and public sectors that controlled large parts of their countries' economies. But these entities were deprived of power, prevented from growing into pillars of a functioning political system, and intentionally retained as vehicles for asserting control over society.[16]

Even the few powerful Arab secular political parties (most notably Egypt's al-Wafd) that, at different periods of the twentieth century, had inspired millions of Arabs and were the standard-bearers of Arab political liberalism, ended up as feeble forces or mere tools in the hands of the countries' regimes. Al-Wafd (the Delegation), which came together to argue Egypt's case for independence from Britain at the Paris Peace Conference of 1919, emerged in the 1930s as the dominant political force in the country. It brought together major landowners, middle-class professionals and bureaucrats in a party that seemed to represent the essence of 'Egyptianness'. Its legendary leader, Saad Zaghloul, grew to be a symbol of integrity and steadfastness, while his house became the 'House of the Nation'. His successor, Mustafa al-Nahas Pasha, was a constitutional lawyer who exemplified respect for the constitution and did not shy away from challenging the royal palace. Al-Wafd's highly secular rhetoric and the fact that its leadership had always included prominent Christian figures cemented it as 'the party of all Egyptians' – the one party whose constituency was larger than that of any religious group (and significantly larger than the Muslim Brotherhood's in the

1930s and 1940s). And yet, by the early 1950s, that venerable party had fallen under the control of a group of big landowners who dominated its leadership and controlled its finances. The legacy of the founding fathers became mere rhetoric. Gradually it was drawn into the orbit of the increasingly despised royal palace. After overthrowing Egypt's King Farouk in 1952, Nasser found it easy to dispense with al-Wafd as a relic of the old regime. More importantly, what was left of al-Wafd's reputation was no obstacle to Nasser's emergence as the hero of independence from the British and the saviour from the palace's exploitation.

The story of the Levant's *al-Methaq al-Watani* (National Pact) was different, but it had a similar outcome. In the 1910s and 1920s, the Pact's leaders, Riad al-Solh and Bishara Khoury, played a decisive role in convincing the leading families of the Christian Maronite and Druze communities on Mount Lebanon, Beirut's Sunni Muslims and groups of other sects to come together under a united country, Lebanon. Though the newly created state was founded on a compromise between these different sects, the National Pact movement created the first non-religious, non-sectarian, secular political entity in the history of the eastern Mediterranean. For some of its leaders, the Pact ushered in the dream of an Arab secular identity transcending the religious and the sectarian. For others, it brought to an end the successive sectarian wars that had plagued the eastern Mediterranean for centuries. Irrespective of the different interpretations, the Pact's role in giving rise to the modern state of Lebanon imbued it with immense potential. The fate of the Pact itself was not of huge consequence: it was the project that mattered. Throughout the 1950s and 1960s, Lebanon emerged as a trading, banking and entertainment hub. Though accused of being overly decadent and commercialized, it embodied the prospect of a successful secular, democratic Arab state. A few decades later, however, that state was mired in a devastating sectarian war that lasted for over fifteen years and ended only with the influx of billions of dollars of Gulf (and especially Saudi) money to 'incentivize' the leaders of many of the fighting factions to lay down their arms.[17] Yet, two decades after the end of the war, Lebanon remains plagued by the same sectarianism that triggered the conflict 40 years ago. The Pact's success has proved illusory.

The destiny of another major Levantine secular political force – the al-Baath (Resurrection) party – was not so different. Al-Baath was created in 1952 in Syria by young Arab philosophers who perceived the previous decades to have been corrupt and decadent. They believed that the Arabic social and political structure needed to be overhauled by assertive, powerful leaders, who were to strive to unite the Arab world against the oppressive, colonial West. And though its political manifesto was weak and was influenced by various forms of European fascism, al-Baath's apparent promise was that, with the huge fillip it received in the 1950s, it had the potential to emerge as a unifying platform upon which a secular form of 'Arabness' could transcend the Levant's traditional sectarianism. But it did not. After half a century of experimentation, al-Baath came to be the ideology behind two of the most brutal Arab regimes in the last half-century: Saddam Hussein's in Iraq and Assad's in Syria.

Arab secularists looked back in despair. Despite an illustrious cultural heritage they had very little historical success to draw upon. They had no political models to inspire them or to present as cases to potential constituencies. Crucially, some of the most alluring fragments of their heritage had been claimed by the regimes that had marginalized and ridiculed them for decades. Now, having finally got rid of those oppressive regimes, they found themselves confronting their ideological nemesis: the Islamists, who had far more resources and a much more compelling rhetoric, especially in conservative, pious societies.

Many Arab secularists did not see their electoral defeats by the Islamists in 2011 and 2012 as mere setbacks in a free and fair democratic process. As discussed in the previous chapter, for many secularists the Islamists had 'stolen the revolutions'. The decision to join with the entrenched powers of the old regimes was based on a stark choice between letting the Islamists 'Islamize' their countries and 'saving them from Islamization'. When I asked a leading Egyptian secular politician why he and his colleagues did not just let the Muslim Brotherhood fail in power, lose the next parliamentary and presidential elections, and destroy its 'Islamist project' by itself, he replied: 'We did not have the luxury of time; the country was being lost.'

Who was losing, and what was being lost? Not only in Egypt, but across the Arab world, the secularists defined their countries' identities as they saw them and thereby imposed their own ideas of nationalism, their own interpretations of history and their own perceptions of national character on their societies. What that leading Egyptian secular politician meant was that (what he considered to be) the essence of 'Egyptianness' was being lost: his partnering with Egypt's state powers was the only way to save that kind of Egyptianness. Given the intensity and speed of the Muslim Brotherhood's attempts to take over most state institutions, and the way they excluded almost all secular forces in the country, he may have been correct. But by insisting that his definition of what Egypt meant was the only possible interpretation of the country's character, he was committing a severe kind of political and social exclusion – equal to that imposed by the Brotherhood when it was in power.

Scores of Arab secularists engaged in the same exclusion. Arab secularists were confounded when Western commentators, especially in the liberal media, attacked them as anti-democrats. Those secularists saw themselves as saving their countries' 'liberal heritage' from the Islamists' transgressions. Whereas Western liberals insisted on the inviolability of the democratic exercises that had brought the Islamists to power, Arab secularists kept referring to the Islamists' use of religious rhetoric and their deployment of money in poor communities with extremely high levels of illiteracy – tactics that, by their assessment, rendered those exercises manipulation of the true definition of political representation. They were correct that most Islamists, especially the Brotherhood in

Egypt, had exploited the poverty and piousness of large social groups in order to secure their electoral victories. But those secularists did not present an adequate alternative to the universally accepted democratic procedures.

The secularists' rationale betrayed their condescension towards large portions of their own societies. Across the Arab world, the most prominent voices justifying the secularists' dismissal of the democratic transitions that had begun in 2011 hailed from privileged backgrounds: well-educated men and women, fluent in various languages, who were equally comfortable in Arab and in Western social milieus. Their definition of their countries' identities as rich mixes of East and West, complex tapestries of various hues, and which included but transcended religion (and especially Islam), reflected the way they saw their societies. But there was a dramatic disconnect between the role played by religion in these views (and in the lives of those secularists), and the place that it actually occupied in the lives of most Arabs. In Egypt and Tunisia, the secularists accused the Muslim Brotherhood and Annahda of violating the notion of a multifaceted, liberal Egyptianness and Tunisianness that, for centuries, had absorbed contributions from scores of cultures. But in the same way, their narrow definition of their countries' identities violated the way in which large sections of their own societies perceived the role of Islam in their lives.

The partnering with the old, powerful institutions of state also placed Arab liberalism once again in the hands of the state. Many Arab secularists found that these institutions were their true allies against the Islamists. But the objectives of those secularists were markedly different from those of the institutions. Whereas the secularists in the opposition wanted to get rid of the Islamists, so as to set their countries on a transition course towards 'liberalism', the state institutions and the power groups that had benefited from the old regimes wanted to return to the political dynamics that had existed before the 2011 uprisings. Many of these state institutions were happy to use the 'liberalism' rhetoric in their efforts to stem the rise of the Islamists.

The security establishments in different Arab countries were particularly concerned by the state fragmentation that the uprisings unleashed. Abdel-Fattah al-Sisi, Egypt's former defence minister and later president, repeatedly emphasized that if the Muslim Brotherhood had continued to rule Egypt, its project and the social polarization it triggered would have dragged the country into the kind of quagmire found in Syria or Yemen. Though they refrained from engaging publicly in politics, several key Tunisian defence officials regarded the outcome of a number of the uprisings (for example in Libya) as serious threats to Tunisia's national security – threats that needed to be quickly contained. The powerful institutions that had controlled most Arab republics for the six decades prior to 2011 attributed the uprisings to a multitude of factors: mistakes made by the ageing presidents of those states, lack of reform (especially economic) over the preceding two decades, the 'inheritance projects' (passing the mantle from a president to his son or stepson), deteriorating socioeconomic conditions, and, for some, foreign conspiracies against their states. Irrespective of the reasons, though, these institutions were determined not to let the forces of disorder undermine their states. For them, this was not just their duty, but their *raison d'être*.

These institutions also presented themselves as saviours from the disastrous economic situations that their countries were experiencing. Through support from Gulf countries, the Egyptian armed forces were able to spearhead at least three major infrastructure projects with huge employment and developmental potential. The Egyptian pound was stabilized, thereby stemming inflation. The notion of having a strong state in control of the political situation encouraged many foreign investors to look again at Egypt. In Tunisia, the technocratic government that replaced Annahda in 2012 and which relied on the Ben-Ali era civil service, supported by various interest groups from that era, tried to effect some economic reforms particularly in public spending. The key point here was not the improvement in economic management, but the stark contrast that existed between the Islamists' unpreparedness to assume power – alongside the impression they gave as

115

being overwhelmed by the gravity of the responsibilities they assumed – and the old state institutions' readiness to confront those challenges.

Crucially, these state institutions deployed the major religious organizations that they had controlled for decades in order to demonize the political Islamists. Dozens of sheikhs opposed the politicization of Islam – its 'deplorable usage by the Brotherhood and its like' – and argued for lenient interpretations of *deen wa dawla* (religion and state). The state institutions did not ignore the questions of identity and the 'threat' that Islamism posed to their countries' social fabric; but, unlike the secularists in opposition (whose rhetoric continued to repeat these mantras), they placed the emphasis on the real concerns of the largest segments of their people: security, economics and the stability of society. While the secularist thinkers and politicians were consumed with nebulous talk about identity and frames of reference, the state institutions and the entrenched power centres presented themselves as the real (and sole) alternative to the Islamists' project.

Those claiming to represent Arab liberalism again looked back in despair. A key objective of the transition processes ushered in by the Arab uprisings was to gradually and peacefully transform these countries from top-down political and economic nexuses controlled by a small set of power centres into liberal democracies. Now, with a heavy heritage of successive failures and with limited opportunity to confront the Islamists on their own, large sections of the selfsame Arab secularists who had contributed to these uprisings brought the transition to a halt.

Leading Arab secularists believed that the 'Islamization project' necessitated a firm stand, a union between all secularist forces – those that were in opposition before 2011 (and during the Islamists' time in power) and the state institutions and power groups that had controlled the countries for decades. That firm stand would disrupt the democratic transitions that started after 2011. But many believed that the disruption would be temporary and would not derail the prospects for democracy in their countries. For many Egyptians, the rationale rested on the premise that the powerful institutions had learnt the lessons of the 2011 uprisings: they would no longer tolerate the immense concentration of power that was seen in the 1990s and 2000s; and never again would an Egyptian president dream of passing on the presidency to his son. These institutions would decisively put an end to the blurring between power and wealth that had afflicted decision-making in the last decade of President Mubarak's reign.

A similar mindset existed in Tunisia. For many secularists, partnering with some of the richest families in the country and with groups that had close links to the Ben-Ali regime was essential if Annahda was to be forced to hand over power – and if ultimately it was to be beaten in elections. The expectation, however, was that those rich power centres and groups would now respect the rule of law: Tunisia, in this view, should never return to the shocking corruption of the decade before 2011.

In Morocco, the PJD's success in the 2011 election and its two spells in government from 2012 to 2015 have convinced many secular parties that the country's political transition needs to continue along the same route that King Mohammed VI had laid down in the early 2000s. The PJD's coming to power and the dynamism that the 20 February Movement has prompted 'should not become the milestones by which Morocco defined its move towards democracy'. And so, according to that view, the palace's prerogatives in politics should not only be sustained, but also protected.

Demographics were also supposed to prevent a return to authoritarianism. Many notable secularists in the Egyptian opposition, or in government in Morocco and Tunisia, have claimed that this 'new generation (the tens of millions of Arabs in their teens and twenties and thirties) is different'. Because of its exposure to the world, the communication technology it is adept at using, and the fact that this generation has already demonstrated its willingness to rebel against oppressive powers, this huge population segment would act as a guarantee that the old establishments would not return to the totalitarianism of the last six decades of Arab history.

This is a risky wager. By consenting to circumvent the political transitions that began in 2011, the secularists agreed (and set a precedent) that any political player could ignore the traditional and generally accepted rules of democracy whenever it considered those rules to be dangerous, or for reasons that it deemed strategic. Those disgruntled Annahda members who felt the party had been unfairly compelled to hand over the reins of government despite its 2011 electoral success, could now organize mass demonstrations against the secular party that won the 2014 election. Brotherhood members resolutely reject the procedures that enabled their removal from power. Dispensing with democratic rules leaves society vulnerable to arbitrariness and various parties' interpretations of what constitutes transgressions on identity or threats to national security.

Relying on demographics could also prove futile. Large sections of young secular activists, who are repelled by both the Islamists and the 'secular elders who sold out', are prevalent in small political parties, universities and scores of civil society organizations. But they have limited mobilization capabilities, access to financing or media support to make them strong. They have performed badly in all the elections in Egypt, Tunisia and Morocco. It is difficult to believe that they will transcend their weakness any time soon.

Some feel very antagonistic. Today we see masses of young secularists and Islamists who are grievously upset at the failure of the 2011 uprisings. Many of them believe that peaceful means are ineffective; and some are increasingly resigned to the idea of using violence to effect a transformative change. But that change, if it happens, would be far from the smooth and gradual one to which the elderly secularists who partnered with their states' old powers aspire.

The revolutionary wave that began in 2011 did not empower the young liberals who triggered it. The most prominent Arab secularists ended up in the same place as they were before 2011: marginalized or co-opted by their countries' powerful regimes. The secularists' fear of the Islamists made many of them abandon some of the most valuable principles they had long held sacred. As with the Islamists, the years since 2011 have led many Arab secular groups into a political wilderness. But the secularists were not the sole group to see immense peril in the rise of the Islamists. The next chapter discusses how several religious minorities in the Arab world perceived and responded to the Islamists' accession to power.

CHAPTER SIX

The Minorities' Fears

On 12 February 2015, the Egyptian Muslim Brotherhood commemorated the anniversary of the assassination in 1949 of its founder, Hassan al-Banna. The group's statement indicated that that act was a key factor in leading Sayyed Qutb to join the group. For decades, the Brotherhood had sought to distance itself from the legacy of the godfather of Salafist jihadism. In his book *Preachers, Not Judges*, the Brotherhood's second General Guide, the judge Hassan al-Hudaybi, dedicated many pages to analysing the thinking and work of Sayyed Qutb without once mentioning his name. Throughout the late 1990s and 2000s, almost all the key leaders in the Guidance Bureau were meticulous in distancing the group from Qutb, without disowning him outright. At the time, Qutb's legacy was at odds with the change in the Brotherhood's rhetoric.

The February 2015 shift in position regarding Qutb is not an isolated occurrence. A few weeks earlier, the Brotherhood had uploaded a statement onto its website in which it announced that it was beginning a 'new phase' that 'would evoke the meaning of jihad', where the group's members would 'ask for martyrdom'. The Brotherhood was gradually altering the basis of its fight against the Egyptian regime from a struggle over legitimacy to a battle between Muslims and those fighting Islam.

Many observers wondered whether this change represented a real departure in the group's thinking towards explicit adoption of armed confrontation, or a mere heightening of the tone in an already acute conflict. The Egyptian regime highlighted the new rhetoric as evidence of the group's 'terror'. But in other circles these statements and new rhetoric were carefully pondered and assessed: in Egyptian (and Arab) Christian communities.

The Brotherhood was different from the Salafist jihadist groups that in recent years have terrorized many religious minorities in the eastern Mediterranean. The new tone confirmed the fears of large sections within these communities that the Islamists – irrespective of the distinctions drawn between mainstream groups and militant ones, and between political Islamists and Salafists (and the variations under this capacious umbrella) – may all be hostile. Millions of Christians who regarded the rise of the Islamists with trepidation homed in on the kind of statements issued by the Brotherhood and others, arguing that they represented the Islamists' real thinking. According to this view, the Islamists' apparent change throughout the 1990s and 2000s, and their rhetoric at that time, were just façades to deceive large constituencies into voting for them; at heart, their project has always been to Islamize their societies, irrespective of the means. A UK-based Egyptian Orthodox man in his late forties explained that 'nothing has changed; it is the same old exclusion of others, a narrow view of our country, that makes them willing to attack and destroy, to impose their beliefs on us'.

Fears are shaped by perceptions. As the largest Islamist groups were driven out of power, two interpretations have become increasingly cemented. On the one side, millions of Islamists see Arab religious minorities as being an integral part of the forces that deprived them of what they believed was their right to rule. Scores of Muslim Brotherhood members have repeatedly remarked on the presence of Pope Tawadrous, the patriarch of Egypt's Christian Orthodox Church, in the group surrounding Abdel-Fattah al-Sisi in July 2013 when he announced the removal of Mohammed Morsi, claiming it to prove that large groups of

Christians had never accepted their rule and had worked to bring it to a quick and humbling end. On the other side, broad sections of Arab minorities, especially Christians, felt that the Islamists' rise to power in their countries was the final straw in the gradual but clear marginalization and exclusion they had endured since the end of the Arab liberal age in the 1950s.

Arab Christians remembered the prominent position they had held in Arab politics, economics, culture and art from the second half of the nineteenth century until the mid-twentieth. At that time most of the urban centres of North Africa and the eastern Mediterranean had a cosmopolitan feel to them, marked by the existence of large communities of Christians, Jews and other minorities, and their active involvement in social life. Christian Arabs, such as Bishara Takla, George Abbayad and Yacoub Artine, led the creation of modern Arab journalism, theatre and secular education.[1] The first press put to commercial use in the region was operated by a group of Lebanese Christian Maronites in the early nineteenth century. Christian and Jewish families, such as the Siddnaouis, the Qattawis and the Shamouns, pioneered modern retail, banking and shipping in the region.[2] Religious minorities also held prominent political positions: Egypt's first prime minister with real executive authority was an Egyptianized Christian Armenian, Nubar Pasha.[3] In the period until the end of the Arab liberal age, several Egyptian and Levantine Christians held the post of prime minister or were ministers with important dossiers.

All of this seeped into the way in which Arab religious minorities, and especially Arab Christians, perceived their identity. The committee that drafted Egypt's 1922 constitution was composed of Muslims, Christians and Jews. It was an Egyptian Christian who argued against allocating quotas in parliament to religious minorities, saying 'they are Egyptians like all others'. In Iraq, Towfik al-Swaidi, one of the country's leading intellectuals in the 1920s and later its foreign minister (educated at the Hebraic Alliance Israélite Universelle school in Baghdad), argued that the state does not have a specific religion. In Morocco, a country ruled (then and now) by a family whose legitimacy rests on its descent from the Prophet Mohammed, Jews have played a prominent role in almost all aspects of cultural and economic life. Religious minorities increasingly saw themselves as part of the burgeoning national identities of that age.[4]

By the end of the 1930s and early 1940s, the notion that modern Arab states would quickly transcend their Islamic heritage and move towards secularism seemed plausible. Many were beginning to think of themselves as Iraqis rather than Sunnis or Shiis; as Syrians rather than Sunnis or Alawites; and as Lebanese rather than just Maronites or Druze. No political system in the region at the time evolved into a fully functioning liberal democracy, but in Egypt and Iraq new constitutional monarchies did start to take shape: the ruling families lost much of their influence and elected politicians began to hold serious sway over decision-making. The dilution in the power of the ruling families meant that political authority in the Arab world began to be separated from religious legitimacy, for centuries the basis upon which almost all Arab ruling families had relied. And the fact that the replacement for religious legitimacy appeared to be (albeit nascent) forms of liberal democracy meant that the emerging foundation for legitimizing power was the formal consent of citizens to be ruled on the basis of genuine representation: free elections. This was a new phenomenon in the Arab world. Allegiance to the ruler and loyalty to the country were being freed from any religious threads. The notion of citizenship rendered citizens equal, irrespective of religion – in theory, at least. For many observers, the Arab world was on the path that Europe had trodden a few centuries earlier, when it restricted the authority of its ruling dynasties and freed the state from the Church's power to grant or withhold legitimacy. The leading liberal thinker and literary critic Taha Hussein believed that many traditionally Islamic societies – Egypt's and those of the eastern Mediterranean being the prime examples – should look to the West, and mainly Europe, as a social model. Here he was not only referring to importing modern education, administration and social structures; more importantly, Hussein and scores of other Arab intellectuals in the 1930s and 1940s advocated limiting the scope that religion played in social life. Hussein hardly ever attacked Islam; he believed, however, that religion is a fluid concept, subject to different and changing interpretations according to the prevailing norms of each age; and so, while it could be the frame of reference of any society, it should not be the framework through which any modern society is ruled. In his view, societies need political systems that transcend diverse interpretations and subjective analyses. He did not spell it out, but one can see how liberal democracy and its foundational aspects of checks and balances, the rule of law and the sanctity of individualism were close to his mind when he wrote his famous book *The Future of Arab Culture*.[5] His ideas triggered a backlash from the religious establishment in Egypt, Tunisia, Morocco and the eastern Mediterranean. But they were also celebrated by large sections of Arab intelligentsia because they were congruent with the changes that Arab societies were experiencing in the 1930s and 1940s. At the time, cosmopolitanism, tolerance and liberal political systems were starting to be taken for granted. It seemed that the future of Arab culture, as Taha Hussein advocated, lay across the Mediterranean, in Europe's experience with modernity. The political systems that were then being shaped were the first in the Arab world in around 1,300 years – in fact, since Islam became the basis of ruling the Arabian Peninsula, the eastern Mediterranean, Iraq, Egypt and North Africa – to be founded not on Islam, but on either constitutional monarchies or parliamentary democracies. Arabness was gradually being detached from Islamism. And for some, it was increasingly associated with Mediterraneanism.

Arab religious minorities celebrated this Arabness. It was no surprise that some of the leading thinkers behind the idea of Arab nationalism were Christians (see chapter 5), especially from the eastern Mediterranean. They saw their region emerging from the cloak of sectarianism and, they reckoned, poised to embrace new identities in which Arab religious minorities would have equal rights to Muslims. The more Arabness got detached from Islam, the more non-Muslim Arabs felt equal in their own countries.

The crumbling of the Arab liberal age did not put an immediate end to that secular Arabness. In its formative years in the 1950s, Arab nationalism anchored its legitimacy in the idea that Arab political unity, mutual history, 'shared destiny' and, of course, the language and culture of the 'Arab nation' formed the overarching identity for all Arabs, Muslims, Christians and others. Theoretically, this idea placed all Arabs on an equal footing, irrespective of religion. Religion had no role in bestowing legitimacy, in defining the state, or in a regime's positioning either internally (before its people) or externally (in its relations with others). It was no coincidence that Arab nationalists enjoyed immense appeal within non-Muslim Arab communities, most notably in the eastern Mediterranean, which for centuries had been plagued by sectarian violence.

The experience of Nasser was particularly promising. The deep affection that tens of millions of Arabs felt towards the man, coupled with his consistent insistence that his project centred on Arabness with no religious connotations, indicated that this secular Arabness could achieve wide consensus in the Arab world. The difference between Nasser and Arab liberalism was that Nasser managed to come to represent millions of middle-class and poor Arabs; unlike Arab liberalism, the appeal of his project transcended the well-educated, the intelligentsia and those who had extensive exposure to the West. The legitimacy of Nasser's leadership, and his positioning as the 'hero of Arab nationalism', cemented the idea that a majority of Arabs were willing to be governed by a secular political system.

But, as we have already seen, Arab nationalism quickly descended into militarist, authoritarian and totalitarian states. This indirectly weakened secularism. Arab liberalism's glimmers of liberal democracy were quenched. Arab states were taken off the route of pluralism, rule of law, and checks and balances. Gradually, the secularism of the Arab nationalists became a tool to confront the Islamists. This necessitated close relationships with the religious minorities in their countries. Nasser had a particularly close and warm relationship with the head of the Egyptian Church in the 1960s, Patriarch Kirollos VI. Throughout his three decades in power, Hafez Assad retained cordial relationships with the leaders of Syria's Shii, Druze and Christian communities, in addition, of course, to those of his own sect, the Alawites. Bourghuiba positioned himself as a defender of Tunisia's tiny Jewish community. As Arab countries fell into dictatorships, the notion of citizenry began to fade. Arab states – certainly Arab republics – based their moral authority on their efforts in the struggle against enemies, whether external (colonialism, the West, Israel, etc.) or internal (invariably the Islamists); or on building hero cults around their leaders. This proved unsustainable. By the 1980s and 1990s, colonialism had disappeared; almost all Arab states had become clients of the West, especially the United States; and for most Arab countries the wars with Israel were a relic of a bygone era. Economic difficulties prevented all non-oil-exporting Arab states from assuming the role of provider; and so even the image of the patriarchal giver crumbled. And it became impossible to maintain any semblance of heroism. Despite the billions of words and images that their state media devoted to them, no Arab leader – whether Assad, Gaddafi, Mubarak, Ben Ali or Ali Abdallah Saleh – could seriously position himself as a hero. The ideal notion of citizenry that had begun in the heyday of Arab liberalism was gone; and the consensus offered by masses of Arabs to legendary Arab nationalists such as Nasser had been abused. Arab nationalism itself became a relic of a bygone era. By the 1990s and 2000s, the concept of Egyptianness, Iraqiness, Syrianness, Libyanness and Tunisianness had been acutely weakened and emptied. And as national identities receded, so religious ones began to resurface.

The religious identities were strengthened by a change in the Arab world's cultural orientation. All Arab nationalist regimes adopted assertive and at times highly pugnacious stances towards the West (often with good reason). These regimes' militarism and the gradual corrosion of their legitimacy meant that they always needed an external enemy and a conspiracy to blame. In many cases there were indeed external conspiracies against these countries; but more often than not, the regimes used their media arms to expound the idea that 'we are targeted', that the 'West does not want us to develop'. So it was not surprising that almost all the states that had experienced the cultural openness and vitality of the first half of the twentieth century gradually dispensed with the idea of looking to the West, and especially to Europe, for inspiration. As a consequence, most Arab societies – especially in Egypt and the eastern Mediterranean, for centuries the ones that produced the bulk of Arab literature and art – started to view the West with suspicion and often aversion. The Arab liberal age's notion that Arab societies' future lay across the Mediterranean, and that the future of Arab culture was in a seamless flow between Arabness and Mediterraneanism, disappeared. Arab societies now looked inwards. The factors that fed openness and liberal thinking were severely weakened.

The 1970s' oil boom exacerbated the disconnect between the Arab world and the West, and especially Europe.[6] The colossal windfalls that had accrued to the Gulf triggered waves of migration from North Africa and the eastern Mediterranean to Saudi Arabia, Kuwait, the Emirates and Qatar. The Arab world's cultural antennae shifted from Paris, London, Rome and Vienna towards Riyadh, Kuwait and Abu Dhabi, at a time when these places were still highly conservative societies with extremely limited global exposure and with a cultural heritage unenriched by any significant worldly interaction. The expanding middle classes of Cairo, Alexandria, Amman, Damascus, Beirut, Tunis and Baghdad were slowly being oriented towards the Arabian Peninsula, and consistently exposed to austere forms of Islam and homogeneous interpretations of what Arabness means – interpretations that merged Arabness with Islamism, and that hardly saw the northern shores of the Mediterranean as a cultural model to be admired, let alone borrowed from.

This significantly helped the Arab Islamist movements. It also brought about a gradual but unmistakable change in the look and feel of Arab societies. In the period from the 1950s to the 1970s, the vast majority of

Arab Jews left their countries. Throughout the 1970s and 1980s, most Arab societies (with the notable example of then acutely secular Tunisia) witnessed an exponential increase in the number of mosques built, Islamic books printed and women wearing the headscarf. Even language changed: *assalamu aleikom* (Islam's greeting of 'peace be upon you') started to replace traditional Arabic greetings.

Religion was gradually, but decisively, becoming the most conspicuous social element in most Arab societies, including in those that just a few decades earlier had been on the path towards westernization. The loss of cosmopolitanism, the change in cultural orientation towards the most conservative parts of the Arab world, the rise of Islamist groups across the region, and the shift towards Islamist social features hammered the final nails into the old concept of equal citizenry regardless of faith. Islamism became a conspicuous and highly powerful current in almost all Arab societies. The idea of an Arabness detached from Islamism seemed to have been buried.[7]

In the late nineteenth century, Evelyn Baring (Later Lord Cromer), the British consul-general in (and effective ruler of) Egypt, is rumoured to have commented that it was extremely difficult to differentiate between Muslim and Christian Egyptians. Almost a century later, it was much easier to do so. Starting with the late 1970s, and throughout the following two decades, there was a noticeable withdrawal of Egyptian Christians from the civil service, administrative bureaucracies and the media. Their percentage share of typically middle-class jobs (e.g. lawyers, doctors and teachers) decreased. The same phenomenon took place, at different speeds, across most Arab societies that had significant religious minorities. Reliable studies that provide measurable benchmarks are difficult to come by, but as is indicated by discussions with several community leaders in various Arab countries and in diasporas in Europe, the presence of minorities (and especially Christians) in sectors such as teaching, law, banking, medicine and higher education has fallen in the last three or four decades by over 30 per cent. Demographics has undoubtedly played a role: in all these countries, Muslims typically have more children than Christians; but the crucial factor has been a withdrawal from the public sphere and a shift towards the Christian communities: tens of thousands of small and medium-sized companies owned by Christians, primarily employing Christians, and targeting other Christian companies and clientele. Minorities across the Arab world have always been overly and disproportionately represented in high-income jobs, such as trading and banking. But in the decades since the beginning of the 1980s this representation evolved into quasi-economic fortifications that had an unmistakably sectarian feel.

A similar phenomenon was slowly taking place in many Arab universities. As student unions and *Ousar* (student families) were increasingly dominated by mainstream Islamist groups, gatherings of Christian students began to appear, and over the years formed noticeable and detached social circles. *Madares al-Ahaad* (Sunday schools) in Egypt, Sudan, Syria and Iraq, at one time small schools focusing on teaching the New Testament and Christian history, evolved in the 1980s and 1990s into major educational centres teaching different disciplines and providing various sports and counselling facilities. Also, in different parts of the Arab world, Christian neighbourhoods, and often villages, began to appear. From their early formative years up to college, hundreds of thousands of young Arab Christians were socializing in exclusively Christian milieus.

Leadership of the Arab religious minorities was also changing. In the heyday of Arab liberalism, the major involvement of religious minorities in society's political, economic and cultural life gave rise to the type of leader who transcended religious affiliation and emerged as a national figure. The National Pact's Bishara Khoury (chapter 5) was the most conspicuous example, but it was not limited to Lebanon (which only came into existence as a compromise between its society's largest sects). The Egyptian politician Makram Ebeid, who for decades was one of the most prominent figures in Egyptian politics and the orchestrator of the country's then immensely powerful party, al-Wafd, was also a notable essayist and commentator on a wide array of issues, including Islamic matters. The Jewish banker and industrialist Youssef Cattaui was a leading force in the transformation of the Egyptian irrigation system, and one of the country's largest patrons of the arts. The Druze leader Sultan al-Attrach, who had fought the French occupation of Syria and Lebanon in the 1920s, repeatedly emphasized that he represented the whole of Syria, rather than the Druze community or the Mount of the Druze region. His family gave the Arab world a number of its leading singers and actors. A Syrian Christian prime minister, Fares Khoury, was instrumental in the creation of Syria's first law school as well as its music conservatoire. Those and other leaders represented the secular, nationalist identities of their countries. Their services went beyond their communities, and in that way they transcended sectarianism and cemented their communities' ties to society at large.

But as these religious communities withdrew in the face of the encroaching Islamism, the leaders who emerged from the late 1970s onwards were compelled to respond to the new social environments. Egypt's Pope Shenouda III (patriarch of the See of St Mark of Alexandria from 1970 to 2012) oversaw a major expansion in the social service network serving Egyptian Orthodox Christians. Iraq's Mar Raphael Bidaweed, perhaps because of his own decades of experience as a 'spiritual refugee' outside Iraq, believed that the future of the country's Chaldaean Christian community lay in strengthening its relationship with other Christian communities in the eastern Mediterranean, and especially with the Maronites in Lebanon.[8]

The rhetoric was also changing. There was a clear distinction now between minorities (especially Christians) and the rest of society. In Egypt, the term *shaab al-kaneesa* (the people of the Church) became ubiquitous in most leading Christian publications, including those sponsored by the Church. In Lebanon, the term *al-massiheya* (the Christians) became not just a religious designation, but signified a return to the days that preceded the creation of the country, when Christians constituted a social bloc with its own interests that were separate from society at large.

The Lebanese civil war strengthened that trend. The conflict pitted the country's various sects against each other, with episodes of horrifying violence between communities of the same faith. But the primary conflict was between Muslims and Christians. Some scenes carried dangerous emotional connotations. Thousands of Christians were killed amidst accusations that they were 'infidels'. At the same time, images of Christian militias rampaging through Muslim camps while carrying pictures of the Virgin Mary were imprinted on the minds of tens of millions of Muslims. 'Killing by identity' (one of the most horrendous episodes of the Lebanese civil war) traumatized many Muslim and Christian families and severed relationships between communities that had lived as neighbours for centuries.

The war devastated Lebanon, but its impact resonated throughout the Arab world. The country that in the 1950s and 1960s had appeared to be an oasis of tolerance and cosmopolitanism (the Orient's Switzerland, as many Arabs affectionately called Lebanon) became the theatre of what seemed to be an unending series of bloody massacres, perpetrated primarily by people of the same nationality, on the basis of sectarian identities – and sectarian hatred. The lesson for many Arab religious minority communities was that seemingly civil and tolerant Arab societies could descend into barbarity; that national identities could crumble in the face of sectarianism; and that centuries-old social fabrics could be torn to shreds.

The Iraq war was another blow. Almost immediately after the US's invasion of the country in 2003, the chaos, upheaval and political struggle resulted in a highly sectarian divide, primarily between Sunni and Shii Muslims. The country attracted swathes of Salafist jihadists who poured in, initially to fight the foreign occupying troops and later to prevent 'the seat of the Abbasid caliph' (Baghdad) from 'falling to Shiism'. The Iraqi economy was in tatters long before the invasion. The various sanctions that the country suffered since the end of its occupation of Kuwait in 1991 and up to the 2003 invasion had devastated almost all economic sectors, including oil. Over 80 per cent of all Iraqi

Christians left the country from the late 1990s to the late 2000s, with a dramatic increase from 2004 to 2008.[9] That a country of Iraq's size could lose the vast majority of its Christians in a single decade came as a shock to all religious minorities across the region. This huge wave of emigration entailed harrowing drama: extended families of doctors, lawyers, teachers, bureaucrats, merchants and other members of the country's once colossal middle class became refugees in ghettos in London, Stockholm and Oslo, rebuilding lives that had been totally shattered. And as the years went by, and as Iraq descended into more sectarianism and violence, most of them lost all hope of returning to their country. The lesson that many observers in the region drew was not dissimilar from that of Lebanon: even old and entrenched religious minority communities in big Arab countries could suffer extreme political and social circumstances.

Amidst all of this, the relationship between these communities and the state changed. The Egyptian Church and the community's leaders were to support the Mubarak regime in elections against political Islam in return for the regime's protection from the rising tide of political Islam. This bargain was more of an understanding than an actual alliance, for the regime hardly needed the Church's support and was capable of imposing its will alone, as well as dictating the electoral results it sought. The regime's dealings with political Islam were also a function of the former's objectives, with little regard to the wants and desires of the Church or of prominent Christian leaders. Yet, that subtle bargain between the leaders of the Egyptian Christian community and the state remained a key feature of Egyptian politics for at least the last two decades of President Mubarak's reign. The same sort of relationship (or subtle understanding) existed between the Moroccan monarchy and the country's Jews; between the Syrian Baathist regime and the country's minority sects; and between the Saddam Hussein administration and Iraq's Christians and other religious minorities. This kind of relationship was the exact opposite of equal citizenry, which flourished for a short period during the Arab liberal age. And the longer that kind of relationship persisted, the more sectarian Arab societies became, and the more detached Arab religious minorities grew.

A deep sense of loss drove religious and community leaders to accept this kind of relationship with their countries' regimes. For most of those leaders, allying themselves with the regime and withdrawing from society was an insurance policy against what they saw coming. Few of them envisaged an uprising that would topple the governing body in their country and usher in the Islamists. But almost all of them realized that those circumstances that had made the Arab liberal age possible were no longer to be found in the Arab world. Cosmopolitanism, openness to the world, tolerance, progressive educational systems, and the vibrant cultural and artistic environments had all been weakened and in many cases totally obliterated. As Islamism continued its social ascent in the 1980s and 1990s, and after the wars and migrations that devastated many Arab minority communities, those leaders looked on the Arab liberal age as a golden period that would not return. They reconciled themselves to the idea that the social presence and influence that religious minority communities had once enjoyed were lost forever. Thus, accepting a relationship with the regimes was hardly an endorsement of those regimes; and nor was it a stance against political Islam. It was a damning indictment of the Arab experience of the previous half-century.

Younger generations, however, saw things differently. Just as Lebanon was the theatre for the most devastating episode of sectarianism in the Arab world in the last hundred years, so the country also witnessed the birth of a new current that sought to transcend that sectarianism. The Valentine's Day 2005 assassination of Rafik Hariri,[10] the most powerful and charismatic leader in Lebanon in the 1990s and 2000s, brought to the forefront a shift that many observers had failed to detect: the fact that Lebanon's two decades of civil and sectarian war had created a thirst for secular nationalism among its predominantly young population. The 'two lost decades', 'the years of grief', and the 'smell of blood and the sight of tears'[11] served as a case study in how sectarianism and the loss of a unifying nationalism could drag one of the Arab world's most culturally diverse, rich, refined and well-educated societies into a suicidal spiral. When the Christian journalist and politician Jibran Tueini took to a podium in Beirut's Martyrs' Square in March 2005 and movingly stated that 'In the name of God, we, Muslims and Christians, pledge that united we shall remain to the end of time to better defend our Lebanon', he seemed to be speaking to, and on behalf of, a new force that was determined to save Lebanon from the religious-identity politics that had ruined it. Tueini's words challenged the notion that the circumstances that had allowed religious minority communities to integrate and prosper and succeed in taking leading roles in society had been totally lost; and that Arab religious minorities were compelled to look at their societies through a sectarian lens to protect themselves from a wave of Islamism that, irrespective of its components, could crush them. Samir Kassir, scion of an old Lebanese Christian family and one of Tueini's friends and comrades in the struggle against sectarianism, argued that the Arab liberal age happened not because of openness to the world, the cosmopolitanism of societies, or the vibrant cultural scene: these were consequences, not causes. Rather, the foundational basis was democracy. By that way of thinking, a return to genuine representation, respect for the law and (crucially) equal citizenry irrespective of religious and sectarian affiliation would put the Arab world (or parts of it) back on the road to political and social liberalism.[12]

The vast majority of Tueini's and Qaseer's followers, the millions who repeatedly filled Martyrs' Square in Beirut in 2005 and 2006, did not have a clear understanding of the history of how the Arab liberal age had come into being, why it ended, and the arguments for how it could return. For them, their movement was against the merging of religion and politics; against any special political role for religious institutions.[13] For the millions of Christians and other religious minorities, this movement was against siding with old, powerful regimes against any political force, Islamist or otherwise. It was the minorities asserting their desire for equal citizenship, not protection. This view was hardly friendly to political Islam: the main logic was that a functioning democracy would either expose political Islam as an extremist movement or would compel it towards becoming an ordinary political player – the religious affiliation of which would be merely a cultural frame of reference, not a doctrine to be imposed on society.

The spark that was ignited in Lebanon was quickly extinguished.[14] But the idea survived. The secularists who had triggered the Arab uprisings were particularly opposed to that subtle relationship between religious minorities and entrenched regimes. The various forces that led the first waves of Egypt's January 2011 uprising maintained that their 'revolution was Egyptian', revolving around a secular understanding of 'Egyptianness', detached from any religious subtexts. This was intended mainly to distinguish their act from the Muslim Brotherhood's political activism; but it also ensured that the Christian groups within the 'revolutionary forces' were independent of the Church and the leading Christian forces in the country. George Ishak and Emad Gad, two of the most prominent Christian faces in Tahrir Square in 2011, repeatedly distanced themselves and their fellow Christian demonstrators from any religious institution. For them, the term 'Christian revolutionaries' was a misnomer: they were 'Egyptian revolutionaries'; 'their religious faith was a personal matter'; 'the revolution was by Egyptians, for Egypt, and against a regime whose suppression and mismanagement did not differentiate between Egyptians, Muslims and Christians'. Many in Tahrir Square dismissed the term *shaab al-kaneesa* (the people of the Church) as a relic of 'the old regime'; some even refused to sit down with leading figures in the Egyptian Church who felt they could offer the firebrand youths advice and guidance. As was the case in Lebanon, those revolutionary Christians wanted a complete overhaul of how their communities were represented and how they dealt with the state.

The rise of the political Islamists between 2011 and 2013 punctured that idea, but did not crush it. As the Islamists took control of the parliaments and presidencies of different Arab countries, it became clear that Arab politics was far from witnessing a separation of religion and state. Yet, many of the young people from religious minorities who had participated in the uprisings stuck with the notion that political Islam had changed. Some in Egypt even joined various committees established by the Muslim Brotherhood's Freedom and Justice Party. Without articulating it, they were subscribing to the view that genuine political representation would compel the Islamists to behave like secular political movements. There was also a sense of camaraderie. Many of those Christian youths considered the Islamists, and especially the young Islamists, their partners in 'their revolutions'. They saw themselves, together, as part of a generational revolution against the old powers that had controlled their countries for decades. This thinking was strengthened as the revolutionary groups – secularists and Islamists – entered into various confrontations in 2011 and 2012 with the powers of the old regimes. After a particularly bloody clash in Mohammed Mahmoud Street near Tahrir Square in Cairo, several youth groups made a point of putting the names of their dead, both Christian and Muslim, next to each other under the banner 'the martyrs of the revolution'.

That perception was reinforced the rapid emergence of the Salafists as a force to be reckoned with. The Salafists, with their highly conservative rhetoric, their insistence on imposing Sharia and their austereness made groups such as the Muslim Brotherhood, Annahda and the PJD seem not only moderate, but (more importantly) closer to how the secularists defined their countries and their identities. The Salafists were a threat: they blatantly differentiated between sections of society on the basis of faith; they wanted to 'purify economies from sin'; and they viewed their societies through a religious prism. The political Islamists, in contrast, were miles ahead in terms of the evolution of their religious views. There was also an element of familiarity. In Egypt, Tunisia and Morocco, just as in Lebanon, tens of thousands of secular and non-Muslim youths had come to know members of the Muslim Brotherhood, Annahda or the PJD well: they were people with whom they had talked and debated; they were known entities, unlike the Salafists, who seemed entirely alien, coming as they did from isolated groups that had hardly any presence in domestic political activism. And so, for those activists from religious minorities, supporting the political Islamists in the face of the old regimes was the correct and principled choice. For them, it was much better than either of the alternatives: the return of the old regimes or the ascent of the Salafists. As the Christian host of an Arab radio show put it to me: 'Imagine what the region would be like if the millions of Islamists voted for the Salafists.'

For a period, the minorities seemed to emerge as kingmakers. The Druze have always wielded immense influence over Lebanon's convoluted politics, totally disproportionate to their demographic representation.[15] Annahda strove to secure the blessing of leading figures in Tunisia's Jewish community. In Egypt, throughout 2011 and early 2012, all political forces bar the Salafists sought to have excellent relationships with the Church. The notion of the Church as the spiritual guide of Egyptian Christians was quickly replaced by rhetoric that emphasized the Church as a key pillar of the Egyptian state and society. Some leading journalists in both the secularist and the Islamist camps argued that it represented the 'essence of Egyptianness'. In the protracted discussions over the country's 2012 constitution, many stressed that any concern expressed by the Church over a clause in the constitution was sufficient reason to drop that clause.

The confrontation between secularism and Islamism compelled minority communities to take sides. The polarization witnessed by Egypt in 2012 and 2013, the Libyan civil war, the hijacking of the Syrian uprising by Salafist jihadists – all this convinced many influential institutions and leaders of large minority groups that the transformation in the Arab world since 2011 had brought nothing but chaos and violence that had not only plunged the region into disorder, but which also posed an existential danger to their communities. Religious minorities watched in horror as the Salafist jihadist group the Islamic State of Iraq and Syria (ISIS) persecuted the religious minorities of the Yazidi community in Kurdistan in northern Iraq and launched a campaign of forced conversion to Islam, killing scores of Yazidis and enslaving their women. Inside Syria, Salafist jihadist groups attacked both the Assad forces and those loyal to the regime, and several non-Muslim groups. In Libya, jihadist militias repeatedly targeted expatriate Christians, seeking to abduct them for ransom. Several jihadist groups in the African Sahara threatened Tunisia's and Morocco's Jewish communities. As many minorities see it: wherever in the Arab world the state has lost control, religious minorities are subjected to persecution in the name of Islam.

Several youth groups inside the large religious communities continued to argue that democracy would be the best guarantee of their communities' safety. Democracy (so the argument went) would bring all peaceful Islamist forces into the political process; would turn the largest segments of Arab societies (including the constituencies of the Islamist groups) against Salafist jihadists, who would be exposed as intellectually bankrupt and bent on causing mayhem; and would enshrine peacefulness. According to this view, sticking with democratic means, even if that entailed being ruled by Islamist groups, would in time give rise to a new social contract – one that would be anchored in equal citizenry in secular states. Such a system, they repeatedly argued, would be the sole guarantee of freedom and safety for all communities, majorities and minorities.

The problem was that this ideal was almost entirely disconnected from the petrifying realities that were unfolding all over the Arab world. If the relatively smooth and peaceful political processes of 2012 and 2013 in Morocco and Tunisia seemed to evidence that ideal, as we have seen, the former hardly had any political transition, and the latter lacked any sizeable religious minority. Egypt, with its large Christian community, was the only model that could have lent credibility to this argument. But it was in Egypt that it encountered fierce resistance from the Church and leading voices in the community. They not only detested the Brotherhood's exclusion of and condescension towards other political groups, fearing the impact of the Brotherhood's project and the Salafists' rise on the way of life of minorities. Crucially, they also believed that the associated social polarization could rend the Egyptian state and break its institutions. For them, Egypt stood on the brink of utter chaos. Some envisaged the possibility of Egypt descending into a Syria-type scenario (a multifaceted civil war). A few incidents were indeed chilling. In 2012, several sectarian confrontations in southern Egypt left dozens of Christians dead; in early 2013, a group of Sunni Egyptians attacked a Shii family and slaughtered most of its members in the belief that they were 'infidels'. These fears were assuaged neither by the assertively Islamic clauses of the 2012 Egyptian constitution that the Brotherhood sponsored and which was ratified in a popular referendum, nor by the visible closeness between President Mohammed Morsi and leaders of the Salafist movement, including some who, a decade earlier, had been major spokesmen for violent Salafist groups. For many leading Egyptian Christians, including senior figures inside the Church, their youth groups that advocated patience and acceptance of the rule of the Islamists were not just naïve: those 'young revolutionaries' were condemning the country to disorder, and their community to an uncertain, but likely bleak, future. By choosing to support the removal of the Islamists from power, and especially by backing the armed forces (the only institution that was able to act decisively) in that objective, they believed they were saving Egypt from an Islamization project that they considered alien to its nature, cultural heritage and historical experience; more importantly, they believed they were saving Egyptian society from anarchy.

The minority youth groups that rejected this line of thinking were marginalized. Many felt despondent. They believed that their leaders had positioned their communities as enemies of the Islamists and, as they saw it, this was a dangerous position to be in. They reckoned that large groups inside the Muslim Brotherhood would believe that many in society (including the Christians) were determined to deny them power, even if it had been gained through democratic means. They feared that few Islamists would reflect on what had led these communities to want to get rid of them so badly and at any cost. Desire for revenge could eclipse introspection. This was a prescient assessment.

But there is another danger. As scores of young people from the major political Islamist groups become radicalized and drawn to Salafist jihadist thinking, violence could escalate, and Arab religious minorities could become even more fearful. Inflamed feelings and the emergence of a religion-fuelled rhetoric could incentivize Salafist jihadist groups to widen their operations and augment their resources. This has already begun to happen in Tunisia (2014) and Egypt (2015). Salafist jihadists in the former believe that Islamism was prevented from ruling and that Annahda's leaders have acquiesced to the status quo. Several of their groups have launched a campaign against the Tunisian state, using the border with Libya as a conduit to smuggle arms and to hide from the security forces' retaliatory attacks. In Egypt, at least two groups emerged after the removal of the Brotherhood, both claiming links to major Salafist jihadist groups in the eastern Mediterranean, and both bent not only on fighting the regime but also on attacking secular and Christian Egyptians. And the more young Islamists become convinced that broad segments of society reject them for their thinking, their beliefs and for who they are, the greater the wave of terror could be. In this scenario, the minorities would feel even more threatened. Some in the minority communities would coalesce around the regimes; the notion of secular nationalism fighting Islamization could be strengthened. But many would find the increasing polarization and the rise of violence too depressing or too costly. Some would opt to leave, either internally (through further withdrawal from society) or externally (with immigration). Major Arab countries could lose substantial percentages of their religious minorities. A key component of Arabism would vanish. And as the social presence of Arab religious minorities declines further, so the dreams of equal citizenry in tolerant, cosmopolitan, liberal societies enjoying genuine democracy would be postponed for a far-off time. Paradoxically, excluding the Islamists could end up strengthening them.

1 A mass demonstration in Cairo's Tahrir Square on 9 February 2011, two days before President Mubarak stepped down after almost thirty years in power. Though preceded by the Tunisian uprising, Egypt's 2011 demonstrations calling for the 'fall of the regime' marked a transformative change in the Arab world that quickly triggered social polarization and turbulent political transitions.

2 Gamal al-Din al-Afghani in 1893, during the period in which he was travelling between Iran, the eastern Mediterranean, Egypt and Istanbul (then the capital of the Ottoman Empire), advocating his views on how Islam could continue to be a social frame of reference at a time of immense change.

3 Friday prayer at al-Hussein mosque, one of Cairo's 'grand mosques', which for centuries have been the focal point of the lives of millions of Egyptian Muslims.

4 A 2014 photo of fighters of the Islamic State of Iraq and Syria (ISIS), the militant Islamist group which had by that point managed to gain control of significant territories in the eastern Mediterranean, larger than several European countries.

5 A demonstration in July 2013 outside the Tunisian Constituent Assembly demanding the ouster of the government led by the Islamist Annahda movement. At the time, the Tunisian political transition that had begun after the country's uprising seemed threatened by social tensions and political violence.

6 Annahda's leader, Sheikh Rached al-Ghannouchi, here leading a prayer in Tunis in 2012, has, in the last two decades, been one of the prominent and creative Islamists trying to reconcile Islamism with secular modernity.

7 On the left, Morocco's Head of Government, Abdel-Illah Bin-Kirane, the first leader of an Islamist party to form a government in Morocco, with the country's King Mohammed VI, whose family – descendants of the Prophet Mohammed – has ruled Morocco for centuries.

8 The journalist and politician Jibran Tueini addresses a Lebanese crowd in March 2005 during the 'Cedar Revolution' that followed the assassination that February of the country's prime minister, Rafik Hariri.

9 Saudi Arabian forces arrive in Bahrain in March 2011 to bolster the royal family's rule against mass demonstrations on the island. The Saudi intervention was the clearest example of the country's assertive response to the transformations that the Arab world has witnessed since 2011.

10 In most public ceremonies, such as this one at the establishment of the Turkish History Institution in 1931, none of the women surrounding Kamal Ataturk, the founder of the Turkish Republic, wore the Islamic *hijab* (veil).

11 President Recep Tayyip Erdogan addresses supporters of the AKP, which, since the early 2000s and until its latest victory in the November 2015 parliamentary elections, has come to represent wide segments of pious Turks in a country that throughout most of the twentieth century was subjected to an assertive, top-down secularization.

12 Millions celebrated the arrival in Tehran of Ayatollah Rouhullah Khomenei, who was to lead the 1979 Islamic revolution that overthrew the secular regime of Shah Mohammed Reza Pahlavi.

13 Students clash with supporters of Iranian President Mahmoud Ahmadinejad and members of the Basij militia outside Tehran University during protests following the country's 2009 presidential elections.

14 President Barack Obama receives a standing ovation before speaking at Cairo University on 4 June 2009. That speech was intended to mark a transformation in the US's strategy and positioning in the Arab and Islamic worlds. The Arab uprisings and subsequent developments have posed serious challenges to that strategy.

15 An aerial view of the Zaatari refugee camp in northern Jordan, the home of tens of thousands of the 3 million and more Syrians who have fled their homeland and settled in neighbouring countries between 2012 and 2015.

As waves of Arab religious minorities (and especially Christians) come to believe that they are targeted and threatened and choose to leave their societies (mentally and physically), the demographic supremacy of Arab Muslims would be cemented. This would be a major boon for Islamism.

CHAPTER SEVEN

The Gulf's View of Islamism

In the summer of 1982, with Iraq's position in the Iran–Iraq war that had started three years earlier deteriorating, many Kuwaitis felt threatened that the Iranian troops then advancing along the Gulf's northern shores could soon reach the borders of their oil-rich emirate. The military developments coincided with a slump in international oil prices; investors began to worry, and the emirate witnessed a mass flight of capital. Within weeks of the Iranian military push towards Iraq, Souk al-Manakh, Kuwait's unofficial, over-the-counter trading market and exchange, in which over USD 100 billion had been invested, crashed, with severe economic consequences for tens of thousands of investors. Almost immediately the Kuwaiti government set up a rescue fund to pay off the obligations of thousands of individual investors.[1]

Economic considerations, of course, played some part in the government's decision to intervene. A significant percentage of the investments in Souk al-Manakh were in the form of post-dated cheques worth tens of billions of dollars that had been issued without supporting funds – a situation that could have threatened the state's banking sector. Aside from financial considerations, however, the basis for the government's decision was the fundamental pillar upon which Kuwait, and all other Gulf states, had been founded: the notion that the emir (the prince) is the sheikh of the tribe and will take care of his tribe's members in their moment of need; the provider who holds ultimate responsibility for his people's wellbeing, from defending them and securing food and accommodation to supporting them in getting married and educating their children; the elder sage who controls all resources and the ways in which these are allocated and distributed.

This positioning of the ruler (and behind him, the royal family he leads) as provider is at the heart of the arrangement on which the politics of all Gulf states have been structured since those states came into existence in the first half of the twentieth century. The citizens of Gulf states enjoy a very high standard of living, especially compared to their neighbours in the rest of the Arab world or Iran. Health, housing, transportation and education services, offered at highly subsidized prices, are light-years ahead of those offered by the public sector in non-oil-exporting Arab countries. Since the major increase in oil prices in 2003, and despite the international economic slump that started in late 2007, the states of the Gulf Cooperation Council (GCC) have achieved an average economic growth rate of 5.8 per cent. The per capita GDP of Qatar and the United Arab Emirates (UAE) is among the highest in the world. And the modernization undergone by Gulf cities in roughly the same period – led by Dubai, which emerged in the 2000s as an international hub for transport, logistics and entertainment – triggered a wave of development, dynamism and commercial vitality that resulted in major and numerous economic opportunities for a significant percentage of the local populations, especially the large merchant families close to the rulers. This consistent – and, some would argue, dramatic – improvement in economic and living conditions came without corresponding demands for increased work, output, productivity or the shouldering of economic responsibility.

In return, the Gulf's populations are expected to acquiesce to their ruling families. As all Gulf states depend largely on the revenues generated by their hydrocarbon (oil and gas) riches,[2] these states have not traditionally needed to impose taxes on their citizens, which in turn has meant that the states do not have to offer any concessions regarding political representation or civil rights. The kings and emirs of Gulf states hold near-absolute power with regard to major foreign policy, fiscal and monetary strategy, security and administrative decisions.

Save for Kuwait, no Gulf state has an elected parliament that genuinely represents the majority of its citizens and that has any significant legislative power or supervision of government. Saudi Arabia has a Shura (guidance) Council, whose job is to 'advise' the monarch and whose members, though drawn from some of the leading tribes in the kingdom, are appointed by the ruling family. There are no formal checks on the executive, and any balance of powers has been created as a result of tribal rivalries rather than through a constitutional process. The sheikhs and the royal families retain very privileged positions in the economy. Members of the royal families enjoy major advantages in securing the sole distribution agencies for international brands, leading major financial transactions and acquiring prized land-banks and real estate. Some Gulf states have managed to bring about a clear demarcation between state assets and those of the royals. In Abu Dhabi, for instance, different professionally run agencies have controlled state assets inside and outside the emirate for over forty years. Since the mid-1960s, when Saudi Arabia took full control of its oil industry, its major oil companies have been run by qualified professional managers. Despite that, across the Gulf, power and wealth have always merged. This has given the royal families various means by which to reward, incentivize and penalize their various constituencies.

That arrangement reflects the type of legitimacy upon which the Gulf's ruling system was built: a religious-tribal mandate given by Islamic theological authorities to specific families that had managed to subjugate particular geographic regions in the Arabian Peninsula. Saudi Arabia offers a clear example. Abdel-Aziz al-Saud, a tribal prince from the Najd region in central Arabia, defeated the al-Rasheed family in 1902 and captured Riyadh, a trading centre in Najd and the ancestral home of his family which later evolved to become the Kingdom of

Saudi Arabia. This political project was anchored in an old alliance dating back to the 1740s between his family and the Sunni Islamic sect that adopted the puritanical ideas of Sheikh Mohammed Ibn Abdel-Wahhab (1703–92), and which managed to build major followings in different parts of the region. All of Abdel-Aziz's sons – from King Saud, who succeeded his father in 1953, to King Salman, who ascended the throne in 2015 – have adhered to Salafist Wahhabism. A grand bargain was struck: the Saudis ruled as absolute monarchs monopolizing all executive and administrative power, and in return the major scholars of the Wahhabi sect[3] were awarded almost exclusive control over the country's religious, judicial and educational systems.[4] This heady pact endowed the Saudi family with a religious legitimacy that they did not possess before. The stories of the formation of other Gulf states and their power structures are much the same as that of the Saudis.[5]

Britain, and especially its colonial representatives in eighteenth-century Iraq and India, also played a major role in the creation of these states.[6] In the face of this foreign influence the new royal families were keen to buttress their legitimacy by emphasizing their tribal heritage and religious credentials. The former was typically achieved by strengthening the rulers' position as the providers for the whole tribe. For example, Qatar's al-Thani family established a tradition in the mid-1970s which awarded every male Qatari with a handsome financial support package for education. Abu Dhabi established the Sheikh Zayed Marriage Fund. Religious sanctioning was achieved by commissioning major Islamic projects and championing ceremonial religious causes. The rulers of the UAE have spent many millions of dollars on endowing the world's most prized Koran-recitation contests. Sheikh Zayed's mega-mosque in a suburb of Abu Dhabi, reportedly built to accommodate more than 35,000 worshippers at a cost exceeding USD 400 million, vies with King Hassan II's edifice in Casablanca, Morocco, for the title of the largest mosque ever built. In the 2000s, the Qatari royal family commissioned the world's largest Islamic art museum in Doha. But the most notable effort to use religion to entrench a ruling family's authority took place in Saudi Arabia in 1986, when King Fahd ibn Abdel-Aziz (1921–2005) assumed the title of 'Custodian of the Two Holy Shrines' – a reference to the Saudi kings' control of the Kaaba, Islam's most sacred shrine in Mecca, and Prophet Mohammed's mosque in Medina. The title continues to be the official designation of Saudi monarchs. Aware that their constitutional and political foundations are recent, arbitrary and somewhat the result of external influence, these states have reached back to the past for both historical and religious legitimacy, and have attempted to consolidate this with vast expenditure.

Gulf regimes have also been keen to associate the ruling families' senior princes (and of course the reigning monarchs) with old Islamic leaders, particularly the caliphs of the Umayyad and Abbasid dynasties which ruled the Islamic world from the seventh to the eleventh century.[7] The reference to the Umayyads helps us understand the basis of legitimacy created and sustained by the Gulf royal families. The Umayyads ended the Islamic tradition of choosing the Islamic caliphs (those who succeeded Prophet Mohammed in ruling the Islamic community) on the basis of religious pedigree, and instilled the notion of hereditary monarchy at the heart of Islamic rule. Unlike their predecessors, the 'four rightly guided' caliphs who ruled over Islam's hinterland in the Arabian Peninsula from the time of Prophet Mohammed's death in 632 to the assassination of Imam Ali, Mohammed's cousin, in 661, the Umayyads established themselves in Damascus, an urban city with many non-Arab and non-Muslim communities, where the social milieu was heavily influenced by the culture of the adjacent Eastern Roman Empire. Over time, and as they entrenched their rule, especially in the then immensely wealthy eastern Mediterranean and Egypt, the Umayyad caliphs began to adopt the ways and traditions of the imperial court in Constantinople. But the crucial development that occurred in the first few decades of Umayyad rule[8] was the separation of temporal rule over the Islamic world from religious authority. The Umayyad caliphs explicitly argued that they were the best and most qualified political and military rulers of the expanding Islamic empire. But they never claimed any religious or theological mandate. What they pursued, typically by means of carrots but often also using sticks (including horrifying episodes of torture), was the *bayah* (pledge of allegiance) of the most notable religious scholars of their time. The *bayah* transformed the Umayyads from kings of the Levant to Islamic caliphs – and with that, and through the repeated endorsement of the religious authorities, came the submission of the vast majority of the people to their rule. The way in which the Umayyads distinguished between religious and temporal power in Islam (one of the key reasons for the later schism between Sunnism and Shiism), and yet retained a religious mandate for themselves, became a template for many Islamic kings – including the Gulf's royals.

The Gulf royals' legitimacy was repeatedly challenged, however. The immense popular support that Arab nationalism had generated in the 1950s and 1960s, and especially during the heyday of Egypt's Gamal Abdel-Nasser, threatened the governing structure of all Gulf regimes. The Arab nationalists, and with them a potent media machine, portrayed the Gulf royals as pawns of the West. There were times, especially in the early 1960s, when the wave of Arab nationalism seemed to be advancing inexorably towards the Gulf. But the defeat of Arab nationalism in the 1967 war against Israel and the subsequent death of Nasser put an end to that danger.

Over the years, Gulf royal families managed to attend to these and other threats. For example, in Oman and Ras al-Khaimah (in today's UAE) there were attempts from within the ruling families to overthrow the existing rulers and seize power, on the grounds that they and the senior sheikhs surrounding them had deviated from the religious responsibility placed in their hands. In Bahrain, the ruling family has repeatedly faced revolts from various constituencies that never accepted its authority. There have also been cases when marginal religious groups challenged the Gulf royals' religious-tribal legitimacy. The most dramatic episode was in 1979, when the Saudi royal family sent commando troops to storm Mecca's grand mosque, Islam's holiest shrine, to end its occupation by a group of religious dissidents who described the Saudi state as corrupt and proclaimed their leader to be the 'redeemer' who would bring that state, and the whole Islamic world, 'back to the path of righteousness'. Challenges were diluted, and as the decades passed, and as national – and personal – wealth was accumulated, so confidence increased. The oil boom of the 2000s, during which prices leapt from around USD 25 per barrel in 2000 to over USD 140 in 2008, swelled national capital reserves, boosted current accounts and resulted in a wave of Gulf investments all over the world, adding influence and prestige to the royal families' international positions. By the end of the first decade of the twenty-first century, the Gulf's governing system seemed solidly secure.

The 2000s, however, saw the emergence of a different type of challenge. Between 1990 and 2010, the Gulf population doubled from 20 million to around 40 million. Literacy rates in the two-thirds of the population under the age of twenty-five surpassed 70 per cent. Female participation in the labour force increased significantly, reaching almost 50 per cent in the UAE – a reflection of a strong trend in female economic empowerment across the region: some of the Gulf's leading merchant families were now led by well-educated and assertive businesswomen. This new generation was exposed to the world in ways that no previous generation ever had been. Again, Saudi Arabia is a good example. By the end of the 2000s, two-thirds of the country's 30 million people were under the age of thirty, and two-thirds of those were in their teens. More than a million Saudis had studied in the West for at least a year. Internet penetration in the kingdom had surpassed 60 per cent, and was above 80 per cent among Saudis under the age of thirty. Over a third of all Saudis who are online access Twitter every month, the highest such ratio worldwide. By the end of 2014, there were over 6.5 million Saudis who were using Facebook; YouTube usage jumped in 2013 by 260 per cent, against an average growth of 50 per cent internationally. Across various social media platforms hundreds of young Saudis expressed their frustration with their political system. Many had serious misgivings about the official interpretations of Islam. In one telling episode, a young Saudi woman was ordered by the religious police to leave a shopping mall because they deemed her make-up provocative and inconsistent with the kingdom's moral values. She filmed the encounter and uploaded the video to YouTube; in less than two weeks, the video had had over 2 million hits. In another case, a blogger triggered a wave of admiration (and condemnation) when he posted an imaginary conversation with the Prophet Mohammed which subtly challenged some of the notions that the Saudi Wahhabi establishment holds sacred. And throughout the 2000s, the kingdom witnessed several campaigns led by women who challenged the state's ban on women driving cars.

In the late 2000s, several universities in Kuwait and the UAE held student union elections. Doha hosted debating events in which young Gulf citizens discussed important social, economic and political issues openly. In Kuwait and Bahrain, several trade associations held elections in which the state's economic policies were dissected. Increasingly, many young activists were calling for a say in how their states are governed.

Gulf media also witnessed a revolution in this period. While Egypt and Lebanon had traditionally dominated the production of Arab news and entertainment, now the largest regional news and entertainment satellite channels were based in the Gulf, with dramatic consequences for freedom of expression in the region. For example, one of the most popular TV programmes on the Saudi-owned and Dubai-based al-Arabiya network is written and presented by Gulf women and focuses on gender issues, including some that in the 1990s and earlier were considered socially taboo. Openness in the media, which was significantly boosted by the wide availability of broadband internet in the 2000s, also provided many opportunities for Islamic scholars, including a generation of young Gulf preachers, to put forward social and political ideas that were alien to the region's religious heritage. For instance, the rhetoric of a few Kuwaiti preachers combined the mainstream ideas of some of the largest schools of Islamic thought with notions imported from Asian traditions. Such intellectual experimentation, especially in Islamic thinking and rhetoric, have had a long history in other parts of the Islamic world (such as Persia, Turkey and North Africa), but was new to the Gulf, where strict Islamic ideologies, based on literalist interpretations of the Koran, have been dominant for centuries.

Gulf art blossomed. A new generation of novelists, painters, sculptors, jewellers and filmmakers, including scores of young women, transformed the region's artistic scene. A Saudi woman won the Arab world's biggest literary prize, while a young Saudi man became the first Arab painter and sculptor in over three decades to exhibit his work in the Metropolitan Museum of Art in New York. A group of Emirati artists in their twenties and thirties created the Arab world's first permanent 'garage-art space'. A Saudi woman was the first female Arab filmmaker to have a movie shortlisted for an Oscar in the foreign film category. All of that revealed a new generation of Gulf citizens who are open to the world, interact with it, create daring cultural productions, question their heritage and are willing to move beyond and discard norms and ideas which, for centuries, had been taken for granted.

It was against this background that the Arab uprisings took place. The Gulf's first response was shock, not only at the scale of the demonstrations across North Africa (and soon in the eastern Mediterranean), but at the response of the West, and particularly the US, to them. After less than two weeks of wavering, the US made it clear that it supported the fall of both Tunisia's President Ben-Ali and Egypt's President Hosni Mubarak, the Gulf's long-time ally. From the perspective of the Gulf royals, the US had quickly abandoned one of its closest partners in his moment of need. It was an extremely alarming message for them. Would the US do the same in their time of crisis? The Gulf royals were not willing to take any chances. For them, the US's position betrayed a new uncertainty that could affect their security calculations. The region's leaders became convinced that they should take their security into their own hands.

The protests were approaching the Gulf. On 14 February 2011, tens of thousands of Bahrainis (out of a total population of some 1.2 million) took to the streets in huge demonstrations that called for a new constitution that would render equal the rights of citizens and limit the privileges of the al-Khalifa family, rulers of Bahrain for the past two centuries. Bahrain has always been the Gulf's weakest link. Though it has one of the freest economies in the Arab world,[9] its oil capacity of only 40,000 barrels per day makes it one of the most feeble economies in the Gulf. Bahrain's vulnerability is significantly exacerbated by the fact that the Sunni al-Khalifas rule a Shii majority population, large sections of which believe themselves to be discriminated against, especially in economic rights. The island has witnessed many Shii revolts over the past half-century, when Emergency Law was continuously in force from 1957 to 2002. But the 2011 revolt was different. It came immediately after the Tunisian, Egyptian and Libyan uprisings. And though its slogans were secular, calling for constitutional and political reform, the revolt's most conspicuous faces were Shii leaders, whose rhetoric combined the secular with the sacred. Hundreds of Shii protestors waved banners depicting the face of Imam Hussain (626–680), Prophet Mohammed's grandson who was martyred in Karbalaa in Iraq in 680 and who represents Shii Islam's ultimate symbol of suffering. The Bahraini regime's response was a mix of coercion and co-option.[10] But the decisive reaction came from Saudi Arabia and the UAE. In the first ten days of March 2011, after an 'invitation' from the Bahraini royal family, a force from those two countries crossed the causeway linking Saudi Arabia with the island of Bahrain to help 'bolster the government security forces'. Within days, the uprising was crushed. This was the first time in many decades that a combined Gulf military force had undertaken an operation in a different Gulf country, against its own citizens, and without any external support. It demonstrated the Gulf royals' determination to act decisively and assertively, even if that was against what seemed to be the position of their long-time security partner, the US.

After making it abundantly clear that they would not accept 'Arab Spring'-style demonstrations in the Gulf, the royal families resorted to their classic modus operandi. In the first half of 2011 the Saudi government announced a package of economic, educational, health and social subsidies and allowances totalling over USD 70 billion. By the second quarter of 2012, the package had swollen to USD 130 billion, more than the entire Saudi national budget in 2007/08. The government also quickly put forward a programme to employ thousands of young Saudis in the country's security and religious establishments – a move intended to absorb some of those who had no chance of securing jobs in the private sector, or even in the state's own administrative structure. Over 100,000 houses were built between 2011 and 2013. The government expanded a programme in which it paid around USD 500 per month to each registered unemployed young Saudi, while offering them training to find a job; by the end of 2013, over a million Saudis were enrolled in the programme. In the UAE, the Abu Dhabi government, the largest and richest of the seven emirates that form the country's confederacy, increased the salaries of all employees in the public sector (the only sector in the whole economy that is not dominated by expatriate workers), expanded the social welfare system (especially to the less privileged parts of the country), and significantly increased spending on amenities and infrastructure. Qatar, whose total population is less than 300,000, announced a welfare package worth over USD 8 billion.

After absorbing the shock of the fall of Ben-Ali and Mubarak, Gulf royals were keen to bolster the non-Gulf Arab monarchies of Jordan and Morocco. With high youth unemployment, a dependency on foreign direct investment, budget deficits, unsustainable food and energy subsidies upon which at least half their populations depend, and deteriorating competitiveness across most of the industries offering mass employment, the two countries needed significant financial support. The Gulf states were ready and willing. In the four years between 2011 and

2014, Gulf states provided Jordan and Morocco with grants, development loans and budgetary assistance exceeding USD 8 billion.

Most observers link the Gulf states' assistance to the royal families' implicit support for other Arab monarchical regimes. The logic goes that the fall of any Arab monarchy would shake all the others' foundations of power, and so there are strong incentives for Gulf regimes to avert any substantial risks confronted by the Jordanian and Moroccan powers. That is true, but the Gulf's responses had another, more strategic basis: the Gulf royals had quickly recognized that Arab political Islamism – which seemed from 2011 to 2013 to be the main beneficiary of the transformation enveloping the Arab world, and which was knocking on the door of the two non-oil-exporting kingdoms – posed a serious threat to their legitimacy.

The rhetoric adopted by Arab political Islam since the late 1990s establishes its legitimacy not on a mandate from a religious authority, nor on divine texts, nor on archaic deals between tribes and religious establishments, but rather on the consent of the people, secured through elections that the world recognizes to be free and fair. This was not only an innovation in the political thinking of one of the most powerful ideologies and political trends in the Arab world: it had the potential to challenge the foundations on which Islam (Sunni Islam, to be specific) had been used in politics for centuries. Theoretically, it marked the end of the system that the Umayyads had established in the Islamic world: the securing of temporal authority through force, legitimized through the allegiance of the most prominent religious scholars of the age. This new model meant that there was now a system of governance that on paper successfully combined Islam with the modern tenets of democracy.

This was particularly threatening to the Gulf, because it seemed to provide a solution to the disjunction between the region's old ruling system and the aspirations of the young generation, by far the largest demographic in their societies. If political Islam managed to reconcile an Islamic frame of reference and respect for religious heritage with genuine political representation and checks and balances, then it would have the chance of emerging as a natural evolution of the Gulf's old system of rule: a system that would not challenge Islamic jurisprudence, would not offend the sensibility of deeply conservative and pious sections of Gulf societies, and at the same time would be enshrined in modern modes of governing that allow the electorate to hold the executive accountable.

This was a real peril that the Gulf royals were determined to tackle. Annahda in Tunisia and the PJD in Morocco appeared to be the parties with the most developed thinking and whose models could marry modern systems of governing with an Islamic frame of reference. Both, however, were restricted by local circumstance. As was discussed earlier, the PJD was not willing to attempt to transform Morocco's political system; thus, from the Gulf's perspective, so long as the authority of King Mohammed VI remained unchallenged, the PJD's rise did not pose a serious threat. Annahda was more problematic, because it embodied that 'perilous' model. But the success of Tunisia's secularists in containing Annahda and thwarting any potential Islamization project meant that Annahda's form of political Islam would not have the ability to take root and expand. The Gulf royals also reckoned, correctly, that Tunisia was unique and would not emerge as a model for any other Arab country. Because of its experience with Bourghuiba's staunch secularism, its cultural and economic closeness to Europe, its historically limited role in any major issue in Arab politics, and its small size, Tunisia was a country that many Arabs would watch but would not emulate. It triggered the Arab uprisings, but its circumstances rendered it different from the large countries in the Arabian Maghreb (Algeria, Libya and Morocco), from Egypt, and from all eastern Mediterranean and Gulf countries. The problem was with Egypt's Muslim Brotherhood. If the Egyptian Islamists managed to forge a successful model that united Islam with democracy in the country that has always been the regional trendsetter, then that new governing model would take a tangible form, would be obvious for all to see, and would inspire others, including many young Gulf citizens.

This 'peril' was exacerbated by an old mistrust between Saudi Arabia's Wahhabis and the Muslim Brotherhood. Saudi Arabia gave thousands of Brotherhood members refuge in the 1950s after Nasser had made the group's existence in Egypt effectively untenable. The secular, republican, firebrand revolutionist was seen as a common enemy. But the closeness of the Saudis and the Brothers proved very short-lived. The Saudi Wahhabi establishment saw the Brothers' ideas at that time as a deviation from the austere, puritanical Islam to which they adhered. They also differed substantially on the Brotherhood's acceptance of the idea of *istitan* (allowing the settlement of non-Muslims in Islamic lands, despite knowing that their way of life would gradually be incorporated into Islamic society). The Wahhabis suspected that some of the Brothers who had come to Saudi Arabia were dealing with foreign powers, which many in their ranks considered a violation of the Wahhabi concept of *baraa* (denunciation of infidels). The differences of the 1950s did not result in conflict; but by the early 1960s it had become clear that no alliance would be established between the Saudi kingdom and the leading force of Arab political Islam. That coolness continued throughout the period between the 1960s and the 1990s. As the Brotherhood became a key opposition to Saudi allies, such as Egypt's President Mubarak, the old aversion hardened into deep suspicion.[11]

Other Gulf powers held that suspicion for much longer. The Brotherhood had a strong presence in Kuwait and the UAE from the 1960s to the 1980s. Thousands of young Kuwaitis and Emiratis who had studied in Egypt and in different Islamic and Western countries were exposed to branches of the Brotherhood. Many returned home convinced by the group's ideas and desirous of spreading their teachings, which they saw as the way forward for their societies. Leveraging their country's vibrant intellectual and parliamentary life, the 'Kuwaiti brothers' developed their own semi-detached branch of the Brotherhood. Contacts with the latter still existed, but the Brotherhood exerted hardly any real influence on the Kuwaitis, who went on to form the Constitutional Reform Movement. After Saddam Hussein's invasion of

Kuwait in 1990, however, the relationship became very strained. The Constitutional Reform Movement's leaders were convinced that the Brotherhood, whether the original Egyptian group or some of its branches (e.g. in Palestine) did not take clear enough positions against the invasion; some suspected that many of their co-Islamists actually supported Saddam Hussein's aggression. This put an end to any real connection between Kuwait's Islamists and the Brotherhood. Unsurprisingly, it left a sour taste in the mouths of many Kuwaitis, especially in the ruling family.[12]

The situation was different in the UAE. A group of Brothers established Jameyat al-Islah (Reform Association), a society with close links to the Brotherhood, in Dubai in the mid-1970s. It proved highly successful. Its leaders managed to convince several of the UAE emirs to give them leading roles in many ministries, especially education and information. For a period in the late 1980s and early 1990s, the Association's publication *al-Islah* (*Reform*) had a huge following. The UAE authorities had no theological quarrel with the Brotherhood, but as the group's influence over the country's schooling system became conspicuous and its periodicals influential, several savvy emirs sensed a burgeoning threat. Some security professionals in the UAE had doubts that members of al-Islah had links to some of the Salafist jihadists that fought the Egyptian and Algerian regimes in the 1990s. The Association and its periodicals were banned, and many of its members or sympathizers, particularly in the education ministry, were removed from their positions. Though most Brotherhood leaders insist that the group ceased its presence in the country, many in the Emirates' security establishment maintain that the group went underground.[13]

These old suspicions were hardly doused when the Brotherhood ascended to the Egyptian presidency. Time and again in his speeches, Mohammed Morsi made it clear that he had grave misgivings about Mubarak's foreign policy, and would oversee a revolution in Egypt's handling of all strategic dossiers in the region. Not only did the Saudi, Emirati and Kuwaiti royals dislike the attacks on their old ally (Mubarak), but they also believed (correctly) that the Brotherhood aimed to use its success in Egypt to establish itself as a regional power with special relationships with major countries. In 2012, Mohammed Morsi and various senior leaders of the group effectively intervened with the leadership of the Palestinian Islamist group, Hamas, to secure the release of an Israeli soldier, Gilad Shalit, who had been abducted by the group. During the negotiation process, US President Barack Obama had several lengthy conversations with the Egyptian president, and by the end a working relationship seemed to have been born. Weeks later, two senior Brotherhood members were received at the White House. Leading American newspapers began to describe Mohammed Morsi as a statesman who had managed to defuse a complicated problem in the Middle East. Only weeks after taking control of the Egyptian presidency, the Brotherhood was beginning to establish constructive cooperation with the power that had guaranteed the security of the Gulf for over six decades. Several influential Gulf princes believed that there was a real chance of a fundamental change in America's calculus in the region. If the Brotherhood appeared to American decision-makers as offering a workable example of a form of Islamic democracy – one that was friendly to the US and willing to liaise with Israel – then it could possibly emerge as a serious American partner in the region.

There were also signs that the Brotherhood was interested in a special relationship with Iran. In his first few months in power, Morsi became the first Egyptian president in three decades to visit Iran, and by the end of 2012 it was clear that Egypt would resume diplomatic relations with the Islamic Republic after a break of nearly three decades, ever since the Iranian revolution of 1979. Morsi's address to the Non-Aligned Summit in August 2012, less than six weeks after his inauguration, was particularly unnerving for many Gulf decision-makers. Speaking in Tehran, he praised the Islamic Republic's democratic credentials and religious values, while at the same time deriding those whom he considered bastions of the old power structure that had dominated the Arab world for at least the previous half-century. It did not matter whether a strategy based on partnering with the US and having a close relationship with Iran was coherent or would work in practice. What mattered for the Gulf was that Egypt was on the verge of becoming an adversary.

Gulf states dreaded the prospect of 'losing Egypt', the largest and most strategically important Arab country, after over four decades during which it had been a close ally of all Gulf states, and especially Saudi Arabia – and at a time of such tumult and transformation across the region. Losing Egypt – especially to the Brotherhood – also carried a worrisome subtext: it could potentially signal that the Gulf powers were unable to support their allies or stand up to Arab Islamist forces. The fall of an old entrenched regime and the rise of a group that just a few years earlier had been illegal could embolden Gulf opposition forces. More importantly, it could inspire young Gulf citizens with a model of political representation that, at least rhetorically, linked itself to Islam. It was noteworthy – and disturbing for the Gulf royals – that several Islamic preachers with large followings in the Gulf were praising 'the Egyptian experiment under the Brotherhood'.

Gulf powers were also worried that the Brotherhood's incompetence, which by the end of 2012 was becoming abundantly clear, could result in economic disaster for Egypt. The prospect of the Egyptian economy going into freefall (by no means impossible in early 2013) was frightening to the rulers of Saudi Arabia, the Emirates and Kuwait. These countries, which host millions of Egyptian migrant workers and which boast hundreds of billions of dollars of foreign currency reserves, feared that an economic meltdown in Egypt could compel them to assume unwanted responsibilities. The danger here went far beyond potentially having to commit billions of dollars in fiscal support for a number of years: the Gulf royals dreaded the possibility that the economic situation could result in the collapse of the Egyptian state structure and the advent of social disorder. And so, from the Gulf's perspective, there was a crucial need to ensure that the Egyptian state would not crumble. The thinking was that this necessitated supporting the state institutions that were able to maintain stability: effectively, the military.

There was also a Gulf-specific dynamic behind Saudi Arabia's and the UAE's extreme suspicions concerning the rise of Arab political Islam, especially the Muslim Brotherhood. The rulers of these countries believed, with good reason, that a number of senior princes in Qatar were extending considerable financial and media support to the Islamists. Al-Jazeera, Qatar's hugely successful pan-Arab TV satellite channel, has always been a strong backer of all Islamic movements in the Arab world, but since 2011 the channel has effectively been the mouthpiece of various groups, and especially the Brotherhood. Al-Jazeera's colossal audience gave the Islamists a powerful and influential media platform with unrivalled reach. Saudi and Emirati rulers suspected that Qatar's support for the Islamists was part of a grand strategy by that tiny emirate to bring about a major transformation in the Arab strategic order. In the previous decade, Qatar had become the main arbiter of almost all major conflicts in the Arab world, from the semi-continuous sectarian paralysis in Lebanese politics, to mediation between various Palestinian factions, to negotiations between North and South Sudan over sharing oil revenues. Qatar's seemingly inexhaustible financial resources were oiling the wheels of various struggles. The shiny new palaces of Doha seemed to have replaced Riyadh's and Jeddah's as the new pilgrimage destination of many Arab (and Islamic) political mavericks. Qatar is also host to the US's largest military base in the Middle East, which not only guaranteed its security, but also meant that it has a unique relationship with the superpower. There have been several hypotheses put forward as to what Qatar's supposedly grand strategy was; in any event, for the Saudi and Emirati leaderships it was hostile to their interests. And although through various intermediaries (especially from Kuwait) they repeatedly tried to convince the Qataris to change course and reduce their support for the Islamists, Qatar's rulers – or at least their key media platforms – remained strong backers of Arab political Islam. Neither Saudi Arabia (especially the assertive late King Abdullah) nor Abu Dhabi (with its firm and shrewd Crown Prince Mohammed Bin Zayed) would accept that they had to bend to the will of the rulers of their tiny neighbour. A political and media war erupted between the two sides, and Egypt was its main theatre.[14]

It was also personal. For at least two decades, President Mubarak had been a close friend of King Abdullah and Abu Dhabi's ruling Zayed family. King Abdullah and several senior Abu Dhabi princes made it clear to many of their visitors, including senior Egyptian politicians, that they abhorred the treatment of the elderly ex-president – especially his imprisonment and confinement to the criminals' box in an Egyptian court, 'while the world was watching'. Some members of President Mubarak's family privately intervened with senior Saudi and Abu Dhabi princes, pleading with them to intercede on his behalf. A few did. For them, this was a matter of personal loyalty, devotion to an old friend and the dignity of an old man, whom many of them considered to have been a successful politician.

Saudi Arabia and the UAE made it quite clear that they backed the removal of the Brotherhood from power in Egypt. Less than an hour after Morsi's removal, Saudi King Abdullah sent a message praising the Egyptian army for 'having saved the great country from a dark tunnel'. In the following eighteen months, the kingdom and its Gulf partners backed up its words with over USD 18 billion in fiscal support for Egypt.

With the Brotherhood's failure and its removal, Annahda's containment, and the PJD's decision to settle for a position as just one party among many in Morocco, the rise of Arab political Islam seemed to have ended. The model of a governing system in the Arab world that combines an Islamic frame of reference with genuine representation and real supervision of the executive by the electorate remained just that – a model. Gulf royals have managed to confront and circumvent one of the most serious political threats of the past century. But though the model never acquired material form in the Arab world, there were non-Arab models that, despite the different circumstances, still seemed to promise a potential meeting between, on the one hand, Islam and the cultural preferences of the pious and the conservative, and on the other, democracy. We discuss the Turkish model in the next chapter.

CHAPTER EIGHT

Turkish Islamism as a Model for the Arab World

At least 15,000 Egyptians, mostly young, holding posters of Recep Tayyip Erdogan and chanting slogans of an 'Islamic caliphate', welcomed the Turkish prime minister as he emerged from Cairo airport in September 2011, less than nine months after the removal of President Mubarak. Wherever Erdogan went in his three days in Cairo, scores of young Islamists surrounded his convoy and waited for him at his destination, hailing him as an Islamic hero.

For millions of Islamists across the Arab world, Erdogan and his Justice and Development Party (AKP) had come to represent the ultimate political success they had dreamt of. In slightly over a decade, that party, led by that man, had come to dominate the politics of the one country in the Islamic world that, for three-quarters of a century, had been subject to a highly assertive programme of secularization and de-Islamization. So too, the fact that the AKP's rise to power and consolidation of authority were far from easy further inspired Arab Islamists; many looked to the AKP's experience as a model to emulate.

Modern Turkey was the creation of a group of Turkish nationalists (the vast majority of them from the Ottoman armed forces) who believed that the Ottoman Empire's defeat in the First World War and its subsequent demise offered Turkey a chance to emerge from the ruins of empire as an independent country, looking forward to a Europe-inspired modernity rather than remaining shackled to an Islamic heritage. These nationalists' ideas rested on those of various modernization movements that had begun in Istanbul in the mid-nineteenth century, when the empire was going through the various political, social and administrative reforms that came to be known as the *Tanzimat* (Organizing Concepts).[1] The First World War not only crushed the empire; it humiliated the Turks. By the end of the war, not only had Turkey lost all its Ottoman possessions, but foreign troops (including those of historical arch-enemies, such as Greece) were on Turkish soil. The Ottoman leadership was conquered, the country's political structure in meltdown. And yet, amid the military defeat, the political chaos and the collapse of the administrative bureaucracy, and despite the presence of foreign armies in various parts of the country, Turkey managed to bring together sections of its armed forces, civil service and civil society to resurrect the skeleton of a central command, which enabled it to fight the invaders, formulate a coherent message to the people who were watching the fall of everything they had known, and ultimately negotiate with the First World War's victors – a political deal that was, by any standards, extremely favourable to a country that was on the losing side. This achievement came about thanks to the efforts of thousands of brave Turkish soldiers and peasants who had abandoned their farms to fight for their country, as well as to the tenacity and courage of at least two dozen military leaders. But at the core of that inspiring episode in Turkish history lay the genius of one man, a senior Ottoman general named Mustafa Kemal Pasha. Mustafa Kemal's military cunning, political savvy, charisma and luck positioned him as the unquestionable leader who salvaged Turkey after its defeat and enabled it to emerge from the First World War as an independent and proud nation. Senior generals in the Ottoman army deferred to him and accepted him as their leader. By the end of the negotiations with the victorious allies, in the eyes of large swathes of Turks, Mustafa Kemal had become the country's saviour.

Mustafa Kemal relished that image. He was a sharp politician, who understood the power of addressing national emotions and using the mass media (radio) to widen his appeal and entrench his image. He also understood the power of the idea of the saviour, the hero, in Islamic and Turkish heritage – the man destined by the heavens to rescue his society. His most significant decision, however, was to assume the role of a Turkish as opposed to an Islamic hero – to become 'Ataturk' (the father of the Turks).[2]

Kemal Ataturk abolished the Ottoman Empire; ended the Islamic caliphate; exiled the Ottoman family; eliminated the office of Sheikh-ul-Islam (the highest official theological position in the Islamic Empire); closed the Sharia courts; brought all schools of Islamic theology training under the control of the secular Istanbul university; banned most Sufi orders, including dervish shrines; replaced the Ottoman Islamic calendar with the international Western one; moved the workers' day off from Friday to Sunday; and crucially, in the republic's 1928 constitution, eliminated the clause designating Islam as the state religion. Ataturk had no qualms about the route that he, and Turkey, should take. This was not a confused man on a quest, or a politician weighing his options. Ataturk was convinced that only the Turkish identity could be a basis for the modern powerful state over which he wanted to preside.

To make that Turkishness distinct, he defined it as the opposite of everything Ottoman. He made it clear that Turkishness was not a cultural concept: one would not be Turkish by embracing the Turkish language, culture and customs, or by living in the country for decades. It was racial: Turkish blood made one Turkish. And so he was one of the key engineers of the major exchange of populations which saw tens of thousands of Ottoman subjects (Greeks by origin) leaving their homes for Greece, and thousands of Turks 'returning to their motherland'. Turkishness was also patriarchal, militaristic and progressive, the antithesis of Ottoman decadence, permissiveness and 'weakness' which had characterised the two centuries prior to the war. Most importantly, Ataturk's Turkishness was secular. It was not based on any Islamic legitimacy, and was not even reliant on the approval of an acquiescent religious establishment, as was the case in secular Arab countries throughout the twentieth century.[3]

Ataturk, and the coterie of 'founding fathers' who surrounded him, installed a top-down political system anchored in a new establishment that incorporated the military, judiciary, the groups entrusted with westernizing language and society, and the group of media advisors whose job it was to promote, directly and indirectly, Turkish nationalism. Decision-making in almost all areas was dominated by this new establishment. The Ottoman tradition of devolving municipal issues to regional governors and social elites was abolished. The new republic had different layers of supervision to ensure that top-down strategies (in all areas) were being followed and executed. And almost invariably, all these monitoring layers reported, at the top of the chain of command, to Ataturk's management bureau, which later evolved to become the republic's National Security Council.

The republic proved highly successful. It quickly cemented its legitimacy, entrenched its secularism, crushed and marginalized the old Ottoman elite, reinvigorated several industries that had been blossoming in the late decades of the nineteenth century, reshaped the country's civil service to become the loyal and effective administrative arm of the republic's ruling establishment, and positioned Turkey as a stable country in the tumultuous world of 1930s and 1940s southern Europe and Middle East.[4]

This strong centralization shared one key feature with Ottoman rule: it dispensed with genuine political representation. Six decades before Ataturk's transformation of Turkey, the architects of the *Tanzimat* had managed to force the Ottoman sultan to delegate significant executive power to the government, which, though never elected, was representative of Turkey's – and to some extent the Balkans' – upper-middle classes. A few decades later, Sultan Abdelhamid II reversed this reform, and asserted the palace's supremacy in all executive (and to a large extent legislative) matters. One of the central characteristics of the last few decades of the Ottoman Empire's life was a struggle between the palace and reformers in the civil society over the extent of the sultan's potency. After acquiring power, Ataturk and his establishment did not side with the civil society's democratic aspirations; they continued the same trend of consolidating their authority. In this respect they clearly did not trust the citizens of the new republic, the progency of a centuries-old Ottoman heritage, with their ambitious state-building project. Ataturk and his establishment decided to become the guardians of their people, the ones who would chaperone them towards modernization. Mustafa Kemal's choice of the title of 'father of the Turks' succinctly and brilliantly captured that patriarchal mindset.

There were some attempts by economic interest groups to acquire power from the secular, militarist Ataturk establishment. The election of Adnan Menderes as prime minister in 1950 offered a chance to change this structure and to set Turkey on the road to democratization. Though he had various connections to Ataturk's party and the group that ruled in his name after Ataturk died in 1938, Menderes was not a representative of that power structure. His core constituency was in Turkey's middle class, and especially among the merchants and traders of Istanbul and Turkey's coastal cities. Though he had an affable style and was a savvy tactical politician, his rule was erratic; he had no consistent economic policy; and at various important junctures he displayed a strong authoritarian streak. This, coupled with interventions by the security apparatus, resulted in successive policy failures for his administration. Public mood turned sharply against him. A wave of demonstrations demanding change – and often explicitly his removal – took place, including in some coastal towns where some of his political partners were quite influential. In 1961, the military removed – and later executed – him.

Menderes was certainly a failure. But the experience of being led by a civilian politician who came to power through a free election, whose constituency transcended Istanbul's upper echelons and who represented large sections of Turkish society, could have shifted Turkey away from the patriarchal governing structure that placed the military – the guardians of Ataturk's state – above society. The Menderes experience was a lost opportunity, especially so given that he was respectful and cognizant of the military's exceptional role in the state. Apart from a few minor episodes, he did not try to challenge the military or other key pillars of the Ataturk state. And so, even as a failed politician, Menderes' time in power could have provided Turkey with a smooth and safe bridge from Ataturk's state towards representative politics. Turkey could have moved away from Ataturk's top-down structure without dismantling the institutions and the state he had built. The decades-long influence of the military, judiciary and some of the state's cultural grandees would have continued, but in a declining trajectory. The voice of the middle classes – and gradually other, lower sections of society – would have become louder and, in time, the decisive factor in Turkish sociopolitics. But with the removal of Menderes, the abrupt end to the relatively democratic process that his reign represented, and especially his and most of his key aides' total elimination from politics, Turkey was returned by force to Ataturk's patriarchal model.[5]

This steering from above continued for over half a century. But it proved increasingly problematic. The positioning of Ataturk as the hero who had saved Turkey and founded the republic was not inheritable, either by Inonu, the president who followed him, or more importantly by the military and national security establishment that guarded the state he had created.[6] In time, the pride felt at Turkey rising from the ruins of the Ottoman Empire became a distant memory, the reverence for the military waned, the nationalistic rhetoric started to sound repetitive and tired, and the state's guardianship role became too prescriptive, and often too intrusive.

Because the westernization effected by Ataturk (and the ruling establishment) was centred on state institutions that were created in Ankara and had found strong support in the well-educated, Western-exposed, middle and upper-middle classes of Istanbul (and to some extent, certain other urban centres such as Izmir), rural, agrarian Turkey (especially the Anatolian hinterland) was always on the receiving end of the dictates of the state's guardians. Rebellion was hardly an option. The vast majority of Anatolia's communities comprised small farmers, retailers and lower-cadre public officials, who depended on the state for almost all their needs, from subsidized food to basic infrastructure. Still, when the state's prescriptive regulations invaded their private lives, the unease of these communities was palpable. The Islamic headscarf, traditionally worn by almost all Anatolian women, was perhaps a simple yet powerful symbol of these communities' insistence on preserving their heritage. It also reflected the way in which Ataturk's laws and regulations interacted with previous reforms, and how these together shaped social behaviour. The mid-nineteenth-century *Tanzimat* indirectly gave rise to openness to the West and ushered in a gradual relaxation of Turkey's hitherto conservative social codes. By the 1880s and 1890s Turkey had an active and often assertive 'social development' movement that encouraged women (including in rural Anatolia) to raise any objections they had regarding 'social restrictions'. When Ataturk created the republic, the majority of Anatolian women wore the headscarf, though many had already discarded the *salvar* (a special type of baggy pants designed to be comfortable enough for working in the fields or markets, yet still concealing any feminine features). Ataturk made it very clear that 'modern Turkish women' were 'liberated', that the headscarf was 'uncivilized', and he consistently appeared at state events surrounded by Turkish women dressed in Western clothes. However, well into the 1940s and 1950s, the headscarf remained almost ubiquitous headgear for Anatolian women.[7] Its prevalence was neither a threat to the state nor an act of social protest against the ruling establishment. It was a symptom of the disconnect between the Ataturk state's view of how society should develop and the cultural comfort zone of wide segments of Turkish society who were unwilling to discard their traditions.

Economics widened that disconnect. Throughout the period from the early 1960s to the late 1980s, Turkey pursued an ambitious and, in various sectors, highly successful industrialization policy. This aimed to reduce Turkey's dependence on Western technologies, especially in sectors that were set to expand due to the demands of the country's growing middle classes: the auto industry, electrical appliances and textiles, for example.[8] In less than a quarter of a century, the contribution of agriculture to Turkish GDP decreased from about 60 per cent to less than 35 per cent; that of industry, including agribusiness, doubled to over 40 per cent. The more dramatic change, however, was in patterns of employment. At least one-third of all workers and labourers in traditional farming communities moved from agrarian-based work to jobs in manufacturing. In most cases this entailed moving from rural lands to the newly industrialized parts of the country, like the area around Istanbul. This major shift in employment patterns sent various ripple effects across society. By the 1970s, the Turkish middle class comprised not only the merchants, traders, civil servants, officers and landowners of Istanbul, Ankara and Izmir, but also (albeit at a lower level) the hundreds of thousands of families of industrial workers.

This new lower-middle class increased their financial means, moved to urban Turkey and in time began to acquire economic assets, especially real estate. But to a large extent, they continued to adhere to the cultural products they were comfortable with. The headscarf is again a salient example: while hardly any veiled women would be seen in Istanbul's old middle-class neighbourhoods, the headscarf was ever-present in the newly rising neighbourhoods on the city's periphery, where the majority of the inward migrants had settled.

This section of society was far more religious than the upper classes that had formed the spinal cord of the Ataturkian republic. This was hardly a surprise: Islam has for centuries been the primary identity of rural Turkey, and especially of eastern and southern Anatolia. Also, throughout the first half-century of the republic's life, the state did not consider any force in rural Turkey to be a threat to its power or to its social narrative. And so, while the state, and especially the military, had been highly assertive and often brutal in its dealings with potential dissidents (e.g. leftist groups in Istanbul and the coastal towns), its attitude to the rural regions was one of benign political neglect. Rural Turkey's exposure to the state was also minimal. Economic, social and especially education policies were implemented in the Anatolian regions, but there were hardly sustained efforts at engaging these regions, at linking them to the state's secularism, at changing their social frame of reference. The state's reach, especially in matters of culture, was always quite limited. Some Anatolian towns, such as Adana or Kaiseriah, had seen significant development in their infrastructure, especially during the years of heavy industrialization; but when it came to social traditions, culture, entertainment and general way of life, the influence of Ankara and Istanbul was distant and barely noticeable.

There was also a subtle condescension towards rural Turkey. Over time, Ataturk's paternal 'guidance of Turks towards modernity' had evolved into a consistently haughty and often contemptuous rhetoric towards the rest of the country, on the part of both the state's institutions and large groups of Ankara's and Istanbul's political and social elite. An old Turkish term, the 'black Turks', acquired a new meaning among the upper echelons of the two cities, referring to vast swathes of their rural compatriots. The social distance that arose between official, upper-middle-class Turkey and the country's rural, agrarian and industrial parts, and the arrogance that often characterized the former's approach to the latter, resulted also in misunderstandings and stereotyping. For many westernized Turks, the 'blacks' were living in the Ottoman darkness. For many rural Turks, the upper-middle-class 'Istanbulites' and their like had lost their identity.

Nothing reflected this social and cultural disconnect more than the attitude to Islam. The Ataturk establishment made it consistently clear that it viewed Turkey's Islamic heritage as a backward social force that needed to be at best reformed, and at worst trounced. Many in its ranks exhibited discomfort with the country's Islamic history, and some pugnaciously opposed any attempt to reconcile the society's secular state with its religious heritage. Meanwhile, for huge numbers of lower-middle-class and poor Turks, especially in Anatolia's hinterland, Islam endured as the decisive force in their identity and culture. Mehmet and Ahmet remained the most popular names. Most ordinary Turks went to mosques, prayed daily and fasted during Ramadan.

Turkey was exposed to a strong wave of Europeanization between the 1970s and 1990s. Over 2 million Turks, primarily from the lower-middle classes and poorer segments of society, emigrated to western Europe, particularly Germany and the Netherlands, and to a lesser extent to Sweden. This was also the period when Turkey opened discussions with the European Union regarding the terms of its candidacy for accession to various European organizations, from the customs union to the common market and the EU itself. The remittances of the millions of Turks who had settled in western Europe became a major source of foreign currency in the Turkish economy. The summer visits by these migrant Turks and their families connected Turkey's lower-middle classes with the ideas, fashions and technologies prevalent in Western countries. The long and often difficult discussions and negotiations with the Europeans compelled the Turkish state to adopt European laws, particularly in trade, taxation and the regulation of competition, in different industries. They also significantly exposed Turkish politicians and the state's sprawling bureaucracy to the machinations, style and rhetoric of various European institutions.

And unlike Egypt, Syria, Jordan and Morocco, Turkey was hardly exposed at all to the strong Islamist winds blowing across the Gulf from the 1970s to the 1990s. The total number of Turks who had emigrated to work in the Gulf was negligible relative to those who had settled in Europe. All these social, economic and political factors caught Turkey in the crosshairs of immense European influence. Yet, while Turkey's upper social segments (and arguably a significant part of its middle class) were increasingly more westernized, this exposure to the West did not trickle down to the customs, traditions and identity of the broadest sections of Turkish society, which clung to their Islamic heritage.

The political representation of this Turkish Islamist orientation was also vastly different from that in the Arab world. Never in the period from the 1970s to the 1990s did Turkey have an overtly Islamist political movement bent on Islamizing the state and society. It never had any significant Salafist movement. On the contrary: historically, Turkish Islamism tended to be Sufist in nature, eschewing jurisprudence, law and practices for the spiritual dimensions of the religion.[9] Turkey never witnessed a struggle between the state and jihadist groups. The country never had any strong official institution that sponsored Islamism, such as the Saudi Wahhabi establishment. And, unlike in many Arab countries, the Turkish regime continued its strict separation between the state and religion.

Turkey's Islamist tendencies expressed themselves within civil society. From the mid-1980s to the mid-1990s, the vast majority of farmers' cooperatives, labour associations and small sports clubs, some relatively independent educational institutions such as vocational institutes and high schools, and the offices of the *mukhtars* (local chieftains) across the country, became bastions of conservative groups hailing from Turkey's southern and eastern regions. The sons and daughters of the increasingly rich farmers, labourers and merchants began to assert themselves in their local communities. This was not intended to challenge the secular state. It was a natural evolution: a new generation, better educated than its parents, was seeking to affect and influence its immediate social and economic environment.

Scores of young men who had started their careers in farming, small-scale trading, entry-level bureaucratic positions or various services targeted at local communities emerged as community leaders. They understood the needs of the increasingly sophisticated farmers and traders much better than the mid-level bureaucrats sitting in Ankara and Istanbul. And unlike those bureaucrats, the young leaders were not imposed by a central authority: they grew from within the communities. Gradually, a new narrative began to emerge, which revolved around representing the 'black Turks' in interactions with the state. They advocated the rights of these groups to forge their own policies, independent of the dictates of the *effendiys* (office dwellers). They made it clear to the farmers, labourers and merchants owning small and mid-sized businesses that collectively they could exert power on decision-making in areas that mattered to them, especially in farming and trade regulation. And crucially, in contrast to the state's rhetoric, which had remained highly secular and ultra-nationalistic, they spoke the same language as their communities: drawing on old traditions, conservative backgrounds and Islamic heritage.

Recep Tayyip Erdogan is the most prominent and successful of those new leaders. He grew up in one of Istanbul's immigrant neighbour-hoods. He worked with local merchants in the area; enrolled in different social groupings; became a small-scale football star in Kasimpasa (a sports club associated with another lower-middle-class quarter); and studied at the state's local high school, as well as at a local vocational school with links to Sufi orders. He then went on to study economics, becoming politically active in the 1970s in various youth organizations as well as in the student union of the Aksaray School of Economics and Commercial Sciences. He was outspoken in his hostility to Western domination of world economics and the West's intervention in the affairs of Islamic countries, and he displayed a clear distaste for Zionism. These positions were not directly hostile to the secular state, but they reflected a political disposition that was very different from that of the Turkish establishment, which prided itself on Turkish NATO member-ship, alliance with the West, and close relationship with Israel. Erdogan exemplified the rise of Turkey's new lower-middle classes asserting their presence at the heart of urban Turkey.

Erdogan won the 1994 local Istanbul elections and became the city's mayor.[10] His association, however, with the conservative, traditional Refah (Welfare) party caused him several problems. Refah, which was founded by two Islamist Turkish politicians (Necmettin Erbakan and Ahmet Tekdal), was the political heir to earlier traditional parties that were banned from politics. To participate in elections, the party had to shed many of its Islam-inspired ideas. Refah had emerged as one of the most important parties in the country in the early 1990s. This reflected the fragmentation of Turkey's political scene, but crucially also the fact that Refah's Islamist tendencies resonated with large groups of Turks. In the 1996 election it won the largest number of parliamentary seats, and Erbakan formed a coalition government. It was to be short-lived. As Refah seemed to attract larger constituencies, especially in Anatolia, the military decided to put an end to that 'threat to the state' in 1997. It forced Erbakan out of power, and a few months later suspended the party. Erdogan himself was imprisoned in 1999 for reciting a poem by the renowned 1920s Turkish activist Ziya Gokalp which the authorities deemed to be 'inciting religious hatred and public disorder'.

Refah's removal from politics sharply highlighted the disconnect between secular Turkey and the rest of society. While the widest segments in the former viewed the ejection as saving Turkey from Refah's 'Islamization project', millions of Turks considered it a brutal assertion of top-down power and a crushing of genuine representation. For many, it was another episode in upper-middle-class Turkey's imposition of its will on the rest: 'white Turkey' squashing 'black Turkey'. Yassir Yasar, one of Erdogan's earliest companions, has described the moment of Refah's suspension as a turning point in the public's feelings towards the 'old structure'.

The military's intervention was futile. The public's feelings meant that the rising middle classes, whether in Anatolia or (increasingly) around and within Turkey's largest urban centres, were not going to accept another marginalization from national politics. The social and economic changes to Turkish society between the late 1960s and the 1990s had effected a complete transformation in the distribution of wealth in the country, and so gave rise to interests that wanted and needed to have a say in how Turkey was governed. After a few years of experimentation with other parties and groupings, a small band of community leaders representing those rising social classes came together in 2001 to form the Justice and Development Party (AKP). In the 2002 parliamentary election, the nascent AKP came first, with over 34 per cent of the popular vote. In the 2007 election it increased its share to 47 per cent. In the 2011 election it grew again to 49 per cent. In 2014, following a constitutional amendment, Turkey held its first ever national presidential election. (Until that time it had been decided by a vote by members of parliament.) Recep Tayyip Erdogan was elected outright through a simple majority in the first round.

The AKP has always been a pragmatic party. Its successful record in a large number of municipalities, most prominently Erdogan's own experience as mayor of Istanbul, has instilled in the party an awareness of the power of being perceived as a doer, as a group of politicians who make things happen, as opposed to the 'Istanbulite elite', the establishment, which the AKP leaders have repeatedly described as being comprised of 'salon speakers'. The AKP's leadership was smart in embracing the economic reforms that Turkey had undergone from the mid-1980s to the mid-1990s.[11] It realized that those reforms resulted in significant fiscal and monetary achievements, and so, as a pragmatic party concerned with delivering results, it continued many of the policies. As these policies (alongside the favourable international economic conditions of the mid-2000s) gave a huge boost to the Turkish economy, so the AKP's leaders took credit for the growth, the creation of tens of thousands of jobs, the new heights in capital market capitalization, the real estate boom and the overall sense of wealthiness that Turkey experienced in the 2000s.[12]

The AKP's success would not have been possible had it not faced weak competition. The country's secular parties continued to adopt a highly nationalistic rhetoric; and those representing Turkey's Kurds remained focused on their ethnic demands. Neither appreciated the incremental but decisive change that had taken place in the country's middle classes. The secular nationalists were still tarnished by the dysfunction and rumoured corruption that had characterized the last two governments they formed before the AKP's rise to power. They also remained detached from the municipalities, professional syndicates, farmer cooperatives and other civil society organizations operating outside Istanbul and Izmir. And so it was almost impossible for them to portray themselves as 'doers' and politicians who could deliver on the ground, as the AKP had consistently done.[13]

The secularists' rhetoric also continued to focus on their core constituency of the upper-middle class, the urban intellectuals and some leftist groups. Surprisingly, throughout the 2000s, and despite the conspicuous social changes that Turkey was undergoing, they did not seem to be actively widening their support base among the rising lower middle classes, especially in eastern and southern Anatolia. As the AKP gradually extended its influence from the legislative to the executive to various state institutions, and even into the military and the intelligence apparatuses, the national secularists seemed reduced to issuing diatribes against the AKP in Istanbul's wealthy neighbourhoods, a few top universities, Bodrum's summer resorts and international gatherings where they could meet Western counterparts and warn them against the 'AKP's Islamization project'.

Western responses varied. While many in academia, think tanks and within official European circles were sympathetic to their fellow 'liberals' – the ones they felt were their natural allies in Turkey – they also looked upon the AKP's experience with admiration. Here was an Islamist party that had risen to power through democratic means, seemed to respect the tenets of the secular state, proved an adept manager of the economy, and – though it had been a tough negotiator with Europe on various dossiers – was respectful of international agreements and the commitments made by previous Turkish governments. For many in Europe, despite their reservations about the party's style of government and Erdogan's rhetoric, the AKP seemed to offer an example of a type of political Islam that was compatible with democratic principles.

Other Europeans were alarmed. Some leading European politicians, most notably in France, were strongly opposed to any significant progress in Turkish accession negotiations with the EU. In their eyes, AKP's conservatism, its return to old Turkish traditions and 'Islamism' were all signs of a move away from westernization and Europeanization.

The US was unmistakably in the former camp. As the 2003 invasion of Iraq became a military, political and financial disaster for the US, and as the neoconservatives' project to democratize the Middle East (discussed in chapter 10) was cast aside as a total failure, so the US saw the AKP's experience in Turkey as the sole success story – a ray of hope in a Middle East that seemed lethargic and immune to the waves of democracy that had transformed central and eastern Europe, Latin America and parts of Africa.

No one recognised the significance of the AKP's experience more than the AKP itself. By the mid-2000s, the architects of its foreign policy began to talk about the 'Turkish model', and of presenting the country as proof of Islam's compatibility with democracy. They positioned their Turkey as a bridge between the West and the Islamic, and especially Arab, world. Between 2006 and 2010 Turkey hosted numerous conferences at which Turkish experts moderated discussions between their Western and Arab counterparts. Turkish foreign policy, under the then foreign minister (and later prime minister) Ahmet Davudoglu, promoted the country as a 'connecting power' with strong links to the West and a 'long history in and understanding of the Arab and Islamic worlds'. Turkish Airlines became the largest carrier connecting European capitals to Arab cities.

The AKP leaders understood that the Arab world was facing a profound political and strategic void. Throughout the 2000s, the region's key powers (Saudi Arabia, Egypt and Syria) were inward-looking, ruled by languid regimes, for whom power and wealth had become inextricably linked. The AKP leaders saw that their form of Islamism, coupled with an impressive economic success story, resonated with wide sections of young Arabs, especially in the lower-middle classes, who lived under autocratic, corrupt regimes, suffered frustrating economic circumstances, and lacked any national project that they could relate to. Erdogan used many public occasions in which he addressed international audiences to send a message to the Arab masses that they should look at, and to, Turkey for political and economic inspiration.

Two factors helped Erdogan. The explosion in the number of Arab satellite channels in the 2000s led to an exponential increase in the demand for content from several markets, particularly Turkey. Turkish social and historical drama became immensely popular across the entire Arab world. Behind the sensational plots and the attractive actresses lay beautiful homes, clean streets and what came across to millions of Arab viewers as a thriving nation and a content society. What made this particularly important was that this was not Europe or the US: it was Turkey, a country to which most Arabs feel historical, cultural and religious connections. It was not surprising that Arab tourism to Turkey more than tripled in the period from 2004 to 2010, and Turkish products (from electronics to cosmetics) increased their market share across the Arab world. Major Arab investors began to take notice of Turkey. In 2007, three of the Gulf's largest commercial banks bid against each other to acquire a banking licence in the country.

The second factor was the chronic Israeli-Palestinian conflict. Erdogan consistently adopted an assertive rhetoric that was strongly supportive of the Palestinians. That contrasted with what came across as Arab indifference. In 2009, Egypt's former president Hosni Mubarak shook hands with Tzipi Livni, Israel's then foreign minister, on the eve of Israel's attack on the Gaza Strip which resulted in the death of hundreds of Palestinian civilians. Saudi Arabia issued customary condemnations. Most Gulf states provided little more than financial support. Erdogan, however, was pugnacious in his verbal diatribes against the Israeli operation, and provided logistical support to various aid agencies helping Palestinian civil society. This consistent posture against Israel earned him a huge following among tens of millions of Arabs.

For Arab Islamists, the AKP's experience was everything they wanted for themselves. Here was an Islamist party that came to power through free elections, and whose rhetoric combined an Islamic frame of reference with a way of operating within a secular country; a party that entrenched its rule and power through a consistently successful economic record that adopted free-market liberal economics with a keen eye for the desires of the country's lower-middle classes; that managed to sideline or co-opt a traditionally powerful secular establishment that had dominated the country for over seven decades; and that was recognized by important international stakeholders, including the US and large European countries, as a key player in the region. For Annahda and the PJD, there were elements of that story that they thought could be imported and implemented within their unique circumstances. Tunisia's Annahda, then still scattered in exile in London, Paris and Rome, admired the AKP's ability to put forward its Islamist frame of reference while remaining within the confines of a decisively secular state, a model they thought could be adopted in their country, which had a strong secular tradition. Even the Moroccan PJD, which resolutely insisted on the uniqueness of Moroccan society, sought to understand the AKP experience in a meaningful and detailed way. Elements of the PJD's campaign during Morocco's parliamentary election of November 2011 bore a striking resemblance to many of the AKP's economic policies and social rhetoric. For the Egyptian Muslim Brotherhood, however, the AKP's success seemed the exact destination they wanted to arrive at themselves. Many of the group's leaders in the 2000s were captivated by that success story. And so, when the 2011 uprising catapulted them into the upper echelons of Egypt's politics, they looked to repeat it, albeit at a very rapid pace.

The moment of the Arab Islamists' ascent came and went. But this did not mean that the AKP lost its status as a model for the compatibility of Islamism, modernity and economic success, as well as Islamism's ability to function in a democratic system. What was lost, however, was the notion that the AKP's experience itself, rather than its ideas, was exportable to the Arab world. Because of the peaceful nature of the political transitions in Morocco and Tunisia, the PJD and Annahda did continue to reflect on some aspects of the AKP's experience. Even after Annahda's transfer of power in 2013 and its later inclusion, in February 2015, as a junior partner in a coalition government, many of its members, especially in the younger cadres, repeatedly met AKP members to study their approaches to municipal work, interacting with a bureaucracy that had traditionally been associated with the secular establishment, and the AKP's campaigning style. But as the Arab Islamists lost power, and as many Arab countries descended into civil war, chaos and polarization, so the question of political Islam's compatibility with democracy and modern systems of governance became marginalized in the culturally most influential countries of the Arab world, most notably Egypt and Syria. Arab political Islam became embroiled in a confrontation between Islamism and secularism and nationalism. The situations in Egypt, Libya, Syria, Yemen and even Morocco and Tunisia, are vastly different from that in Turkey in the 2000s. For the majority of Arab Islamists, the struggle now has become one of existence and survival, rather than how to match an Islamic frame of reference with the tenets of democracy.

The AKP itself became embroiled in that polarization. It (and President Erdogan in particular) allied itself with Arab Islamist forces against the latter's opponents. In the eyes of most of the AKP's leadership, groups such as Annahda and the Egyptian Muslim Brotherhood had come to power through free elections, so compelling them to hand over power (or in the case of the Brotherhood, removing them entirely from the political scene) was a violation of democratic processes. They refused to accept the argument put forward by various Arab secularists (including many visitors to Istanbul) that these Islamists' projects portended great danger – from the potential fragmentation of several countries, to highly disruptive social circumstances in others, to the strengthening of jihadist groups across the region. The AKP also adamantly refused to accept the accusation that any of the large Islamist groups, especially the Egyptian Muslim Brotherhood, was aggrandizing power, marginalizing all their opponents (including the secular youths who had made their ascent to power possible), inciting hatred, or threatening national security.

The AKP's support for the Egyptian Muslim Brotherhood, Tunisia's Annahda and the Palestinian group Hamas, and what appeared to be a strategic alliance with Qatar (one of the key backers of several large Islamist groups) set it directly and squarely against the Saudi, Egyptian and Emirati regimes. President Erdogan seemed to relish the confrontation. In various media interviews, speeches in his presidential campaign of summer 2014, and in his address at the September 2014 UN General Assembly, he lambasted the intervention of the military in Arab politics in a direct reference to the Egyptian regime led by the former defence minister (and later president) Abdel-Fattah al-Sisi; and he scoffed at undemocratic regimes in a not-so-subtle reference to the Gulf royals. After Qatar was pressured by its Gulf neighbours to eject the Egyptian Muslim Brothers who had fled to it in late 2013, Erdogan welcomed them in Istanbul. Turkey hosted an array of satellite TV channels linked to various Islamist groups, and especially to the Egyptian Muslim Brotherhood. These channels have used Turkey as a base in campaigns that have focused almost solely on attacking Egypt's al-Sisi administration and the secularists who supported the removal of the Brotherhood from power. Istanbul also became a financial hub for various Islamist groups which fund and clear transactions there. This was particularly helpful for the Brotherhood after the Egyptian authorities designated it a terrorist organization in December 2013, rendering it impossible for the group to operate publicly in the country.

Personal perceptions have also played a role. After their successive electoral triumphs, Turkey's AKP leaders see themselves as experienced politicians who have built their credibility bottom-up, through successes in local, municipal and national elections. They have come to regard the Gulf's dynastic political system and the decisive role played by military establishments in different Arab countries as the antithesis of their experience. Furthermore, top-down politics (whether dictated by royal palaces or national security councils) remind the Turkish Islamists of Turkey in the 1980s, under General Kenan Evren, a period in which they, and the previous generation of religiously conservative Turkish activists, were aggressively excluded from politics. There have also been elements of personal drama. President Erdogan shed tears on a live TV show when his interviewer read out a letter that a leader of the Brotherhood had written to his daughter, who died in the Egyptian authorities' breaking of a sit-in by Mohammed Morsi's supporters. For many of the AKP's leaders, supporting the Arab Islamists, and especially the Brotherhood after its removal from power, became a personal and moral issue, a point that transcended international relations and regional positioning.

Personal feelings and perceptions aside, the AKP's confrontation with the largest, richest and most powerful Arab states put an end to its reach in the Arab world. Egypt expelled the Turkish ambassador and terminated the two countries' cooperation in several major infrastructure projects. Saudi Arabia, Abu Dhabi and Kuwait, by far the largest Arab exporters of capital, significantly curtailed their investments in Turkey. And apart from Turkish TV drama, which has continued to flourish across the region, many Arab markets have become almost closed to the largest and most competitive Turkish companies. The Arabs took their offensive to international organizations. In October 2014, Arab lobbying at the UN General Assembly resulted in Turkey losing its hitherto guaranteed temporary seat on the UN Security Council.[14] And the AKP was on the receiving end of a major negative media campaign, led by influential pan-Arab newspapers and satellite channels, which depicted Erdogan as a newborn Ottoman sultan, obsessed with expanding his influence and imposing his brand of Islamism on the region.

More important than drawing the enmity of the largest and most powerful Arab countries' regimes, the AKP's strident support of the Islamists, particularly the Brotherhood, led significant numbers of Arab secularists to view the AKP as a mere Islamist force siding with 'its brethren', rather than as a bridge between Islamism and secularism. The largest sections of Arab secularists were not convinced that the Turkish Islamists' position stemmed from respect for democratic values. For many, the position of the AKP and of Erdogan betrayed either a false rhetoric or an utter misunderstanding of their fundamental problems with the Islamists', and especially the Brotherhood's, Islamization.

This was exacerbated by the fact that the stance of the AKP and Erdogan as defenders of democratic values was increasingly frayed by developments at home. Many local and international civil society organizations accused the Turkish police of repeatedly using excessive force in dispersing protests, and charged the AKP with using its influence to fire leading journalists critical to it from prominent positions in newspapers and on TV stations. There was a prevailing sense, especially in Turkey's urban centres, that the power of the AKP, and especially President Erdogan, was increasingly going unchecked.

The AKP's image has become synonymous with that of Erdogan. After over a decade at the helm, with unrivalled authority over the most influential parts of the executive, Erdogan has amassed such extensive power that the collegiality that characterized the AKP in the early 2000s has been lost. Almost all the party's founders have been marginalized. The new leaders who emerged from the mid-to-late 2000s, most notably Ahmet Davudoglu, are bureaucrats, academics or professionals, rather than politicians who ascended through the party's internal ranks. Those new leaders owe their political rise to the party, and especially to Erdogan.

President Erdogan is also increasingly seen as dismembering the Ataturkian state. The complaints of the secular Turks shifted from the generic ('the AKP has taken over all state institutions'; 'Erdogan is creating a Turkey modelled on Putin's Russia'; 'he wants a new pious generation to dominate the country') to the specific (Islamic schools were on the rise; barriers against political representation were increasing; and the government was adopting socially intrusive rhetoric, such as against birth control).

President Erdogan seems to hold strong views regarding Turkish identity and how the Turks should look at their history. In 2012 he attacked the hugely successful Turkish soap opera *The Magnificent Century*, which revolved around the private life of the Ottoman Sultan Suleiman the Magnificent, as an utterly inaccurate representation of the era and the man, warning about how it could impact the way in which young Turks perceived their heritage. At the core of his passionate rhetoric against the series lay his view of himself and the political movement he led as the genuine representation of what real Turkey – and at its core, its Islamic identity – is, as opposed to the secularism that was imposed on the society for decades.

All of this demonstrates Erdogan's view of his mandate. To a large extent, he sees his rise to power through the prism of the old Ottoman (and in some views, Islamic) concept of the *vellayet* (or *wellayah* in Arabic). According to this view, a decisive, just and righteous ruler is mandated by the people, and graced by God, to put the nation on the right path. The ruler is to assert the 'right' values in society, to guide it by 'his wisdom' and his ability to distinguish between right and wrong. In Erdogan's case, he has been reforming the Ataturkian state: infusing Turkey's 'natural Islamic identity' into the state's fabric (without discarding the separation between the sacred and the secular), enshrining genuine representation in the country's politics, and crucially taking the state's power from the unelected Ataturkian establishment of 'white Turks' and bringing it to the 'masses'. Thus, Erdogan has been on a mission to rectify a historical injustice against ordinary Turks. Strategically, he has been correcting the calamitous mistake of abandoning Turkey's Ottoman heritage and disconnecting it from the Islamic world.

In response to his detractors and opponents inside and outside Turkey, President Erdogan repeatedly emphasized that he had the 'votes of the majority' of the people. But a truly democratic political system transcends free elections. At its heart lies inclusion, accepting the 'other' and having checks on major concentrations of power. And so, the model that was increasingly associated with Erdogan began to gain many of the features of the regimes in the Arab world that Erdogan has been attacking.

Aside from the dilution of the AKP's democratic credentials, the party has also been losing the very thing that made it hugely successful, and a model for other Islamists in the region. It has grown beyond the lean political organization that won the 2002 and 2007 elections, evolving into a colossal social, political and economic machine with various arms, attached associations, business interests allied with many of its leaders, and civil society organizations with different links to it. This has strengthened its presence within some key conglomerates, such as professional syndicates. But the AKP has also been losing its agility and its focus on 'delivering'. Various new committees that were established over the years in Ankara and Istanbul emerged as a new internal bureaucracy that had much more influence over priorities, the modus operandi and public messages than local branches. The young cadres who surrounded the party's founders in the early 2000s have been marginalized and replaced by a new generation of functionaries. A major split has occurred between a camp surrounding Erdogan and another around Abdullah Gul, one of the AKP's leaders and former president of Turkey, who made it clear that he opposed the party's external positioning as well as many of Erdogan's internal policies. For the first time in over a decade, the AKP has lost its cohesiveness and its united view of where the party should be going.

The AKP has also lost its most powerful ally in the country's civil society: the Islamist Gulen movement. The group that the Islamist scholar Fethullah Gulen established in the 1980s as a *cemaat* (community) to bring together religious and socially conservative professionals had, by the early 2000s, grown into one of Turkey's largest providers of social services, with special focus on education. It controlled over 70 per cent of the schools that prepare students for university admission exams which, in early 2014, had some 2 million students enrolled in them. The Gulen movement always maintained its distance from national politics. Its focus was on supporting ambitious students from conservative backgrounds to attain the best education that Turkey could offer. An experienced Turkish journalist described the group to me thus: 'They did not seek to infiltrate the establishment, but to transform it from within.' Throughout the 2000s, there was a clear meeting of minds between the AKP and the Gulen movement. Both were conservative groups with an unmistakably Islamist frame of reference. The Gulen movement's support was particularly helpful to the AKP in the country's diverse media scene and business community. The relationship broke down, however, in 2013 over major differences concerning the direction of Turkish Islamism and disagreements regarding Erdogan's policies. The two sides became engaged in a bitter political war. The AKP has arguably outgrown its need for the support of a civil society group. But that an old alliance, and one with the country's largest non-political Islamist group, could break down so rapidly revealed that the AKP was losing its social touch.[15]

The more the AKP becomes synonymous with President Erdogan, adopts more Islamist stances and views, evolves as an enemy of the Ataturkian state, continues its paternalistic approach to society and loses all connection to secular Turks, the more Turkish (and Arab) secularists will invoke it as another failure of political Islam. The argument is already advancing: the Islamists can present well-drafted manifestos that talk of the compatibility of Islamism with the tenets of plurality, inclusion and respect for national, secular states. Exploiting historical injustices and using religious rhetoric, they are able to build large constituencies. Because of their long experience of running community services, and because their leaders usually come from lower-middle-class backgrounds, they know how to translate their election victories into policies that placate large segments of the lower-middle classes. But, the argument goes, in time their commitment to democracy will waver; they will always reduce it to the concept of elections and nothing more; they aggrandize power at the expense of others; and crucially, they recast their political struggle as a moral and religious one.

Islamists, of course, see it differently. Within the AKP itself there is another interpretation of the party's experience in the last few years. Some of the groups that surrounded Abdullah Gul believe that the AKP will, sooner or later, outgrow Erdogan's dominance. They see Recep Tayyip Erdogan as having been the most charismatic and transformative Turkish leader since Kemal Ataturk. It was normal for a man like him to come to dominate his party, which came into existence only a decade earlier. These people argue, however, that after leaving the scene Erdogan will become, like Ataturk, the father of a movement, a man who gave immense momentum to an idea, as opposed to the domineering figure he was during his time in office. Some Islamists from the Gulenist camp subscribe to the same view, though they are less charitable towards Erdogan. They believe that the social changes that paved the way for the rise of the AKP have given Turkish Islamism a sustainable social, economic and political base. In their view, Erdogan's concentration of power and his disregard for wide sections of the population have tarnished 'one implementation' of that Islamism. Once he leaves power, other Turkish Islamists will put forward different, more accommodating, pluralist implementations. Others believe that the AKP will gradually lose its ability to dominate Turkish politics, and that soon it will be forced into governing coalitions with parties of different ideologies. The AKP's failure to achieve a majority in the country's June 2015 parliamentary election might be the start of such a trajectory.

There will be other chapters in the story of Turkish Islamism. But that aside, the version put forward by the AKP and Erdogan in the last few years has failed to sustain itself as a model for the largest of the Arab world's social segments. Not only did the moment of the Arab Islamists' rise to power come and go; the moment in which the experience of the AKP (and Erdogan) seemed to provide an inspiration for many Arabs also arrived, and then evaporated.

CHAPTER NINE

Iranian Islamism as a Model for Arab Islamists

In February 2011, as hundreds of thousands of people camped in Cairo's Tahrir Square to call for the removal of President Mubarak, Iran's Supreme Leader Ayatollah Ali Khamenei, effectively the ultimate religious and political authority in the country, stated that 'these revolutions, this Islamic awakening, are a war between two wills, the will of the people, and the will of their enemies'. Throughout the year he repeatedly described the Arab uprisings as 'Islamic revolutions', the expression of the desire of the region's young people for Islam as their identity and the system they aspired to realize. Khamenei was savvy enough to gloss over the distinction between Iran and the Arab countries, and between Shiism (the Islamic sect that most Iranians follow) and Sunnism (the one that the majority of Arab Muslims adhere to). Neither did he elaborate on what an 'Islamic system' might mean. But his message was clear: just as the Iranian people chose Islam as their identity and political system, so the Arabs were now doing the same. He depicted the young Arabs' revolts not as countering oppressive and lethargic ruling structures, but as an episode in the confrontation between those for and against *hukmu Allah* (God's rule).

Khamenei's utterances were not mere reflections of a man's perceptions or hopes. The Arab uprisings offered Iran a historic opportunity to extend its influence across the region. Egypt's President Mubarak, one of Iran's bitterest regional enemies, was removed. The Muslim Brotherhood wanted to improve Egypt's relationship with Iran. Iran also held multiple talks with Tunisia's Annahda. And for a while (in 2012 and early 2013), it seemed that Morocco's PJD was flirting with the idea of developing the country's links to Iran.

Iran was becoming a crucial – if not the decisive – power in the hottest wars in the region. Between 2012 and 2015, it lent at least logistical support to the Shii Houthi tribes and militias in Yemen, enabling them to take over the capital Sanaa and effectively control the most strategically important parts of the country. For the first time in at least half a century,[1] the Iranian-backed Houthis were in control of almost all the key regions on the border with Iran's arch-enemy, Saudi Arabia.[2] The revolt against the Shii–Alawite Assad regime in Syria, which began in March 2011 as a series of peaceful demonstrations, quickly descended into an extremely violent sectarian struggle. Salafist jihadists flocked to fight in Syria. Iran encouraged its Lebanese client, the Shii organization Hezbollah, to logistically and militarily support the Assad regime. Less than two years after the beginning of the revolt, however, Iran was directly and deeply involved in the war there. Hundreds of Iranian 'experts' from the Revolutionary Guard (the Iranian armed forces' most sophisticated division) and thousands of fighters and volunteers from various Iranian military units were leading forces in the fight against the rebels and the Salafist jihadists in the country. Syria's Assad regime became beholden to Iranian assistance. Throughout 2014, a few senior figures in the Iranian Shii religious establishment quipped that Iran controlled Damascus, Sanaa and Baghdad.

Controlling Baghdad was a consequence of the US invasion of Iraq in 2003. The war ended half a century of military rule in that country, and at its centre the command of the secular Arab nationalist Baath party, the Iraqi branch of which was headed by Saddam Hussein, the man who had invaded Iran in 1980 and triggered a war between the two countries which lasted for eight years and cost almost a million lives. In the early years following the American invasion, the US led a systematic de-Baathification of all Iraq's key institutions, beginning with the military forces and the country's civil service.[3] This, coupled with the country's descent into civil war in the mid-2000s and the rapid brain drain that Iraq suffered in the years after the invasion, resulted in a dramatic shift of power in the country. For at least six decades – since the rise of the Baath party to power in 1958 – Sunni Iraqis had controlled the most powerful state institutions; but by the mid-2000s, Shii Iraqis, some highly assertive (such as former prime minister Nuri al-Maliki) were in command. This gave the Shiis, who constitute the majority of Iraq's population, the first chance in many decades to achieve political representation commensurate with their demographic weight. The following decade witnessed the entire Iraqi political system become dominated by politicians, families and militias that had various connections to the country's largest Shii 'religious references' or social groups, many of which in turn had diverse links to Iran. A large number of figures in Iraq's new establishment were Shii refugees or political dissidents during Saddam Hussein's era, whom Iran had supported, hosted or financed. At times, especially in the period from 2010 to 2013 during al-Maliki's reign, Tehran became by far the most important player in almost all key decisions in Iraqi foreign and domestic affairs. Two decades after the end of the Iraq–Iran war, Iran's bitter enemy seemed to have become an Iranian satellite.

Something similar happened in Lebanon. Following the assassination of Prime Minister Rafik Hariri in 2005, Lebanon seemed on the verge of sliding back into a civil confrontation between its multitude of sects, a reminder of the civil war that consumed the country from 1975 to 1989. Various political blocs representing Sunni, Christian and Shii constituents positioned themselves for the impending conflict. Amidst the fluid alliances between the different sects, Hezbollah emerged as the unrivalled power in the country, controlling key state institutions, having an effective veto on the formation of any government and the election of any president, operating large stakes in strategic economic sectors such as telecommunications, and wielding a military power that dwarfed the

Lebanese army. For years Hezbollah has vacillated between being a client of the Iranian Islamic Republic to maintaining some distance from policy-making in Tehran. Some saw the group as a mere tool of the Islamic Republic; others as a fully fledged partner. Irrespective of the dynamics of the relationship, Hezbollah's colossal influence over Lebanon's politics and economics placed Lebanon within Iran's sphere of interest.

The Iranian Islamic Republic has always positioned itself in opposition to Israel. Ayatollah Rouhullah Khomeini, the godfather of the revolution that ended the rule of the Shah of Iran in 1979, the most revered Shii authority of the twentieth century and the Islamic Republic's first Supreme Leader, saw Israel as 'Little Satan' to the US's 'Great Satan'. Almost immediately after toppling the shah, Khomeini cut off all diplomatic relations with Israel, effectively terminated Iran's hitherto extensive economic links to Israel, and adopted a highly antagonistic rhetoric against the Jewish state. Though his relationship with the Palestine Liberation Organization wavered, he retained extensive links to other Palestinian factions. Later, after his death, the Iranian Islamic Republic became a close ally and backer of the Islamist Palestinian movement Hamas. The leaders of Iran have consistently sought to use their enmity with Israel to position themselves as patrons of Arab causes. That enmity was heightened by Israel's intense opposition, especially in the 2000s, to Iran's nuclear programme. As Israel launched diplomatic, intelligence and cyber campaigns to derail the Iranian programme, Iran painted a particular picture of the strategic struggle: the Islamic Republic standing up to the Jewish state, a positioning that resonated widely and positively across the Arab and Islamic worlds. This coincided with the emergence of Hezbollah as Israel's main regional opponent, especially after it managed to withstand a major Israeli military campaign in 2006 and emerge with its power structure, leadership and stranglehold over Lebanese politics intact. All of this boosted Iran's standing in the region.

Even after the moment of the Islamists' rise had passed, Iran's aspirations to expand its influence did not diminish. Its reach in Yemen, Iraq,

Syria and Lebanon, and its stance as a force against Israel, all imbued it with confidence. Ali Khamenei stopped describing the Arab uprisings as 'Islamic'. But Iranian strategists looked at the region around them with relish. In a decade, since the mid-2000s, Iran's influence and ability to shape its neighbourhood and threaten its opponents – whether Israel or leading Sunni Arab countries such as Saudi Arabia – have increased substantially.

This resonated with the premise upon which the Iranian Islamic Republic was founded. Khomeini hardly saw his mission as toppling the shah, overthrowing an oppressive regime or installing democracy. For him, the 'revolution' was 'Islamic'; the revolutionaries were 'his followers'; the system of governance that was to be imposed on the country was 'Islam'; and crucially he represented the will of the people. The last point had different meanings for different people. Khomeini was the only Iranian politician who managed to unite the country's Islamists and secularists under the idea of fighting the 'oppressor' (the shah's regime).[4] Almost all the key groups that had made the Iranian revolution possible (including many secular socialists) deferred to him. In this sense, he represented the will of the people, at least for a while. For Khomeini, however, he represented the desire of the people to have an Islamic system – a system that in his definition was one that would not defer to the people at all. His political vision revolved around the notion of *welayat al-faqih* (the rule of the learned scholar or the jurist). He resuscitated that old concept in Shii tradition, expanded on it, imbued it with new meanings, and interpreted it as giving the *faqih* (the jurist, the learned 'imam' of the age) unrivalled, unquestioned authority over all facets of his followers' lives. To locate this theological concept in a political system, the term (and position of) 'Supreme Leader' was invented and bestowed upon Khomeini. He did not object to having free elections, through which presidents and MPs were to be elected. But in this theological-political architecture, all Iranians, including elected officials, were to submit to the jurist, the imam, who ruled not just on the basis of his theological knowledge, but had a semi-divine mandate. In this system, the imam represented the will of the people through their submission to his theological superiority, not by way of electoral mechanisms through which they might choose or depose him.

Khomeini was close to eighty years old when he landed in Tehran on 1 February 1979. Because of age, his personal aspirations were limited.[5] His religious and political ambitions, however, were colossal. Khomeini's vision transcended Iran. He was aware that the Shii underpinnings of his *welayat al-faqih* system would inhibit its adoption by the majority of Sunni Islamic societies. But he held a deep conviction that his success in toppling the shah ('the king of kings' who had commanded the fifth-largest army in the world) using only his sermons and 'letters to the faithful' (which were clandestinely circulated throughout Iran for at least four years prior to the 1978/79 revolution) was the beginning of a transformation of the Islamic world. In various conversations and interviews, he commended the role that several Islamic scholars had played in bringing Sunni and Shii Islam together.[6] It is highly doubtful that Khomeini ever thought his system would be exported to Egypt, Syria, Morocco, Malaysia, Pakistan or any of the large Sunni Islamic countries. But the notion of the rise of Islamic scholars to command their societies seemed to him not only possible, but an Islamic obligation.

Not only did Khomeini overthrow one of the most powerful secular regimes in the Middle East.[7] He also came to represent, albeit briefly, the aspirations of the largest groups in his country. Further, he seemed able to incorporate the tenets of democracy into his vision for how Islamic societies were to be governed. By allowing elections and yet subjecting the victor to his theological system, and by ensuring representation and curbs on the executive power, and yet keeping himself beyond any checks and controls, he was marrying seventh-century Islam with twentieth-century political representation. For ardent Islamists (the vast majority of his followers), he was 'the imam'; for those who abhorred the shah's autocracy and extreme abuse of human and political rights, he was the man who had won the hearts of tens of millions of Iranians. Khomeini used rhetoric that could hardly be considered 'democratic': his pronouncements were largely anchored in theology or represented his conviction that he personally embodied 'the will of the people'. But when it suited him, he would use the consent given to him by the people against his enemies. And so he often remarked, with acid irony, 'When did the Arab or Saudi kings subject themselves to democratic tests?'

Herein lay the threat of the Iranian Islamic revolution and republic. Even though Khomeini's Shii concept of *welayat al-faqih* was not exportable to any Sunni country, his complicated amalgamation of some political representation, fiery revolutionarism, dramatic appeal to millions of people, and their consent to be ruled according to a system based on some understanding of Islam, made him (and his model) a genuine threat to many non-democratic regimes presiding over pious, conservative societies.

Khomeini's specific reference to Saudi Arabia was intentional. The Saudi leadership saw the danger that the Iranian Islamic Republic posed to its rule, especially given that Saudi Arabia's Eastern Province (the location of over 80 per cent of Saudi oil) has a substantial Shii population. Saudi Arabia became a major supporter of Iraq's Saddam Hussein in his war against Iran's Islamic Republic. This was not merely a function of 'Arab brotherly support': the Saudis wanted to stem the expansion of Iran's 'Islamic revolution', and Saddam's Iraq was the willing and determined vehicle. The war exhausted both Iran and Iraq; in addition to the enormous human toll, it left both countries semi-bankrupt. Khomeini died shortly after war ended.

Iran entered the 1990s tired. The inconclusive end of the war left a bitter taste in the country's mouth.[8] Tens of thousands of families had lost fathers, sons and breadwinners. Iran did not acquire any territory; it did not improve the lot of Iraq's Shiis; it did not overthrow Saddam Hussein or crush his Arab nationalist regime; and it did not advance the 'Islamic revolutionary tide' that many of Khomeini's lieutenants had repeatedly talked about. Actually, the tide seemed to have lost momentum even inside Iran, leaving behind a drained society that was weakened and poorer than it had been when the revolution rocked the shah's throne in 1978.

Iran in the 1990s felt different from Khomeini's time. The economic boom that the West, and especially the 'Great Satan', witnessed in that decade, the exposure that the internet delivered, the transformative effect of satellite channels, and the overall optimism that characterized those years reached Iran. Suddenly, a significant percentage of Iranians had sources of information about the outside world other than official state media. The Iranian regime had no response to the burgeoning realization of millions of Iranians that the West was enjoying not only abundance and buoyancy, but more crucially, a sense of confidence. That was particularly acute in the case of the United States, as the Clinton years gave strong momentum to 'brand America' across the entire Middle East. While Iran seemed tired and impoverished, the West and the 'Great Satan' seemed content. Khomeini's famous sentence of 1979 – broadcast repeatedly on Iranian TV – that 'we do not fear sanctions, we do not fear military invasions, but we fear the invasion of Western values and immorality', began to ring hollow.

Economics hardly helped Iran's Islamists. Throughout the 1980s, the first decade of the Islamic Republic's life, Iran witnessed a significant deterioration in economic freedoms, market openness, private sector competitiveness, labour rights and overall economic progress. That was primarily due to the dramatic exodus of high-end Iranian talent and private Iranian capital after the fall of the shah, as well as the collapse of foreign direct investment in the country. That oil prices fell throughout the decade by over 70 per cent (to single digits) did not improve the republic's finances. As the 'revolutionary tide' had receded, passions had cooled off and Khomeini had left the scene, the average Iranian began to compare his economic circumstances before the eruption of the revolution and a decade later. Many came to the conclusion that both they and their country were much worse off.

Corruption exacerbated the problem. Throughout the twentieth century, Iran's various leaders had exploited the country's economy. But the Islamic Republic was supposed to be different: the rule of the religious jurists was supposed to bring fairness, integrity and rectitude. And yet various of the ruling religious establishment's leading figures and members of their families emerged as significant economic power centres, without any clear explanation for the sources of their new-found wealth. There were several cases of blatant abuse of power in favour of acolytes and political allies. And then there were the systematic state interventions in the economy that many Iranians, the heirs to a vibrant mercantile culture, found highly distasteful. One example among many was 'Setad Ejraiye Farmane Hazrate Emam', the economic entity that Khomeini had created in 1979 to manage and sell properties abandoned in the chaotic times of the revolution. Sedat had expanded throughout the 1980s, and by the mid-to-late 1990s had become one of the most powerful economic actors in the country, with hundreds of billions of dollars in assets and, more significantly, dominant market shares in an array of sectors ranging from financial services and farming to the production of birth-control pills. This colossal economic player, and a few others, operated beyond any supervision save for that of the Supreme Leader.

Khomeini's successor, Ali Khamenei, could not match the revolution's godfather. Khamenei, who was elected in 1989 by the influential Assembly of Experts, a group of leading Shii scholars with a wide mandate to devise and interpret which policies were congruent with Shii jurisprudence, had the religious expertise, political savvy and years of experience to ascend to the most powerful position in the country. That he was arrested five times during the shah's reign and had suffered an assassination attempt that paralysed his right arm only helped his candidacy.[9] But the man lacked Khomeini's charisma, appeal and the almost magical spell that Khomeini could cast on the crowds. This deprived the Islamic Republic of arguably its most valuable asset: the people's willingness to accept an intensely deficient form of 'democracy' because of their utter faith in the *faqih*.

Khomeini's aspirations to export the Islamic revolution came to nothing. But, almost a decade after his death, a group of his followers aspired to bring about a reformation of the system he had built. In Iran's 1997 presidential election, Mohammed Khatami, hitherto a barely known Shii scholar and philosophy professor who had only once held a minor ministerial post, won 70 per cent of the popular vote in an astonishing 91 per cent turnout. The jovial man, with a near-constant smile, charmed young Iranians, women and a substantial percentage of the well-educated middle classes who flocked to vote for him, humiliating scores of conservative figures in Iran's Islamic establishment who considered him a lightweight contender with hardly any chance of ascending to the presidency. In his campaign, Khatami suggested significant changes to the political system, social code and role of the religious establishment that had existed in the country since the 1979 revolution. He and the circles of 'reformers' that had coalesced around him during the election campaign advocated relatively tolerant regulations regarding women's rights, gender mixing, press freedom, openness to civil society and a 'dialogue between civilizations' with the West, and suggested a gradual reduction in the powers of the Supreme Leader.

Some observers saw Khatami and his fellow reformers as challengers to Khomeini's system – politicians working from within the machine in order to undermine it. Numerous media reports portrayed Khatami and his allies as combatants in a fight against the conservatives, especially the 'old guard' that surrounded Khomeini's successor as Supreme Leader, Ali Khamenei. Khatami's campaign, his electoral victory and the various reforms he set out to implement in the first few months of his presidency were repeatedly presented to international observers as an utterly new phenomenon in Iranian politics after the revolution. Often these reforms were seen and depicted as attacks on the regime from within; and so, for many in the Western media and in Europe's political salons, Khatami and his allies became the contenders deserving of the West's support. Pictures helped. Numerous newspapers and TV stations contrasted Khatami's cheery smile and friendliness, especially towards Western reporters, with Khamenei's stern expression and aloofness. One became 'our friend', the other 'the enemy'. These views were partly wishful thinking and partly a mistaken reading of what Khatami and his allies wanted. Those reformers wanted neither to challenge the regime, nor to weaken its command over the state's institutions. Neither were they interested in defying Khamenei. They wanted to bring about gradual change that would strengthen the regime and cultivate it from a 'revolutionary tide by an exceptional leader' (Khomeini) to a sustainable social and political structure. They believed that the regime had no option but to develop, and they wanted to set in motion a process of change from within. To a large extent, they had set out to save Khomeini's system from itself.

Unlike Khomeini, Khamenei and the most prominent figures in Iran's Islamic regime, Khatami hardly ever spent time in Qom (the seat of learning of Iran's Shii Islam), preferring instead to tour local bazaars, schools and businesses in far-flung places across the country. He introduced significant economic reforms.[10] He lobbied the Guardian Council and the Supreme Leader to change the press law, allowing more than a hundred new publications to appear in Iran, many of which evolved into serious critics of the regime. Though he did not change the strict regulations affecting civil society organizations in the country, he did make it clear that he welcomed criticism – not just of the government and the presidency. He emphasized that Iran respects free speech and the right to express oneself without fear or inhibitions – something Iranians had not heard since the outbreak of the revolution.

These measures were hardly pandering to liberal, secular Iranians. In several speeches, as well as in his book *Islam, Liberty and Development*, which he released in his first year as president, Khatami accused secularists of intellectual detachment and of being cut off from the fabric of Iranian society. He emphasized the piety of the Iranian people and the country's 'Islamic identity'. He was also far from being enamoured of the West, accusing it of trying to 'dominate' the world, not just politically and often militarily, but crucially through 'inconsiderate promotion of values' which had already proven 'deficient'. Throughout all of this, and even in his economic initiatives, Khatami and many of his key allies kept returning to one word, 'moderation': a middle-of-the-road approach to enforcing Islamism without repressing rights and values; a middle-of-the-road economic outlook that could engage the economy and the world without losing control of the state's autonomy and its ability to assert its vision over society; a moderate social contract through which the Islamic Republic could move beyond its initial revolutionary fervour towards settling within the traditional, centuries-old fabric of Iranian society.

The reformers presented this new direction as part of the thinking behind the economic and social developments they had put forward. They refused to separate their policies from the macro view they had for the state and society. The new press freedoms, relaxation of the social code – even the initiatives in fiscal, monetary and investment domains – were all part and parcel of a new orientation that was open to the world, as well as to Iran's various historical experiences.[11] It proved highly popular among large groups of young urban Iranians, women and sections of the country's middle classes. Nothing confirmed this popularity more than Khatami's re-election as president in June 2001 for a second term. Even in ultra-conservative Qom, Khatami managed to secure the vast majority of the youth vote, taking around 70 per cent of the ballot. Posters depicting his smiling face became a common scene in Tehran's middle-class neighbourhoods, in Shiraz's markets and in the northern cities which, for centuries, had been touched by Azeri, Armenian, Turkish and Russian influences. Despite the traditional waning of popularity that afflicts most politicians after a few years in office, Khatami remained at the centre of most reformers' aspirations. Even when his administration's performance disappointed, such as in the government's far from impressive response to the effects of the devastating earthquake that hit Iran in 2003, most Iranian NGOs and liberal media pointed their fingers at various state institutions, sparing Khatami and the reformists around him from any serious criticism.

The reformers' solution was not to eliminate the religious layer, but to widen the Islamic Republic's frame of reference, in order to include in its ingredients elements of what Iran had had prior to the 1979 revolution. They wanted to add 'Persianness' to the mix. That was an innovation. A significant part of Khomeini's appeal to large sections of Iranians had been his intellectual and religious purity, his utter disregard for anything he deemed to be outside the boundaries of Islamic, and especially Shii, traditions. And so, for over two decades, the Islamic Republic, and with it Iranian politics and public life, had been almost entirely devoid of the traditional features of Iranian culture, the rich heritage of one of the world's most sophisticated civilizations. Asked once about Iranian history, Khomeini dismissed it as a 'background'; for him there was only one identity – Islam.[12] The 1990s' reformers wanted to connect the Islamic Republic with its Persian heritage. That was neither a challenge to Khomeini's thinking, nor an attack on the existing system, but rather an evolution that the reformers deemed necessary. In almost every major speech in his first two years in office, Khatami incorporated references to Iranian culture, to the country's collective memory, to the society's group identity that was distinct from the republic's Islamism and Shiism. Examples of this new intersection between religion and Persianness ranged from increased funding for artistic productions steeped in Iran's traditional arts, to the state's renewed and enthusiastic celebrations of the Nowruz (Persian new year) festival – something Khomeini and Khamenei had consistently frowned upon.

Incorporating Persianness in the state's fabric was a prelude to the fundamental change that the reformers sought: more plurality within the republic's decision-making system. They wanted to widen the interpretation of the notion of *welayat al-faqih*. Instead of one person, the Supreme Leader, having the ultimate say on all important matters, the reformers wanted initially to include several credible Shii *maraje* (references) in deliberations on major policies. They wanted to open the system to the acknowledgement that Shii scholarship and theological hierarchy extended beyond the strict and narrow interpretation laid down by Khomeini. The next step, they reckoned, was to move beyond the Shii establishment. Their vision was that, at a later stage in the republic's evolution, ultimate decision-making would involve collaboration between several Shii authorities, who would guarantee the Islamic nature of the state, and the MPs, who represented ordinary Iranians.

This was the first time since the founding of the Islamic Republic that an alternative view of its nature (and future) had been presented, albeit subtly and using very cautious wording. It was also the first time that an attempt had been made to move beyond Khomeini's distorted form of democracy towards reducing the *faqih*'s prerogatives and empowering the elected lawmakers. By trying to integrate Persianness into the Islamic Republic's fabric, by trying to move its system of governing away from religious absolutism towards more genuine representation, and by aiming to connect Shii Iran with its rich and resplendent heritage, the reformers sought to advance the system that Khomeini had created a quarter of a century before into a more comprehensive – more Iranian – one.[13]

This model had some potential for being exported beyond Iran. The 1990s' reformers, and at their centre Mohammed Khatami, had come to power through free elections – something that most Arab countries in the 1990s (and today) lacked. They seemed to have a huge following among middle-class Iranians, entrepreneurs, women and youth – demographics with aspirations and interests similar to those of their Arab counterparts. The reformers wanted neither to crush the system in which they were operating, nor to foment revolution. They wanted to evolve it slowly and cautiously, making it more politically and economically open, more inclusive and so more durable. This also resonated with many in the Arab world, and especially in the traditionally conservative Gulf societies. The reformers' rhetoric was neither reactionary nor steeped in seventh-century Islamism; it adopted prevalent, and even Western, ideas and terms. It aimed to marry the national (in this case, Persian) with the Islamic. And it did not define itself as exclusively Shii. Without necessarily intending it, Iran's 1990s' reformers boosted the appeal of the Islamic Republic inside and outside the country. In 1998, the viewers of *Ala al-Hawa* (*On Air*), the most successful pan-Arab TV talkshow in the 1990s, selected Khatami as its man of the year. After almost two decades of ignoring the Iranian political system, several Arab universities and think tanks commissioned studies on the reforms being made to the Islamic Republic's governing structure. Even in Europe, many commentators, especially in the continent's liberal media, reminisced about the old glamorous Iran that the revolution had crushed, and hoped that the reformers' rise symbolized the gradual return of that lush heritage to challenge Khomeini's austere political and social code.

Yet, once again, the potential to export a form of Iranian Islamism beyond Iran's own borders foundered. This time, however, it was not due to entanglement in a war, nor as a result of economic circumstances or the loss of an immensely charismatic leader. It was because the Islamic Republic's guardians wanted the reformers to fail. Ali Khamenei, the leaders of the Republican Guard, the most influential scholars in Qom and the Council of Guardians – none of them suspected the reformists of sedition or of wanting to subvert the republic. They did not believe that the reformists – most of whom, notably Khatami, had emerged from within the establishment's own ranks having served for years in its various theological, legislative and executive branches – intentionally posed any threat to the system. Their conviction, however, was that, even with the best of intentions, the reforms they had put forward would disrupt the power structure that had existed in the country for quarter of a century. In their view, the Islamic Revolution's main achievements in that period had been rising above the forces that wanted to destabilize it, crushing the remnants of the shah's regime, dissociating Iranian society from that 'corrupt period', and laying the foundation of a genuinely Islamic, Shii social and political order. Disturbing that power structure, even with the objective of developing it into a form that would be more palatable to certain segments of society, would, in their view, shake its very foundations.

The conservative forces in the Islamic Republic saw the reformers as sacrificing the true identity of the system for the sake of achieving the recognition of those who, 'in their hearts, have never, and will never, accept it'. To those conservatives, the republic's identity was established by an almost divine intervention, 'blessed by the imams'; the system was laid down after a 'sacred revolutionary struggle against the forces of impiety and irreverence'; and, as the true guardians of the Shii state, it was their responsibility to protect it. Others went further. Some leaders of the Basij (a highly conservative group with close ties to various parts of the Iranian military, which was formed, under Khomeini's patronage, from Iran–Iraq war volunteers) regarded the reformers, and the Iranian citizens who challenged 'the Shii order', as heretics who had rejected Islam, or at least had deviated from the 'true path'. To them, the reformers were not trying to bring about an evolution of the country's political system; they were attacking the 'imams' heritage'. It was telling that in many of the Basij's marches against reformists, such as their repeated confrontations with students in and around Tehran University in the 2000s, they chanted their allegiance not to the Islamic Republic as a state, not to the Supreme Leader, but to Imam Hussein, Prophet Mohammed's grandson, who was martyred in the battle of Karbalaa (one of the defining events of Shii Islam).

The attempt to infuse the Islamic Republic with Persianness was particularly troubling to many conservatives. They did not see Persianness as a rich heritage ranging from philosophy to science to art, and from which they (and the reformers) could pick and choose what could complement the Islamic Republic's system. Rather, it was a reminder of the few decades before the Islamic revolution. The conservatives largely confined their country's non-Islamic heritage to the shah's (and his Pahlavi dynasty's) interpretations of it – interpretations that were imposed on Iranian society between the 1940s and the 1970s. The two Pahlavi shahs who ruled Iran from 1925 to 1979 were vastly different men. Both, however, sought to place Iran firmly in the modern – and in their view, Western – world. The elder Pahlavi's approach entailed a systematic weakening of the Shii religious establishment. His son, Shah Mohammed Reza Pahlavi, whom the 1979 revolution deposed, was less assertive and strong-willed than his father, but his westernization drives were more ostentatious – from legendarily sumptuous weekend parties to a highly westernized court protocol, to almost advertised liaisons with international models. He even went out of his way to position his family's reign as the continuation of Iran's '2,000-year-old uninterrupted empire', though it had begun as a coup by a junior officer supported by the British army. Throughout the 1960s and 1970s, Persianness was reduced to manufactured glamour, phony state narratives and pretentious displays of wealth that betrayed insecurity and a need for acceptance. The conservatives in the Islamic Republic loathed that Persianness. For them, it was precisely the corruption that the Islamic revolution had 'risen' to purge and destroy. And so the majority of them were unwilling to tolerate a new attempt, even from within the establishment, to reconnect with any aspect of it.

Many also regarded diluting the pure Islamic nature of the republic and infusing it with Persianness as a detachment from Shiism. One of the fundamental pillars upon which Khomeini had built his message, especially in his years in exile, was his claim that Iran, and for that matter most of the Islamic world, had for centuries deviated from true Islamic society. His view went beyond rejecting westernization, many aspects of social modernization and openness to cultural imports from outside the Islamic world. He regarded the birth of the modern Iranian nation as well as that of all modern states in the Islamic world as a historical sin, for they contravened the divine order of the rule of Islam. In this perspective, the Islamic revolution was a divinely-ordained correction of Iranian history, which returned it to the only righteous rule: that of God. Here, Iran was not seen as an independent, rich, multilayered civilization: it was the centre of Shii Islam. Many Iranians and lovers of this rich country regarded that view as narrow and limiting. Yet for its supporters, including swathes of conservative Iranians, it was not only 'correct', but also a grandiose identity that filled them with pride: their country leading a new Islamic order that would restore God's rule to the Islamic world.

There was also a social dimension. The vast majority of the conservatives' leaders hailed from Iran's lower-middle and poor classes. The Iranian revolution was, for them, a combination of the establishment of a divine order through the overthrow of the sinful and immoral shah's regime, with the empowerment of the country's poor, who had suffered for decades. That the reformers' supporters belonged primarily to Iran's urbanized upper-middle class made the reformist movement seem, at least to many conservatives, alien. It did not connect with their way of lives and how they perceived Iranian society.

The reforms also threatened entrenched economic interests. For example, a number of reformers wanted to give parliament real powers to question the Republican Guard's financial interests in different economic sectors, as well as its economic ties to foreign entities, such as Lebanon's Hezbollah. For many conservatives, that was a danger that needed to be crushed.

The reformers' thinking also seemed to hurt the conservatives' foreign policy objectives. For at least two decades, the Islamic Republic had been Hezbollah's patron. This gave Islamic Iran, and especially the powerful conservatives in the regime, considerable influence in Lebanon, the most vibrant country in the eastern Mediterranean. It cemented the Islamic Republic's strong relationship with the regime of Hafez Assad in Syria. And it served as a route for Iran towards Israel's backyard. Yet, it was sectarianism that defined that patronage. With its immense political influence, its presence across various sectors of the Lebanese economy and a foreign policy that was almost independent of the Lebanese state, Hezbollah was (and continues to be) the political representative of a significant majority of Lebanon's Shiis. Iran's Islamic Republic had expanded its sponsorship to one of the region's oldest Shii communities – one whose contributions to, and influence over, Shii theological and political thinking far exceeded its demographic size. The connection to Hezbollah was paramount in order to entrench the Islamic Republic's credentials as the heartland of global Shiism. In the same period, and especially during and immediately after the war with Iraq, the Islamic Republic also became a refuge for, and backer of, hundreds of Iraqi political dissidents, the vast majority of them Shiis opposed to Saddam Hussein. Here too, sectarian affinity was a chief reason for Iran's openness to those dissenters. And so, the more the reformers infused Persianness into the state's political order, rhetoric and ultimately legitimacy, the less the regime would have been able to use Shiism as a basic pillar of its foreign policy. The funds, arms and logistical support that various parts of the Shii establishment, including the influential Republican Guard, had for years been supplying to Hezbollah and other groups would increasingly have come under scrutiny from the reformers.

And then there was the loyalty to the Khomeini legacy. Irrespective of the reformers' care not to offend the sensibilities of the millions who continued to revere Khomeini, many in the republic's conservative elite saw their political reforms as, at best, attenuating the fruits of the man's lifelong struggle, and at worst, as attacks on the man they regarded as the historical deputy of the twelfth Shii imam, the founder of the true Islamic state and the personification of their faith. They were not willing to allow anyone, even with 'good intentions', to disrupt the man's ultimate achievement: the political system he envisioned and brought to fruition.

The conservatives struck back. In January 2004, weeks before the country's parliamentary elections, the Council of Guardians banned over 2,200 candidates from standing (roughly 40 per cent of the total). These included seventy-five sitting MPs. Several groups closely associated with the Revolutionary Guard, such as the Clergy Association, launched an intensive media campaign against many reformers, including Khatami. The result was a major victory for some of the most conservative forces in Iranian politics, which took around 60 per cent of the parliamentary seats. In Tehran, which for the past decade had been the centre of the call for reform, the conservatives were guaranteed to win after most leading candidates were either prohibited from participating in the election or decided to boycott it. Shirin Ebadi, a prominent lawyer and later recipient of the Nobel Peace Prize, argued for the 'futility of competing in such an environment'. Not one of the city's thirty parliamentary seats went to a reformer.

Throughout 2004 and early 2005, the Basij intensified their presence in some of the reformers' main constituencies, such as Tehran University. In several cases they broke up peaceful demonstrations by students, civil society organizations and women's activist groups. The Islamic Iran Participation Front, an amalgamation of many reformers, lost over 20 per cent of its parliamentary seats as a result of what many considered to be systematic state efforts to crush the party.

The final blow came in 2005 with the election of Mahmoud Ahmadinejad, the ultra-hardline former mayor of Tehran and former revolutionary guard, as president. After two terms in office, Khatami was constitutionally barred from running a third time. The reformers' main candidate was Mehdi Karrubi, who had spent the previous two decades within the clerical Shii establishment and had risen to become the speaker of parliament. Ali Akbar Rafsanjani, a former president and one of the founding fathers of the Islamic Republic, also ran as a centrist who belonged to the 'order that protected the country since the revolution' but had the clear intention of bringing about major political change, especially in the power structure surrounding the Supreme Leader. Both lost to Mahmoud Ahmadinejad. Voters gave this relatively unknown former engineer over 7 million more votes than Rafsanjani. Ahmadinejad made it perfectly clear that he not only opposed the reformers' rhetoric, ideas and thinking, but saw their attempts as 'attacks' on the country's identity and national security.

Official media, especially TV stations close to influential figures in the regime, consistently depicted many reformers, as well as the vibrant youth groups in universities and some civil society organizations, as at best deluded and immature, or at worst as agents of Western (and especially American) conspiracies. These, however, were political tactics to keep the reformers and their supporters on the defensive. Much more effective was the casting of the reformers as urban, upper-middle-class intellectuals who were detached from the desires, frustrations and aspirations of ordinary Iranians. In a way, the regime was playing the same card that the reformers had previously used: shifting the narrative from ideology to mere socioeconomics. Just as Khatami had focused in his first year in office on fiscal, monetary and investment reforms, so the conservatives now tried to portray the reformers' social and political ideas as the concerns of a privileged few – as issues and causes that betrayed their detachment from 'what the people really care about' (i.e. improvements in the standard of living, better education, transportation, finding jobs and stemming inflation). Suddenly, throughout 2004 and 2005, it seemed that some of the most conservative media outlets in Iran had shifted their focus from their decades-old theological thundering towards a socialist rhetoric, steeped in 'the wants and needs of the over-whelming majority of Iranians'.

But Ahmadinejad did not have the support of the entire conservative bloc in Iran's ruling elite. Some saw him as a lightweight. Many, especially inside the Republican Guard's leadership, feared his populist approach, which often seemed uncontrollable. A few advisors close to Ali Khamenei harboured concerns about his 'adventurism', which they (correctly) predicted would cause 'unneeded complications in Iran's foreign policy'. For many conservatives, including Ali Khamenei, however, Ahmadinejad emblematised lower-middle-class and poor Iranians. Unlike Khatami, Karrubi and most leading reformers, and unlike most of the regime's elder statesmen, including Khamenei, Ahmadinejad's outlook, style of clothing and speaking, and the overall way he bore himself resonated with wide groups of poor and lower-middle-class Iranians. He lacked the reformers' urban sophistication and finesse, and the elders' detachment and haughti-ness. He was genuinely a man of the people, belonging as he did to the largest section of ordinary Iranians, for whom Shiism infused their iden-tity and their way of life, and for whom the main concerns in life were much simpler than ideology, foreign policy or exalted attempts to mix Shiism with Persianness. As one elderly Iranian woman put it to me, 'he understood us because he is one of us'. This underpinned his appeal. In addition to the populist policies that he repeatedly advocated on the campaign trail (including handing out cash to every adult Iranian), Ahmadinejad positioned himself as a representative of the second genera-tion of the Islamic revolution who aspired to return to the purity and values of the revolution's early years.

Ahmadinejad was not really a success. His record did not live up to the huge hopes of many poor and rural Iranians in 2005. But nor was he a failure.[14] And, crucially, from the perspective of the conservative elite that had supported him, he delivered. The reform wave lost momentum. All the prominent reformers were sidelined. Ahmadinejad managed to build and sustain a large support base that was at odds with the constituencies that backed the reformers.

Ahmadinejad's re-election in 2009 prompted allegations of electoral fraud.[15] Anger rose, especially in Tehran, where tens of thousands took to the streets to reject the results. Confrontations between the students and youth groups who rejected his re-election, and his supporters, including thousands of Basij members, resulted in the worst public violence in the country in decades. The Iranian authorities reacted nervously. Some newspapers were closed; severe restrictions were placed on accessing the internet; and scores of reformers were arrested. Ali Khamenei made his position conspicuously clear. He not only congratulated Ahmadinejad on his win, but described the protestors as 'ill-intentioned provocateurs, and enemies who wanted to spoil the sweetness of this celebratory event'.

The protests reflected the frustrations of many Iranians, especially the well-educated urban youth, about the dilution of reforms and the marginalization of the ideas that had come to the fore in the late 1990s and early 2000s. But these frustrations failed to resonate with the largest group of Iranians, who indeed supported what Ahmadinejad represented. The conservatives succeeded in their mission. For the majority of Iranians, the reforms became marginal issues – the concerns of politicians and the aspirations of the upper classes. The conservatives managed to dissociate the reformers' political ideas from the social and economic desires of the majority of Iranians. The success here was not that of Ahmadinejad. For many inside the establishment, he was expendable. The function that he had undertaken and fulfilled perfectly was to accentuate the social difference, the divergence in priorities and, crucially, in values, between the reformers and most Iranians.

This put an end not only to the Iranian Islamic Republic's most important project to bring about an evolution from within, but also to the possibility of its development as an Islamist model beyond the country's borders. As the reformers fell from power and Iran returned to the absolutist theological system of the 1980s and most of the 1990s, the appeal of the reformers' experiment dissipated. Whereas the attention of many Arab Islamists (and secularists) in the early 2000s had been drawn to Khatami's presidency and his attempts to introduce modernity into the country's arcane theological system, as well as to his efforts to unite nationalism (Persianness) with strict Shii Islamism, the return to the old system was not really of interest to any large Arab Islamist group. To some extent, many young Arabs (Islamists and secularists) felt sympathy for the Iranian youths who had protested against the 2009 electoral results. Those young Iranians who opposed the Iranian religious establishment seemed to be the ones worth admiring and learning from. Iranian Islamism lost its second chance to connect with those in the Arab world who had been watching it.

This was not how the conservatives saw it. For them, defeating the reformers was a major internal success. And now, after the Arab uprisings, they found the region open for them to widen their influence. By 'controlling four Arab capitals' (Baghdad, Beirut, Damascus and Sanaa), Tehran's conservative Islamists exported their Islamism to countries in which Shii Islam, for centuries, had had a strong presence. Iranian Islamism was now the backer, patron and, to a large extent, the frame of reference of the most powerful political actors in four countries in the eastern Mediterranean and the Arabian Peninsula. It seemed that, two decades after his death, Khomeini's vision of a wave of revolutionary Shii Islamism was materializing.

But whereas Khomeini had envisaged winning hearts and minds (as he had done in Iran through sermons and 'letters to the faithful'), his successors have been using billions of dollars, heavy armaments and thousands of fighters to support dictators, such as Bashar Assad, or to back Shii communities, such as those in Iraq and Yemen. Khomeini's vision of a revolutionary wave based on 'seas of believers', bringing about a new regional order in which the 'jurists' rule by semi-divine mandate, has nothing in common with his successors' hegemonic behaviour. These differences have deprived the new expansionary wave of Iranian Islamism of the most powerful asset of Khomeini's project (and that of the reformers): the appeal to masses of non-Iranians in the region. Despite his austere look and rhetoric, his disregard for modernity, his inability to connect with the life that the vast majority of middle-class Iranians (and non-Iranians) lived, and regardless even of his status as a Shii scholar, Khomeini represented a model that scores of Arab Islamists looked to with respect, and often with awe. The reformers lacked the old man's charisma, but their project represented a model that many Arabs, in the late 1990s and early 2000s, attended to, and admired. The new Iranian Islamism's reach and influence has been limited to segments of Arab Shiis. It lacks any resonance with others: it has triggered neither respect nor admiration.

What it has triggered is alarm. In the same way as Khomeini's revolution scared his neighbours and prompted them into action (Iraq invading Iran, and most Gulf states taking assertive stances against the Islamic Republic), so the new expansion of Iranian Islamism has galvanized Iran's key opponents. Saudi Arabia and Abu Dhabi led a strategic confrontation against Iran's presence in the eastern Mediterranean and the Arabian Peninsula. They backed Sunni politicians in Iraq, supported the rebels fighting the Assad regime, launched a military campaign against the Houthis in Yemen, and have been the main sponsors of Hezbollah's opponents in Lebanon. They also took several measures, particularly using their influence in the international energy market to inflict economic pain on Iran. Jordan's King Abdullah repeatedly warned of a 'Shii crescent' reaching from Iran to Iraq, to Syria, to Lebanon. Egypt's al-Sisi administration declared its commitment to 'the Gulf's security', in a direct reference to its apprehension at expansionary Iranian Shiism.

This cold war has exacted a toll on Iran. The Iranian currency lost over 40 per cent of its value from 2013 to 2015, and the country's fiscal situation has been deteriorating.[16] The war in Syria has dragged on, and

Iran has found itself committing increasingly substantial resources, including some of the best-trained officers in the Revolutionary Guard to serve in the country. And there is no clear exit strategy in sight.[17] Resources are limited, responsibilities are mounting, and allies' and clients' expectations are escalating.

Nor was all quiet on the internal front. President Hassan Rouhani, who won the 2013 presidential election, was a long way from being able to exercise real control over Iranian national security or foreign policy. But he made it clear, inside and outside Iran, that he had doubts about the futility and ultimate outcome of the Islamic Republic's various entanglements in the region. Unlike the conservatives who controlled the levers of power, he saw expansionary Shii Islamism as a threat that could spread the republic's resources thin.

This coincided with various demonstrations in 2013 and 2014 calling on President Rouhani to 'deliver for the people'. Reformers inside the republic's institutions who had been marginalized for the previous decade began to reappear. The group that surrounded Rouhani's foreign minister, Mohammed Javad Zarif, tried (with limited success) to forge an Iranian, not merely a Shii, regional positioning, and an internal explanation of Iran's objectives in its immediate neighbourhood. Many activists, university professors and representatives of youth groups repeatedly urged Mohammed Khatami to consider a comeback and a potential tilt at the presidency in 2017. In Tibriz, for the first time in many years, the city celebrated the birth of its most celebrated son, the poet Hafiz, whose work merges Sufism with love and lust, and which most conservatives consider quasi-blasphemy.[18]

There was also jockeying in the run-up to the looming succession. Though in good health, by 2015 Ali Khamenei was approaching eighty years of age and was noticeably less active than he had been a few years earlier. The Revolutionary Guard's top cadre, and especially the charismatic leader Kassim Suleimani, had become the most influential voice on many national security issues. Though Suleimani seemed to have the Supreme Leader's full trust, he was seen by many inside in the theological establishment as a new type of leader who had built his credibility in the battlefields as an exemplary soldier of the Islamic Republic, rather than as a theological authority. His often decisive role in key geopolitical issues (most recently the Syrian war) and the overall influence that the Revolutionary Guard had amassed in Iranian politics, demonstrated a change within the religious-political establishment: a gradual tilting towards the Islamic Republic's military arm and a slow but discernible weakening of its theological base. That generated resentment from many inside the Shii establishment, whether in Qom or in the circles surrounding Khamenei.

'There won't be an Iranian Gorbachev', said a senior media advisor close to the leadership of the Revolutionary Guard. That was how wide sections of the conservatives viewed the possibility of the return of the 1990s' reformers. Many conservatives were growing concerned about any kind of internal dissent. Their fear was that the checks that were placed on the reformers in the 2000s could be missing this time around; that a new wave of 'loosening control' could come at a moment when external enemies were 'sharpening their knives and Iran is vulnerable'. The conservatives feared a gradual loss of control, not only over decision-making at a time when Iran was committed in various external struggles, but over the country itself. And so they tried to cement their power. From late 2012 to the end of 2014, the electoral law was revised to strengthen the powers of veto that the Council of Guardians and other conservatives bodies have over presidential and parliamentary candidates. Regulations concerning protests, freedom of expression, digital media, blasphemy and respect for courts became stricter. The police arrested many journalists, often on vague charges related to views expressed in messages exchanged by mobile phone. Several local and international non-governmental agencies reported a significant increase in attacks on women who did not adhere to the Islamic Republic's strict dress code; some had acid thrown over them. The conservatives heightened their control over large media outlets, especially TV stations. The Persian Service of the BBC – by far and away the most watched news source in the country – suffered repeated 'technical' problems that disrupted its service. There were significant changes in the faculty of several universities, including Tehran University, to minimize the risk that these institutions might turn into hotbeds of activism, as they had been between 2005 and 2012. Even in Qom, several prominent scholars, including some who were traditionally considered conservatives, were sidelined, often excluded from leading forums and replaced by less experienced colleagues with a limited following, but whom the Republican Guard considered 'reliable'.

Iran's conservatives aspire to stem the country's financial losses, maintain the successes scored in the eastern Mediterranean and the Arabian Peninsula, retain their control over the office of the Supreme Leader, and curtail the chances of any internal challenge. This is a tall order. However, if they achieve it, they will secure the Islamic Republic for the foreseeable future. There will continue to be fresh challenges to the political leadership, the religious-political establishment and the notion of *welayat al-faqih*. Almost certainly, the rigidity that has characterized the system of governance will be relaxed and some reformers will be able to make some gains. But the regime, with its strict theological command of the country and its expansionist aspirations for the region, will persist. It could even manage to preserve some of the influence it has secured recently in Iraq, Syria, Lebanon or Yemen. But irrespective of that, it will remain unable to inspire the vast majority of non-Shii (or secular Shii) Arabs.

But such an outcome is far from certain. Overstretching, resource drain, internal divisions (especially regarding the succession) and the prospect of failing to consolidate external gains could shake the religious establishment. The new reformers could absorb the lessons of the reformers' experience in the late 1990s and early 2000s. This time, they could perhaps include in their constituencies sections of the lower-middle classes; they could be more assertive and could widen their support so as to be able to withstand confrontations with the religious-political establishment. Iran could, as the reformers have sought, move gradually and smoothly – or indeed suddenly, through a shock to the previous three decades' system – towards a new form of Islamism that transcends the absolutist *welayat al-faqih*. The reformers could develop a new Iranian Islamism that does not revolve around a small group of theologians or militants, but which resonates with the country's rich heritage. The July 2015 deal between Iran and the West to regulate the country's nuclear programme offers Iran a chance slowly to alter its regional positioning and its wider international stance. As a consequence of the deal, Iran will gain access to over USD 100 billion of assets that were frozen in the West. This could stimulate the economy, and crucially it could incentivize many inside Iran, including within influential circles, to re-examine the country's foreign policy of the past three decades (and especially since the Arab uprisings). In this scenario, Iran could re-emerge as a model for an Islamist experience that has withstood a long internal division, survived cold and hot regional wars – and yet, despite it all, has managed to find a new and more sustainable model for its internal political system and regional positioning.

Both scenarios will entail long and protracted confrontations between the conservatives and the reformers. Resources will be wasted, passions will be roused and society will endure a long period of polarization. In a way, it will be Iran's turn to undergo what several Arab countries have been experiencing since 2011. In this case, Iran will not offer a model for the Arabs; rather, several Arab experiences will provide case studies for Iran to learn from. Either way, Iranian Islamism will not provide a model for significant sections of the region's societies.

CHAPTER TEN

Islamism and the West

The National Security Strategy 2002, issued to huge fanfare by the White House as the pillar of America's engagement with the Arab world in the aftermath of 9/11, stated that there is 'a single sustainable model for national success: freedom and democracy'. The underlying rationale was that extremism (the kind that led to the terrorist attacks on US soil) should not only be confronted with the 'shock and awe' of military power (as was the case with the US's military campaigns in Afghanistan and then Iraq in 2002 and 2003), but primarily through engendering genuine political representation and inclusiveness in the Arab and Islamic worlds.

This was not a new idea. Several American theorists working on the Middle East had been advancing that proposition since the early 1990s. The thinking was that the modern Arab state, which had typically appeared after the First World War and been cemented in the aftermath of the Second, was falling into decay. The political systems, the decision-making processes, the type of leaders in most Arab states (especially the republics) and those countries' economic difficulties had all set them on a trajectory towards implosion and chaos. Their youthful demographics and the key role played by religion in their society had formed a perilous mix that fuels radicalism. According to this view, the US's support for these countries' regimes was expected to yield diminishing benefits and increasing problems. This thinking impelled American decision-makers to reconcile the US's values and its interests in the Middle East. The US needed a new regional strategy by which to bring about change and to pave the way for the emergence of new regimes which, in the medium to long term, would manage to steer their societies towards real political representation and economic development. Failure to do so would render the region liable to a period of extreme political and social turbulence.[1] The terror attacks of 11 September, and the predispositions and convictions of leading figures in George W. Bush's first administration, lent major momentum to this thinking.

America's long-term Arab allies, Egypt and Saudi Arabia, were not amused. In various private discussions, President Hosni Mubarak and Saudi Arabia's Crown Prince Abdullah, then the state's effective ruler, were treated to President Bush's views on 'democratization'. During his visit to Bush's ranch in Texas in April 2005, the crown prince listened patiently to the president's elaboration on why there was a crucial need for a change in the Arab world. The fact that fifteen of the nineteen 9/11 hijackers were Saudis compelled Abdullah to listen patiently to the American 'suggestions': Saudi Arabia held its first ever elections to form representative municipal councils. And President Mubarak allowed Egypt's 2005 parliamentary election to be the freest in over half a century, primarily to placate American urgings for the need for inclusive genuine representation. But these measures were purely cosmetic, with hardly any impact on the regimes' concentration of power: the leaders were hardly about to alter the power structures undergirding their systems simply to comply with the US's new strategy for engaging with the Arab world. American politicians were not blind to that; there was a clear realization that the country's new national security imperative in the Arab and Islamic worlds would not be implemented in any of its large regional allies. As a former senior official on the US State Department's Policy Planning Staff put it, 'we knew they were nodding, not listening'. Iraq was where that thinking was to be tested, and where the National Security Strategy would be implemented. With its power structure demolished, it was the country that was ripe for experimentation. The Bush administration saw its efforts in Iraq as the case study for how democratization could transform a dictatorship into a sustainable democracy.

It did not. After years of sustained American political, military and economic efforts in the country, over USD 800 billion of direct expenditure, and the deployment of over 150,000 American troops, central authority in Iraq fell, the country descended into recurring episodes of civil war, and the weakened idea of Iraqi nationalism was replaced by virulent sectarianism. The new basis for the US's strategic engagement in the region proved acutely lacking. The US leadership, across both the Republican and Democratic parties – and crucially, also within the military – realized that the cost in blood and treasure of sponsoring and spreading democracy in the Arab and Islamic worlds was extremely high. Many came to regard it as a futile exercise.[2]

The central foreign policy commitment of Barack Obama's presidential campaign was to end 'the war of choice, Iraq', and to dispel the view, held by millions of Muslims across the world, that the US's 'war on terror' was one against Islam. In June 2009, speaking in Cairo University's Grand Hall at an event hosted by al-Azhar University, President Obama emphasized that he was addressing the entire Islamic world, and that his message marked 'a new beginning' in the US's relationship with Muslims. He stressed the shared values of America and Islam and the fact that millions of American Muslims thrive in the land of rule of law and equality. He made a reference to the US's commitment to democracy, stating that the US 'would extend a hand to those who cling to power . . . if they are willing to unclench their fists'. It was supposed to be a balanced message: the US would not assume the burden of spreading democracy proactively, but it would continue to put democratic values at the heart of its interactions with Muslim countries. The words were carefully chosen in order to balance the need for pragmatism after the Iraq debacle with the avoidance of appearing to have completely given up on the idea of a democratic Arab and Islamic world. But the message was convoluted. The US was clearly weary after its long and expensive engagements in Iraq and Afghanistan. It was conspicuously trying to extract itself from what was publicly proclaimed to be one, if not two, disastrous wars. The Obama administration's main objective, especially in its early years in office, was to deliver on its priority domestic projects, such as revamping the US's public health service. And so it reconsidered its global strategy, especially in the tumultuous Middle East.

Arab leaders assumed as much. On the day of his meeting with President Obama, after the address at Cairo University, President Mubarak, though suffering from lower back pain, was in a good mood and expected a smooth discussion with his American visitor. He was right. The two presidents' discussion revolved around the strategic scene in the Middle East and the Israeli-Palestinian peace process. In President Mubarak's eyes it was business as usual. Interactions throughout 2009 and 2010 confirmed that the US had indeed returned to its classic way of operating in the Arab world: anchoring relations in the premises and dynamics of geopolitics and energy economics. Gone was the pressure that countries such as Egypt and Saudi Arabia were subjected to from the Bush administration to push for democratic measures.

Most American strategists, especially within the Obama administration, believed that the missionary zeal that had characterized US foreign policy in the 2000s was not just futile, but conceptually wrong. They believed that the US needed to pursue a long-term strategy that served its strategic interests in the region without losing sight of its values. Short-term interventions of the sort undertaken by the George W. Bush administration, even if partly founded on a grand ideal, were poised to fail. The new thinking was based on a vastly different view of how the Arab and Islamic worlds ought to evolve. It went as follows: the more the US engaged in the region by giving political advice, urging leaders to gradually 'unclench their fists', advancing regional and international trade, and pushing economic reforms that would lessen the state's role in the domestic economy, the more empowered these countries's private sectors would become, the higher would be their growth rates, the more rapidly cash flows would circulate, and the faster economically independent, relatively well-educated middle classes would emerge. These increasing middle classes would, in time, build sizeable economic assets that they would need to protect. This, in turn, would result in demands from this expanding section of society for rule of law and the independence of the judiciary. These, also in time, would weaken the power of the executive authorities, the leaders who had been 'unclenching their fists'. And so, at some point in the future, this would result in a dilution of the concentration of political power that had characterized these countries for decades (if not centuries), and a new system would take hold – one based on checks and balances and separation of powers. That argument centred on the gradual and consistent introduction of economic reforms, and a slow move towards some political liberalization.[3] It did not call for revolution, for the removal of existing regimes, or for deconstructing political-economy structures.

The Arab uprisings both validated and negated this approach. The US's old allies – Ben-Ali, Mubarak and others – proved much weaker than experts at the CIA or the State Department had thought. The shock caused by the wave of demonstrations extending from Casablanca to Manama made the old strategy of acquiescing to the region's ageing autocrats seem idiotic. The rapid fall of Ben-Ali and Mubarak drove home the message that sacrificing the US's values in order to work with these and other autocrats was at best a mistaken approach, and at worst a historical sin. Some in Washington went so far as to say that the Arab uprisings vindicated George W. Bush's project of spreading democracy in the Arab world. The view that the 'Arabs are special' (effectively, that their historical experiences had rendered their societies scarcely fit for democracy) and that the successive 'waves of democracy' that had liberated central and eastern Europe, Latin America, most of Asia and increasingly parts of Africa would never reach the Arab world were dismissed as racist and 'obviously wrong'.[4] For most Western observers, democracy was displacing autocracy in the Arab world; economic mismanagement had finally blown up in the face of the region's corrupt regimes; a growing Arab middle class was demanding not just its economic but also its political rights; and a new generation of Arabs, powered by new technologies, had revolted against the oppressive power structures that had dominated the region for decades. From that perspective, it seemed logical that the West – and at its heart, the US – would put their money on these middle classes and this new generation. Less than two weeks after millions had taken to the streets in Cairo and other Egyptian cities to demand the removal of President Mubarak, the Obama administration publicly called on him to step down. A month-long series of demonstrations, and what appeared to be a new social phenomenon driving them, prompted the US administration to abandon one of its oldest and closest allies in the Middle East. A former secretary for information under President Mubarak described the feeling as 'withdrawing the blanket to reveal a naked sleeper'; his point was that relying on the West, and especially the US, was never a sound strategy because it was 'unreliable'. In the US, however, there was a sense of historical validation – and for some, of comfort: finally the country had been liberated from the difficult position of constantly having to try to square its interests in the Middle East with its values.

The view in Europe was different. Over the decades, Europe had lost most of its influence in the Arab and Islamic worlds. Throughout the 2000s, the EU was the largest trading partner of almost all Arab countries; some European companies, primarily those involved in energy, derived a significant percentage of their revenue from their operations in North Africa; a few European countries had significant military links to Gulf states; and some European politicians had developed close relationships with various Arab dictators, primarily to secure economic benefits for their countries. But, relative to the US, Europe's involvement in the strategic issues of the Middle East was quite limited. And so in Europe, the disconnect between strategic interests in the region and democratic values was less pronounced than in the US. Europe's view of the Arab uprisings was based less on squaring realpolitik with values, and more on viewing its own past in the Arab world's present.

At a dinner in Brussels in November 2011, a stone's throw from the headquarters of the European Parliament, a senior figure in the European Commission compared the fall of Mubarak to that of Nicolae Ceausescu in Romania in 1991. Throughout 2011 and 2012, leading European politicians, including several prime ministers and foreign ministers, repeatedly drew comparisons between the Arab uprisings and the fall of communism in central and eastern Europe. In 2013, at a working breakfast at the German embassy in Prague attended by several Arab activists, a representative of the German foreign ministry boasted that 'here, in this same room where we gather today, tens of European freedom fighters like our Arab friends took refuge in 1991'. For many European observers, the Arab uprisings were revolts by a young genera- tion seeking freedom from the clutches of ageing dictators. Prominent activists from Egypt, Libya, Syria and Tunisia who had played a conspicuous role in their countries' uprisings, were hailed as 'revolu- tionary leaders'. In early 2012, at a private dinner in Cairo, a former Polish deputy prime minister, who years earlier had been a senior figure in the Solidarity Movement that led the Polish struggle against commu- nism in the 1980s, compared several Arab activists to the Czech Republic's legendary freedom fighter Vaclav Havel and to his own leader Lech Walesa. The prevailing narrative revolved around 'freedom fighters fighting dictators', 'a new generation fighting oppressive states', 'those who want democracy' against their 'authoritarian regimes'. For Europe, the Arab uprisings were reminiscent of the continent's experi- ence two decades previously; and so, from that perspective, it was an 'Arab Spring'.

The rise of the Islamists shattered that narrative. The secular activists who had enchanted the West proved to have negligible constituencies in their societies; even in their countries' urban centres they hardly secured any significant parliamentary representation. What made matters worse was that many of these activists seemed condescending towards their own societies. At a meeting between two prominent Egyptian activists and a European delegation comprising several members of the European Commission, the activists warned the European officials that if 'Europe failed to support us, the Islamists would continue to win; the people do not understand much; they will just vote for them; you should help us'. There came regular and increasingly demanding requests for support. In 2011, large numbers Egyptian, Tunisian, Libyan, Syrian and Moroccan activists asked European diplomats for their help in propagating their views among influential decision-makers in Europe. Dozens of visits were duly arranged, and activists spent hours with European leaders and officials ranging from desk officers at ministries of foreign affairs to prime ministers. At least fifteen young Arab activists were invited to address the European Parliament between 2011 and 2013. The requests for support evolved into appeals for help in securing important slots in Western media, and none-too-subtle requests for financial backing. Hundreds of civil society organizations were set up, especially in Egypt, Tunisia and, to a lesser extent, Jordan and Morocco to legalize the financial support that many liberal activist groups expected to receive from Western donors. On the other hand, the Islamists did not ask for any support, but were constantly trying to explain their views, programmes and agendas. And the more detailed the discussions between Western – especially European – officials and secular activists, the starker became the contrast between them and the Islamists. One group was forever asking for help; the other was positioning itself as a partner for the future.

There was also a clear distinction in terms of economic thinking. Most of the prominent secular activists exhibited strong socialist and redistributive economic tendencies. At a meeting in Cairo, one of the most senior members of the European Commission's leadership was surprised to hear a young Egyptian activist explain to her that the '2011 revolution's demand for social equality' meant openness to nationalization of private economic assets and reversal of privatizations completed over a decade before – rhetoric which she felt was reminiscent of that of old-fashioned members of European labour unions. This was the exact opposite of the overtly capitalistic narrative of groups such as the Muslim Brotherhood and Annahda. Of course, secular activists in Egypt, Tunisia and other countries in the region included many who believed in free market economics: many were themselves successful business entrepreneurs. But by and large, the most prominent figures who had the most interaction with Western (and especially European) officials were rather inexperienced in economics or business, and were not quite attuned to the changes in economic policy that the world had witnessed in the previous two decades. The conclusion that many European counterparts drew was that the young secularists who represented 'the Spring' were far less prepared to lead than the vastly experienced Islamist movements.

The Islamists also found a sympathetic ear in the powerful European parties with a Christian heritage. Some sections of these parties held mixed views about the existence of Islamists on Europe's southern shores. But several influential groups inside the Christian democratic parties believed that the Islamists were the only ones in their countries with a major social constituency, and that they were credible counterparts in dealings with the Arab world. Many believed that by embracing democratic means – such as elections and coalition governments – the Islamists were well on their way to undergoing the same development that the Christian Democrats had undergone several decades earlier. The Islamists quickly recognized that this view offered them an opportunity to create an important ally in the West. It was notable that the Brotherhood and Annahda were especially respectful towards, and laid on their best hospitality for, European politicians belonging to parties with a Christian background. In one instance, the Egyptian Brotherhood and groups attached to it put together a jam-packed agenda for a visiting former European Christian Democrat prime minister, during which he met three of Egypt's most revered religious scholars and heard their views on 'Islam's stance on democracy'. Hardly ever did such interactions result in a deeper understanding of the theological arguments or of the development of modern Arab Islamism; what they did achieve was some sort of confirmation for the Europeans that they 'could work with the Islamists'.

Arab Islamists also welcomed and encouraged dealings with European civil society organizations that had clear religious backgrounds. Annahda, for example, developed a close relationship with a UK-based organization that had been founded by a senior member of the Anglican Church. This relationship resulted in various initiatives, conferences and joint activities during which Annahda members (and later Islamists from other Arab groups) were invited to address civil society organizations in various European capitals. Here also the European Christian Democrats were influenced by their experiences in central and eastern Europe. Many saw the Muslim Brotherhood's opposition to Mubarak and Annahda's activism against Ben-Ali as somehow reminiscent of the role that the Catholic Church had played against communist rule, particularly in Poland. Though Arab Islamists had no figure to match Pope John Paul II, leaders such as Rached Ghannouchi skilfully wove religious overtones into their discussions with Western interlocutors on their countries' political transition. To the ears of European Christian Democrats, this sounded like a vague sense of religious commitment that had evolved beyond 'medieval thinking' and which was now on the road to becoming 'similar to us'.

American conservatives were less enamoured of the Arab Islamists. In conferences and gatherings organized by leading international think tanks between 2011 and 2013, several Republican senators held lengthy discussions with members of the Muslim Brotherhood, Annahda, the Moroccan PJD and Kuwait's Islamic Constitutional Movement. The atmosphere was generally friendly, the various exchanges accustomed the individuals to one another, and familiarity brought relative understanding. But there were still important bones of contention. Unlike in their interactions with their European counterparts, the Islamists' exchanges with American interlocutors (especially Republicans) repeatedly revolved around the US's influence over the Arab world and its support for the region's authoritarian regimes in the preceding decades.

This invariably introduced tension into the discussions and the partici-
pants focused more on the conflicting explanations for the recent past
than on the future.

The Islamists' interactions with their American counterparts were also
taxing in terms of time and effort. Most large Islamist groups were
familiar with European politics – either through personal experience
during their years of exile, or because of the relative simplicity of decision-
making structures in European countries. Most of them, however, found
American politics, its various webs of influence and power, and its
complicated lexicon difficult to understand. I was once asked by a
member of Annahda's parliamentary bloc to explain why some American
visitors found the term 'liberal' unpalatable, whereas it 'is the basic ingre-
dient of European politics'.

The most contentious point, however, was Israel and how the Islamists
viewed their countries' relationship with it. This was a particularly salient
issue in the case of the Egyptian Muslim Brotherhood. Its rapid ascent to
power raised concerns in Israel and the US about the group's commitment to the peace treaty that Egypt had signed with the Hebrew state in
1979: although the Brotherhood had made it clear at various levels that it
would honour the Egyptian-Israeli Peace Treaty, still a suspicion lurked.
It was not particularly helpful for the American-Islamist relationship that
a few years earlier, the rhetoric of many of the leading figures inside the
Islamist groups regarding Israel and the Jews had been pugnacious and
at times derisive. Mohammed Morsi's advisors found it difficult to come
up with an explanation when they were asked by two American senators
as to why, during a public address to some supporters a few years previously, the president had described the Israelis as 'sons of pigs and
monkeys'. Suspicions were intensified when, in 2012 and 2013, several of
the legislatures of 'Spring countries' proposed laws to criminalize the
'normalization of relationships with the Zionist entity'. Annahda's relationship with the US and many Western countries was put under threat
when an early draft of the Tunisian constitution included a paragraph
that committed Tunisia to supporting the Palestinian people against

'racist movements such as Zionism'. Although Annahda had neither proposed the wording nor supported it in parliamentary discussion of the constitutional text, the party was indirectly blamed as the new political force whose rise enabled the emergence of blatant anti-Israeli sentiments.

American conservatives were also aware that Israel, especially the Likud party and right-wing groups, had acute concerns regarding the rise of Islamist groups in the region. They were repeatedly reminded that the Palestinian Hamas, which continues to use force against Israel, is but an offshoot of the Egyptian Muslim Brotherhood, and that many leading Islamist scholars and politicians continue to approve of and sanction such violence.

The diversity of the American political system, however, allowed various degrees of cooperation with the Islamists. Mohammed Morsi's administration proved a willing American partner when it came to mediating between Israel and Hamas. Morsi no longer referred to the Israelis as 'sons of pigs and monkeys'; he adopted the rhetoric of a statesman whose country had signed a peace treaty with Israel and who, because of his years in the Muslim Brotherhood, enjoyed Hamas's trust. The Obama administration started to involve the Morsi administration in various international relations dossiers in the Middle East. One of Morsi's most senior foreign policy advisors was invited to a two-hour meeting at the White House, including a chat with President Obama. Leading figures in the US State Department believed that they had a solid understanding of Middle Eastern politics, enabling them to make a judgment call regarding the Muslim Brotherhood: their conclusion was that the US could work with it. State Department members (especially within the Policy Planning Staff) were convinced that the Egyptian Brotherhood could eventually be cultivated as an American ally, with favourable consequences across the region and especially for the Arab–Israeli peace process, which had been stalled for at least a decade. Several visiting American policy-makers were particularly impressed by the Brotherhood's leadership. A few listened to details about the Renaissance

Project (chapter 2) and deemed it an acceptable framework and agenda for a Brotherhood-led government. The US replaced its ambassador in Cairo, by far the most senior American diplomat in North Africa, with an envoy who had spent several years as ambassador to Pakistan immediately prior to taking up her new post. For many, the message was clear: the US expected Egypt and, behind it, large parts of the Arab world, to be led by Islamists in a political environment in which jihadists, rogue Salafists and military establishments competed over fragments of power and economic spoils.

Europe was more undecided about how it could deal with the Islamists in its southern neighbourhood. Between 2011 and 2014, the EU High Representative for Foreign Affairs and Security Policy and her representative in the eastern and southern Mediterranean developed working relationships with all the large Islamist movements in the region. They repeatedly helped to smooth tensions and mediate between various groups at moments of crisis, whether in Egypt, Tunisia or Libya. Professionals from various EU social and economic programmes visited their counterparts in the Muslim Brotherhood, Annahda and the PJD, and in a few cases met the leaders of some of the largest Salafist parties. Senior bankers from Europe's main development banks listened to the ideas and plans that various Islamist groups had for their countries. And yet, at the official level, there remained a strong sense of unease regarding the way in which the Islamists had replaced the secular groups that had spearheaded the Arab uprisings. A few senior decision-makers regarded the Islamists' rise as a 'winter' replacing the 'liberal Spring' of 2011. This was noticeable in the way many European bureaucracies interacted with the Islamists. Whereas bureaucrats were encouraged to widen and deepen their relationships in the Arab world to include the myriad rising Islamist groups, European leaders in office tried to avoid any association with the Arab Islamists: only a very few were willing to visit the capitals of the 'Arab transition countries' and hold discussions with Islamist leaders. Even diplomatic missions kept their distance from the rising Islamists. While almost all the larger European countries' ambassadors to Cairo, Tunisia and Rabat developed working relationships with the large Islamist groups in those countries, to the best of my knowledge virtually all of them restricted their encounters to official meetings, conferences and the odd workshop organized by an international think tank. And those encounters were far less cordial than those with the leaders of the secular parties.

Despite their sophisticated appreciation of the Islamists' electoral power, most European decision-makers had a limited understanding of these groups' style of thinking, their development over the past few decades and the ways in which they had operated before (and after) the Arab uprisings. And so Europe took its time to assess, understand and ruminate. Its immediate responses were channelled towards social and economic support mechanisms. The European Commission established various new support initiatives and financial facilities under the auspices of its Southern Neighbourhood Programme; it directed the European Investment Bank to accelerate the implementation of its investments in the Arab world; and European countries strongly supported expansion of the operations of the European Bank for Reconstruction and Development into the southern and eastern Mediterranean. The UK, France and Germany were pivotal in the creation of the Deauville Partnership between the G7 and the countries of the 'Arab Spring', which was intended to become a platform for exchanging ideas about 'political and economic transition' and a conduit for raising financial support for these 'transition countries'.

Both the preparedness to partner with the Islamists and the cautiousness towards them were founded on a faulty understanding of what had been taking place in the Middle East. The West failed to see that the Arab uprisings were vastly different from central and eastern Europe's struggle against communism; that at heart these uprisings and what followed them were not battles between freedom fighters and oppressive regimes; and that the leading activists who became Europe's key interlocutors in the region were not the faces of large-scale revolutions by a new generation against what had gone before. Gradually, the West began to realize that the cold and hot wars unfolding across the Arab world were rooted in deep social polarizations and opposing identities and visions for the future of these countries.

In summer 2011, a senior member of the Vienna Institute for International Affairs commented that 'it took us [the West] four centuries to realize who we are, to be able to forge a workable form of our different heritages; we should not expect you to complete this task in a matter of a few years'. Since then, I have heard different Western interlocutors make the same point. It is an understanding that shows an appreciation of the conflicting identities that have been pulling Arabs, Turks and Iranians in different directions. It imbues the situation with historical complexity, and thus calls for much-needed patience. But it is mistaken in seeing the struggle as one that began with the Arab uprisings in the second decade of the twenty-first century. It fails to grasp that this search for identity, the struggle over the direction of the societies and over the minds of generations of Arabs (and Turks and Iranians), started when those societies opened up to Western modernity in the first few decades of the nineteenth century, and has been going on ever since; and that the Arab uprisings just lifted the lid to reveal the region's existing critical differences regarding these issues, which had simply been suppressed for decades.

These historical and social perspectives were clear in the thinking of many Western scholars and writers who focus on the Middle East. But they were acutely lacking in Western policy-making circles. This became obvious after Annahda, despite its election victory, was effectively compelled in 2013 to accept a bureaucratic government; and especially after the Egyptian Muslim Brotherhood was removed from power in summer 2013. In both cases, European policy-makers focused on procedures rather than the underlying social currents. Western politicians' rhetoric shifted from praising Annahda's moderation, to sympathy with the young secular demonstrators who demanded its removal from executive power, to praising Tunisia's smooth democratic transition after Annahda's withdrawal from government. In Egypt, there were also shifts from urging the Brotherhood to be more inclusive and less condescending when it was in power, to sympathy with the demonstrators who called for Morsi's resignation, to sympathy with the Brotherhood when it was ejected from the political scene.

With few exceptions, the vast majority of Western politicians looked at events from afar, seeing adherence to or rejection of democratic notions and procedures as the main yardstick by which to judge the success or failure of any country's transition. The situations were either black or white: how 'democratization succeeded in Tunisia and failed in Egypt'. These perspectives ignored the deeper conflicts in each of these countries and in the region as a whole which had been triggered by the rise of the Islamists. There was astonishment at why millions of Egyptians were celebrating the military's removal of the country's first freely elected president. The view, especially in Europe, remained rooted in the idea of the 'Spring' – that is, the struggle of activists against antiquated state structures. It was a limited view that ensured that the West's, and especially Europe's, official reaction to developments in the Arab world continued to shift erratically with the rapidly unfolding developments.

The West's confusion took place at a time when Middle Eastern politics were becoming even more complicated. The period from 2013 to 2015 ushered in new developments that transcended failures of democratic procedures or social polarizations. The spread of the Salafist jihadist Islamic State of Iraq and Syria (ISIS) over the plains extending from eastern Syria to western Iraq increased the two countries' fragmentation, terrorized the region's religious minorities, exacerbated the emigration of Christians, drew Turkey into unfolding regional conflicts, sharpened the Kurds' desire to gain full independence from Iraq, and resulted in the dislocation of over 4 million people. At least 1.5 million of those became refugees in neighbouring countries, particularly Lebanon and Jordan. The two countries were increasingly unable to cope with the inflow of refugees, who put significant pressure on domestic infrastructure and local host communities.

In North Africa, another crisis was unfolding: post-Gaddafi Libya descended into a multitude of low-intensity wars. The Libya quagmire was becoming a global security crisis, as various political groups and militias, some with links to militant Islamist groups, vied for control over billions of dollars parked in banks across the US, Asia, Europe and Africa. And gradually, since 2013, the country has become a key point of departure for thousands of Arab and African migrants willing to risk their lives to cross the Mediterranean to the southern shores of Europe. The West has offered some support to Jordan and Lebanon to enhance their ability to absorb the waves of refugees. But that support, predictably at a time of financial austerity, has paled against the scale of the problem. Also, fear of Mediterranean migration carried significantly more weight with Western (especially European) decision-making than did the human and moral impulses to intervene and help. But Western leaders also faced another dilemma. The Gulf royal families, and especially the immensely rich Saudi and Abu Dhabi families, who were leading the fight against large Islamist groups in the region, were using their influence in Western capitals to lobby governments to restrict these groups' activities in their countries. In the UK, the Saudi and Abu Dhabi governments placed significant pressure on the government to investigate alleged links between the Muslim Brotherhood and terrorist organizations. Many found it difficult to antagonize two of their top arms buyers.

After spending a decade hunting the terrorist organization al-Qaeda from Afghanistan to Iraq, Western governments (especially the US) found themselves having to deal with the return of terrorism to the Middle East. An alliance led by the US, but including Saudi Arabia and the United Arab Emirates, launched an aerial campaign against ISIS and worked on amassing a force of Iraqi Shiis and Kurds to mount a ground offensive against the group. The EU spearheaded a UN task force to mediate between various Libyan political factions and militias. The prime objective was to limit the fledgling arms trade in the country's south and east, and to prevent Libya becoming a safe haven for

Salafist jihadist groups from across the eastern Mediterranean and North and East Africa. Throughout all of that, it became crystal clear that not only have the initial hopes of the 'Arab Spring' crumbled, but that from the Western perspective the region has become host to an assemblage of threats. To confront these threats, many Western decision-makers have arrived at the conclusion that they have to rely on their tried and trusted local 'allies' – the old regimes against which the 2011 uprisings erupted – however undemocratic and oppressive they might have been. These regimes were 'the ones with the experience, the resources and the will to confront the multitude of threats that are emerging from the Middle East'.

This reliance was cemented by the West's diminishing financial resources after the 2008 crisis and its consequences in the US and Europe. The West had limited funds to commit to the Arab 'transition countries'. The different facilities that the EU Commission put in motion after the Arab uprisings came to less than USD 6 billion. The Deauville Partnership gradually lost momentum: three years after it was launched, the total amount of funds it had raised was less than USD 5 billion, a fraction of the initial USD 36 billion commitment.

For the US in particular, certain economic developments reduced its overall commitment to invest time, effort, money and blood in ensuring stability in the Middle East. Because of the exponential increase in the production of shale oil in the US, for the first time in over five decades the country was returning to oil self-sufficiency, with the potential of becoming a major exporter. This significantly reduced America's incentive to engage in every major crisis in the Middle East, especially after the traumatic Iraq and Afghanistan experiences.

The Arabs' interest in the West, and especially in the US, was also declining. Egypt's al-Sisi administration and Tunisia's secular Nidaa-Tunis party, which won the 2014 parliamentary and presidential elections, realized that relying on the approval of the US and Europe (as Mubarak and Ben-Ali had done) was a misguided strategy. And so they deliberately sought to strengthen their relationships with Russia and

China. President Sisi's most important international visits in his first year in office (2014) were not to Washington but to Moscow and Beijing. There he entered into 'partnerships' with Russia and China, including several deals committing the two countries to significant infrastructure investments in Egypt. Saudi Arabia, UAE and the Gulf states began to seriously diversify their arms buying, increasingly focusing on Russian and Chinese weapon systems. After all, the economic reality was that Asia had become by far these countries' most important energy-importing market.

The Islamists also came to see the West as unreliable. Many in the second and third tiers of the Muslim Brotherhood's leadership believed that the US and some European countries condoned the Brotherhood's removal from power. They repeatedly argued that the West 'has a veto against an Islamic government in the Arab world'. The same view was increasingly shared by famous sheikhs with huge followings, who reminded the hundreds of thousands of their listeners, whether in mosques or on YouTube channels, that the US and Europe, which claimed to be the guardians of democratic values, 'were hypocrites who would not follow through on their rhetoric, especially when it comes to defending Islam'.

The rhetoric became tense, and the anger swelling within young Islamists was directed both at their countries' secularists and national-ists, and at the 'hypocritical West'. Prominent figures in the Islamist movement, especially in the Brotherhood's leadership, dismissed that thinking, at least in private. They knew from various interactions with Western observers and policy-makers that the West had conflicting interests and limited resources. The main outcome of that consideration, however, was that many senior figures in Arab Islamism came to think of the West less as a power that needed to be convinced of their bona fides, and more as a physical refuge from persecution – a region in which they could rebuild their economic resources and from which they could launch their media campaigns. It was notable that almost all the Muslim Brotherhood figures who were engaged in the UK's inquiry into the group's activities were less concerned with lobbying the British authorities than with legal arguments that strengthened the group's position. Some of the scholars close to the Brotherhood who fled Egypt after the removal of Morsi and settled in the US have become active campaigners in the media against the al-Sisi administration and its Gulf allies, but they have generally refrained from lobbying the American administration or the US Congress, believing that the effort would yield limited, if any, results.

Leaving power and accepting a technocratic government, by 2013 and 2014 Annahda, whose entire leadership had spent two decades as political exiles in London, Paris and Milan, had come to the same conclusion: that the West's ability and willingness to bring about material change in the region's local politics had diminished considerably. According to one of Annahda's most promising young leaders, who speaks fluent English and French: 'Dealing with them [Western counterparts] is more public relations than real politics.'

This situation will prove temporary. Because of its location as the geographical conduit between Europe and Asia, its indispensable role in global energy economics and, crucially, its demographics (close to 200 million people in their teens and early twenties), the Middle East will continue to impose itself on the thinking and agendas of Western decision-makers, social leaders and observers – as a partner, an opportunity and a peril. Irrespective of how the Islamists and secularists see the West, Western strategies towards the region cannot continue to waver between a partial understanding of what is taking place there, moralistic posturing and short-term expediencies.

As the battle for and against Islamization rages across the region – politically, socially and often militarily – the West need not adopt a definite stance on the conflict, so much as mull over how it relates to it. At the heart of the issue is the West's perception of Islamic societies and of Islam itself. And there is no single perception. Because of their long, complicated, rich and fraught experience with Islam and Islamic societies over more than thirteen centuries, Western societies have developed

myriad conceptions and perceptions of the religion and its social manifestations. But within influential decision-making circles in the West
(and when public political correctness is cast aside), these various ideas
tend to contract into two dominant positions.

The first argues that Islam, by its nature, goes beyond being just a
faith system: at its core it is a social and political framework. Here,
Islamism is not the project of political Islamists such as the Muslim
Brotherhood, Annahda or the PJD; it is the term given to the manifestation and application of Islam in life, which (this view argues) is a necessity in the religion. According to this perspective, all the attempts of the
past 150 years to separate the religion from the state and to enrich
Islamic identity by infusing it with various cultural and nationalistic
components have been aimed at restricting Islam to being just a faith
and a value system. These attempts could be compared to the West's
trajectory between the sixteenth and eighteenth centuries in separating
church from state and creating new national identities distinct from,
and ultimately stronger than, religious ones.

The difference here, so this view holds, is that unlike Christianity,
Islam by its very nature demands to be Islamism. Separating Islam from
Islamism is an absolute must for the Islamic world. And indeed, those
who hold this view see the evolution of the Islamists in the region as
proof of the slow and incremental progress of such a separation. They
are quite confident that, at some point in the future, the Islamic world
will leave Islamism behind, retaining only Islam as a religion (and
perhaps even that will be diluted as the role of faith in people's lives
shifts, similar to what has happened to Christianity in the West in the
last two centuries). But until Islamic societies arrive at that destination
(secularism), in this view political Islamists stand as the genuine representation of the majority in these societies, because their combinination
of a religious frame of reference with politics corresponds to their societies' stage of evolution.

While typically sympathetic to the Islamists, the Western politicians
and observers who subscribe to this view argue that the Islamists will

not ultimately succeed because their societies will move beyond the need to combine a religious frame of reference with domestic politics. The argument goes that if the Islamists stay in power, they will fail. Their societies will come to see that Islamization is not the answer to their social and economic questions; they will recognize that this Islamism (like any religious political ideology and social frame of reference) inhibits social progress, and so will ultimately throw the Islamists out of power. Removing them by force and depriving them of political representation, however, would itself hamper that process of 'progress' and prolong the time it takes for Islamic societies to arrive at the stage that the West is at now. And so, according to this view, Islamism is both a mere reflection of the Islamic world's lagging behind and the very ideology that should be tolerated, because at this stage it is a genuine representation of the state of the Islamic (and especially Arab) world.[5]

Other decision-makers and observers start from the same premise, but arrive at a very different conclusion – the second dominant perception of Islam and its manifestations. They agree that Islam is inherently a political project and a social frame of reference, and that Islamism is a necessary manifestation of Islam. They reflect on the various attempts over the past 150 years to separate the religion from the state and to enrich the Islamic identity by infusing it with various cultural and nationalistic components, and argue that these attempts have failed because they lacked the support of the majority of Muslims. They do not regard that lack of support as being associated with the social and economic factors that were prevalent at various times over that century and a half: for them, the attempts failed because any separation of Islamism from Islam negates the nature of Islam. Thus it would ultimately be rejected by the majority of Muslims.

This view acknowledges that these attempts 'have of course led some Muslim groups to become like us', and that they have set other groups on a path that will lead them to social and political situations that are comparable to where the West is now. But its advocates argue that the majority in Islamic societies have not (and will not) traverse that path.

And so the genuine representatives of Islamic societies are (and will continue to be) groups that invoke Islamism. Since 'they will never be like us', the West ought to see the Islamic world through 'our historical experience with it'. Islam, here, becomes 'the other', which for centuries was 'the enemy'. Islam also becomes Islamdom: a comprehensive religious, social, political and cultural entity that should be taken as a whole. For centuries it was the enemy of Christendom, and indeed it is the opposite of the Judeo-Christian tradition and should now be seen as a threat to the West.

According to this view, political Islamists could develop their thinking and operations to win elections and ascend to power; they could change their rhetoric to deceive the elite of their societies, who have become 'like us'. Some of those Islamists genuinely believe that their Islamism incorporates forms of liberalism and can tolerate many rights and freedoms. But, the argument goes, whether they are deceiving others or are themselves deceived, their Islamism has not evolved, because it is incapable of evolving. Islamism here is not a stage in a long socio-political journey: it is an obstacle to the development of these societies. But because it is intertwined with Islam itself, the barrier is so entrenched that it is extremely difficult to remove. The conclusion is that Western-style liberal democracy is doomed to fail in the Arab and Islamic worlds for the foreseeable; that the West should neither tolerate Islamism nor interfere in the Arab and Islamic worlds' long and protracted wars to determine both their identity and the shape of their future; and if secularists crush the Islamists, this will indeed exacerbate the social polarization and the rise in violence. But 'it is not our [the West's] fight' – especially since 'they' (the Islamists) and Islamism embody all that is 'at odds with us'.

The first perspective encourages engagement with the Islamic world and the Islamists, as well as support for 'their' development and progress, and regards the shift in the 'historical trajectory of progress' as the peaceful route towards freeing the Islamic world of Islamism. The second distances the West from the Islamic world and is content to see

Islamism marginalized or persecuted – to see it not just as a symptom of the Islamic world's lagging behind, but as the essence of the danger that that world poses to the West.

Both views are condescending, have failed in the key moments when the West has had to engage with the implications of Islamism, and will continue to create Arab and Islamic enemies for the West. Crucially, both are Western-centric. Despite their different interpretations and policy implications, they look at Islamism through the prism of the West's own historical experience; they analyze it from within the West's current value system; and they devise policies towards it to lead to results that the West deems amenable. This is hardly surprising: policy-makers, irrespective of their own views, seek to secure and maximize the benefits to their own societies. The Middle East should not expect the West to devise its policies for any other objective. But Western-centric perspectives fail to see the bigger picture: that Islamism cannot be understood solely through an assessment of the 'nature' of Islam; nor can it be understood through a comparative analysis of the historical trajectories of Middle Eastern and European societies; and certainly it cannot be understood by focusing only on the thinking and means of operating of the Islamists (whether the political, the peaceful Salafists, or the Salafist jihadists). Because it is a social battle – over identities, frames of reference, the role of religion, the nature of governance and the meaning of being Arab, Turkish or Persian – understanding Islamism necessitates seeing it through many lenses and from many perspectives. Because the Middle East's experience of Islamism has been shaped by, and is unfolding through, the actions of Islamists of various stripes (as well as those of secularists, powerful institutions and different alliances between diverse powers in the region), any one viewpoint will always be deficient. And if that viewpoint starts from the Western experience and worldview, it is bound to lead, as we have seen in the last few years, to repeated mistakes, false impressions and misapprehensions.

The blame for this misconstruing of historical experience and social dynamics lies not only with Western decision-makers and strategists.

Over the past seven decades, the gap between the West and the Arab and Islamist worlds in terms of scientific progress, economic development, social standards of living and the quality of governance mechanisms has widened to shocking levels. And whereas there have been serious and highly sophisticated analyses in Western academia of 'what went wrong' in the Arab and Islamic worlds,[6] the immense gap has led many practitioners (especially in decision-making circles in politics, international relations and international development) to assume a Western superiority, and then to go about explaining it. This is not racism, cultural bias or even intellectual laziness: the gap has been so immense that many, almost without premeditation, came either to assume the trajectory idea, or to look with acute suspicion on the one key component that distinguishes the societies: Islam.

As the Western-centric perspectives prove deficient in explaining the immense transformation currently unfolding in the Middle East, multifaceted explanations will gain momentum. But understanding Islamism will become even more complex, because its pace of change is increasing. Their ejection from power and the rise and spread of new types of Salafist jihadism are already forcing the Islamists to confront new challenges – challenges that are vastly different from those they slowly addressed in previous decades. The next chapter looks at the most difficult of these.

CHAPTER ELEVEN

The Dilemmas of Islamist Thinking Now

Many members of the Egyptian Muslim Brotherhood, especially the leaders in exile, reflect on what Mohammed Morsi could have done had he ruled longer. Numerous young Annahda and PJD cadres see the period from 2011 to 2013 as a moment of possible transformation that came and went. Tunisia's successful political transition has transformed the country from one of the region's most oppressive states into a burgeoning plural democracy. But for many Islamists, the opportunity to reverse Tunisia's staunch (and in their view, imposed) secularism was lost. Their narrative centres on the premise that they were forced to agree to operate under many restrictions at the precise moment when they could have empowered the 'Tunisians' innate piousness' to assert itself against the secularism with which the majority of Tunisians have never identified. Annahda's official rhetoric intelligently adheres to the vernacular of any party functioning in a secular democracy. It compares its current role in government and its open presence in society to its persecution and marginalization before the country's 2011 uprising, and concludes that it has achieved the best that could have been achieved in a short space of time. But survival and a limited role in government are very different from reversing a social framework (secularization) that they see as alien to their society – and which some in the movement consider 'sinful'. In the same way, the acquiescence of the PJD's leadership to be one party among many in a political system orchestrated by the Moroccan palace clashes with the ambitions of many in the country's Islamist movement (and especially within the Adl w'Ihsane group) to deny the monarchy its Islamic pedigree. Many Moroccan Islamists believe that the PJD's acceptance of the status quo cemented the country's stability, but deprived them of the chance to return Morocco to 'genuine Islamic rule'. All these perceptions and ideas centre on fleeting moments in which the Islamists thought they had opportunities to transform their countries and make their Islamism real. In all of this, many are trapped in nostalgia for what never came to pass.

This nostalgia blurs into anger. Within various Arab Islamist groups, there is a strong narrative that the events of the years between 2011 and 2015 have confirmed the 'duplicity of the liberals'. Despite the major social polarizations that their countries have witnessed in the last five years, many Islamists have arrived at the conclusion that the 'liberals' who, for decades, championed liberal democracy were the first to betray its tenets when they (the Islamists) won. Some Islamists, especially the most prominent leaders such as Rached Ghannouchi, are careful not to confer mass judgements. They understand the complexities of the immense social upheaval unfolding in the region. Few figures inside the Islamist movement acknowledge the colossal mistakes that many Islamists made, and subtle interpretations and sober analyses have now become rare, particularly among the younger factions of the Islamist movements. The prevailing thinking simply demonizes the 'liberals' and assumes the higher moral ground.

There is also escapism into history. Some of the most influential thinkers in the Arab Islamist movement – for example, Sheikh Yusuf al-Qaradawi, the Egypt-born and Qatar-based scholar who, for over a decade, was president of the International Council of Islamic Scholars – reduce the Islamists' experience in the last century and a half to a mere confrontation with the secularists. In this sense, the Arab uprisings signalled the failure of 'Arab liberals and socialists' and marked the beginning of the 'Islamists' age'. According to this interpretation, the secularists had ruled the Arab world (and Turkey and Iran) since its first encounter with modernity in the nineteenth century, and more than 150 years later it was clear that they had failed. It was time for the Islamists to ascend to power and correct what had gone wrong. When those Islamists lost power, most of the prominent figures in Arab Islamist thinking did not pause to wonder why large groups in the Arab world had turned against the Islamists so rapidly. They focused instead on the Islamists' confrontation with the powerful nationalistic institutions that fought them. Quickly their rhetoric acquired Islamic tones and vocabulary that equated the Islamist groups with Islam and painted the nationalistic institutions in demonic hues, despite the huge support for those institutions in their societies. Several popular Salafist sheikhs (with huge numbers of Facebook and Twitter followers) blamed the Islamists for not being assertive enough with 'the enemies of the religion' when they were in power. The dominant theme became that the Islamists' march from the early nineteenth century to the beginning of the twenty-first was their preparation for the resurrection of the Islamist project that had long been suppressed by the secularists, and that was supposed to begin with their accession of power.

Social polarization, different identities and frames of reference clashing with each other, opposing views of national security and a readiness to confront acute economic challenges – all those were dismissed as secondary issues. The new narrative set the Islamists' rise and fall in a much longer historical context. In it, the fall of the Islamist caliphate at the end of the First World War constituted a calamity that was to be reversed. The displacement of Islam as the basis for political legitimacy – and its relegation to the status of a background cultural framework or a component of a rich social fabric – was an affront to God's rule that was to be ended. The Islamists' rise to power was the start of making these 'sins' right – the dawn of a new age of Islamism. According to this view, the removal of the Brotherhood from power in

Egypt, the political attacks on Annahda in Tunisia and the need for it to hand over power to a technocratic government were seen as strikes against Islamic rule.

It was the first time in decades that different Islamist groups across the region had perceived a collective attack – not just on their political activism, economic infrastructure and social reach (e.g. in universities and syndicates), but even on their existence and ideology. This strengthened the mood in favour of a historical narrative that interpreted their loss of power as but one episode in the long struggle against secularism. The Egyptian Muslim Brotherhood saw the al-Sisi administration as its enemy; some in Annahda homed in on specific figures in Nidaa-Tunis, the secular labour unions and the country's leftist movement as the reasons behind their loss of power; groups in Morocco's Islamist movement demonized key figures in the country's ruling establishment; and several Islamist commentators considered the late Saudi King Abdullah (who had vigorously backed various secular, nationalist forces in the region) as the architect of the fight against their groups. But across the region, a wider perspective was emerging that transcended the politics of specific countries and individuals, and that saw the period from 2012 to 2015 as a battle to extinguish Islamism. The culprits in this narrative were not only these regimes, elites and royals; they included large social groups – those who 'rejected Islam'.

This is dangerous, and primarily for the Islamist groups themselves. The most important achievement of Arab Islamism was the evolution it managed to accomplish in the 1990s and 2000s: it moved from its old ideology-focused worldview accepting modern political systems and nation states, and becoming a player in national (rather than religious) political milieus. Although the Islamists' experiences in power had revealed immense deficiencies in how they came to apply that new thinking, the inherent transformation remained valid. Across most of the Arab world, political Islam, as it was seen in the mid- and late 2000s, continued to be regarded as a powerful political force with major constituencies. The experiences of the Arab Islamists in the years after 2011 should have led to some soul-searching within the large Islamist groups as to what went wrong with the implementation. What has happened, however, is the exact opposite: victimization has given way to antagonism and fiery anger. This new perspective, which reduces the Islamists' experience of the past few years to a mere ideological struggle in which they have suffered injustice, threatens to reverse these groups' evolution and take them back to an earlier point on their path.

Repression and exclusion drive people towards rigidity and revenge-seeking. The rhetoric of scores of young Islamists now reveals that many see themselves as Islamist Edmond Dantes (the victim of injustice in Alexandre Dumas's famous 1844 novel, *The Count of Monte Cristo*), though the villains here are not individual conspirators but entire social groups. Victimhood and a desire for revenge help groups come together and manage adversity. But it is escapism that stifles renewal. Most Islamist groups, political and Salafist, are returning to command by theologians, rather than the kind of political and economic leaders seen in the 1990s and 2000s. Most of the Brotherhood's new leadership in exile comes from factions in the organization that are referred to as 'Qutbist' – a reference to Sayyed Qutb. This does not necessarily mean that they actively advocate violence; it does mean, however, that they see large sections of society as at best 'in need of guidance' or at worst as morally and religiously corrupt. This thinking entrenches the idea that they, the Islamists, are moral leaders who hold 'the truth' and are mandated to transform society, rather than to operate inside society and within their established systems. This is one of the key reasons why many in the Muslim Brotherhood's leadership have major reservations about Annahda's and the PJD's experiences in power. Some see the two parties' reining in of their ambitions to fundamentally change their countries as acquiescence to *dalal* (deviation from the righteous path). This thinking draws the wrong lessons from the experiences of the last few years.

This ideological narrative also reduces the Islamists' ascent to power to a question of ideology. This minimizes the scale of their success. The Islamists' rise was a result of their evolution as political movements, their strong organizational structures, their social reach and, in several cases, their major financial resources. For millions of their constituents – those who have repeatedly voted for them – the Islamists were the political leaders that they wanted at the helm of their society. The way they identified with Islam helped their image and certainly made them more favourable to conservative, pious social segments. But it was not mere ideology that catapulted the Islamists to power. And so, by reducing themselves to their core Islamist ideology, the Islamists are not just taking themselves back to an earlier point in their long evolution: they are also lessening the meaning of their recent political successes.

This ideological narrative is similarly incompatible with powerful trends that are shaping the future of Arab societies. Across the Arab world, demographics, economics and urbanization are increasingly transforming lives. Not many young Arabs are willing to accept blind obedience to authority, whether religious or secular. The level of activism that triggered the Arab uprisings appears to have been diluted, lost or subjugated. But beneath the façade of stability in some countries, or the chaos and civil war in others, there is immense anger among young people over the way in which their 'revolutions' have failed to achieve the objectives they started out with. As a result of this anger, many of the countries that today appear stable will witness new waves of demonstrations and revolts against their regimes. And some of the countries that are now mired in civil war will see new social confrontations unfolding, triggered not by sectarianism or internal divisions, but by youths who will try to salvage what is left of their states. Economics serves to exacerbate the anger: almost all non-oil-exporting Arab countries confront acute economic conditions, worse than those in the period before 2011. Amidst the coming wave of revolts, no power (secular or Islamist) could build constituencies by demanding blind obedience. The Islamists' return to their old ideology-focused worldview and rhetoric helps them to coalesce now, but it will not help them broaden their support among rebellious youths who have limited respect for authority.

Strict ideology damages the Islamists in another way. Across the Arab world, we are now seeing large groups of young Muslims who are increasingly open to innovative understandings of Islam. There is a notable revival of Sufism in North Africa and the Gulf. Many youth groups, in countless internet chatrooms and on Facebook pages, are discovering marginal (often esoteric) schools of Islamic theology. Some are coming up with their own interpretations of what Islam as a faith means to them. Religious groups that aim to play a leading role in their countries' public lives – let alone those that aspire to rule – need to be open to different ideas and flexible in the way they respond to people and groups with whom they disagree on key issues such as belief. Backward-looking frames of reference will clash with a forward-looking creativity that is trying to merge the old with the new. The more the Islamists cling to a victimization narrative, coalesce around a desire for revenge and demonize large social groups, the more they return to their ideological origins and the more they become detached from some of the most interesting developments in Islamic theology.

Urbanization exacerbates the Islamists' problem. Almost all Arab countries are witnessing rapid rates of migration to the cities. At the end of 2014, Greater Cairo became an 18 million-strong metropolis. Casablanca has doubled its population in less than two decades. Even in Tunisia, which has one of the slowest population growth rates in the Arab world, the number of residents in the capital Tunis has increased significantly as tens of thousands seek work in the city. Urbanization gives rise to a multitude of problems. One of these is the emergence of unplanned poor suburbs and shanty towns. As already discussed, throughout the 1980s and 1990s these were strongholds of many Islamist groups as well as the hunting grounds of Salafist jihadists. But this is changing: most Arab countries have begun to take serious measures to significantly improve living conditions in their shanty towns, and to integrate them into larger communities. Internal migration has already given rise to a newly urbanized generation that was brought up in the cities. And with this urbanization comes an encroachment of

Western modes of living, social interactions and consumption. Some in this new generation will continue to be torn between these 'alien' norms and the conservative values of their parents and grandparents. But the majority are more likely to be quite comfortable with these norms and lifestyle. This has already become obvious in Morocco, Egypt, Tunisia, Jordan, Lebanon and other places in the Arab world. Islamist groups that return to strict conservatism and an insistence on old patterns and features of religiosity will not only fail to build a constituency within this young generation, but will also fail to maintain their presence in areas and within populations that traditionally numbered among their strong supporters.

Changes in the Salafist movement will also compel the Islamists to rethink their escapism into old ideology. We discussed in chapter 3 the increasing divisions and marginalization of various Salafist parties and how many are returning to a situation similar to that pre-2011: large pious and highly conservative communities that have limited interaction with their societies and are not really represented by any political authority. The difference now, however, is that these communities, or at least many in them, have become politicized; they have been mobilized to vote in successive elections and referendums; they have been courted by an array of politicians calling for 'Islamic constitutions', 'Islamic states' and 'Islamic societies'; and they have witnessed the fierce confrontations between the Islamists and the secularists. These pious groups are not homogeneous in the way they interpret Arab politics of the last few years: some are now convinced that political Islam is a failure and that religion's place is in the home and in the mosque; others have become disillusioned with those who came to 'represent Islam', and believe that 'we all need to wait; let our societies heal'; and yet others continue to follow the Salafist political parties that have emerged in the past four years.

But some are riled by the retreat of Islamism. New voices that appeared in 2013 and 2014 – obscure sheikhs who are building large followings through YouTube channels – attack the biggest Islamist

groups and condemn them as 'frauds'. These new Salafist voices interpret the Islamists' experience, not only in the few years since 2011, but
also in the last two decades, as an 'offence against Islam'. They believe
that the large political Islamist groups erred when they moved away
from the insistence on total imposition of Sharia, when they accepted
nation states, and when they rejected the rule of religious leaders. Their
way of thinking aims to take Salafism away from its detachment from
society and quiet piousness, and to infuse it with assertiveness. It is not
hard to imagine that some of the followers of this Salafism will cross the
line of Salafist jihadism (militant Islamism). But the problem here is not
just the possibility of violence: the failure of political Islam (and its
demonization and persecution) could potentially give rise to new types
of radicalism that, even if not violent, could still divide many Arab societies. The political Islamists' retreat into a narrow, self-serving victimization and a strict ideological mind-set would feed that radicalization.

The Islamists should also realize that their time in power, brief as it
was, did not provide any answers to some of the most difficult questions
that Islamism has always triggered. In several cases it actually further
complicated these questions. The Islamists have always looked at historical episodes in Islamic history as ideal epochs. The first three decades
of Islamic history – from the time the Prophet Mohammed called for
Islam in Mecca until the early years of the caliphate of his cousin and
son-in-law Ali – have always been regarded by all Islamists (and most
Muslims) as the 'rightly guided' era – the 'purest' in Islamic history. That
era has continued to inspire the Islamists since at least the beginning of
the decline of the Ottoman Empire in the late seventeenth century. This
is the age of the 'righteous predecessors' that the Salafists consider to be
the truest representation of Islam's essence, and a model for how
Muslims should live. Other Islamists look to the time of the Abbasid
dynasty (and especially during the ninth century) as 'the golden age of
the Islamic civilization'. This was when the Islamic caliphate was arguably the most powerful and richest state in the world, as well as the
world's preeminent centre for science and the arts.[1]

Islamists who invoke Islamism's acceptance of 'others' (and especially Christians and Jews) habitually stress how Islamic rule in Iberia (the Andalusian era) demonstrates the ways in which Islamic regimes could (and should) maintain an inclusive social milieu in which all citizens are equal, and in which science, art and social harmony thrive.[2] Many Islamist thinkers reflect on the second half of the nineteenth century as the time when Islamists (and thinkers such as al-Afghani and Abdou) put forward ideas that incorporated modernity without sacrificing the 'Islamic nature' of state and society's frame of reference. However, the problem with all of this is these Islamists' backward-looking perspectives. Irrespective of the romanticization of these eras (which were hardly examples of utopian social harmony), they were all the products of social, political, economic and cultural circumstances that differed vastly from those that shaped and continue to shape today's Middle East. Invoking these 'ideal' historical epochs could, at best, inspire observers; at worst, it could mislead them. Either way, in reality these past examples do not correspond at all to the present.

After their long experience, and especially in the last two decades, most large political Islamist groups have come to accept plurality. This acceptance was derived to some extent from the inspiration that the Islamists have drawn from these idealized historical epochs. The Islamists' acceptance of plurality was often more pronounced than that of many secularists in the Arab world. But their acceptance of plurality in societies with a Muslim majority hardly ever translated into acceptance of civil liberties as equal to the tenets of Islamic law. The vast majority of Islamists never put internationally recognized civil, gender and human rights on the same footing as Sharia rules. Many Islamists deflect this point by emphasizing that, short as it was, their record of respecting civil and human rights has been much better than that of the majority of Arab secular regimes. But the invocation fails to resolve the underlying issue: that the Islamists' acceptance of plurality and some civil liberties has always been conditional, subject to their own interpretations of what could (or could not) be tolerated under Islamic rules.

This is hardly a sustainable governance framework for plural societies with significant non-Muslim communities, let along for Muslims who do not want to be at the mercy of subjective interpretations of how and when religion ought to be invoked to curtail their rights.

The Islamists' acceptance of modern nationhood and nationalism is also fraught. The majority of Islamists have moved beyond the idea of restoring the Islamic caliphate – and not as a result of the emergence of Salafist jihadist groups that wreak havoc in the name of resuscitating it. Rather, it is because, in the course of their long historical experience (and especially after their wrangle with Arab nationalism in the 1950s and 1960s), the largest political Islamist groups have come to realize that the idea of the Islamic caliphate negates today's prevailing social and cultural conditions. However, the majority of Islamists have not abandoned the notion of *seyadat al-Islam*: Islam's sovereignty and its superiority over any other religious and man-made framework. This exacerbates the conditionality problem highlighted above. It means that beneath the acceptance of equal citizenry and secular nationality as the basis for an individual's belonging to any society lurks the idea that any non-Islamic social or political framework is threatened by its status as inferior, if not flawed.

Islamism also continues to cling to some naiveté that is inconsistent with its long and rich experience. In discussions many political Islamists (and scores of Salafists) repeatedly invoke *al-Imam al-fadel* (the righteous leader), *al-madina al-fadila* (the ideal city) and the notion that 'Islam is the solution'. Some groups continue to use these slogans in elections to mobilize the masses. A few founding fathers of political Islam derived these terms in the early twentieth century from medieval schools of Islamic philosophy (especially from the age when it interacted with Hellenic philosophy), and tried to imbue them with meanings that related to twentieth-century Arab societies. This had some merit in the 1920s and 1930s. But after the Islamists' past eight decades' of experience, and especially the serious social problems they faced and were embroiled in, such emotionally charged terms have become meaningless, even delusional. Effective soundbites, perhaps, but they and the thinking behind them have nothing to offer societies that are confronting acute social and economic difficulties and which need tangible and implementable solutions.

Some of these problems in Islamist thinking now stem from the fact that the most influential Islamist commentators in the world – those with the largest constituencies and the widest reach – are Arabs, who have limited exposure to non-Arab Islam. The experience of the Turkish AKP aside, the most prominent Islamist thinkers seldom write or speak about the experiences of Muslims in the US, Europe, Asia or Africa. This limits the pool of ideas that Islamist and Islamic thinking can draw upon, and restricts its chance of benefiting from developments outside the wider Middle East. One example is the role of women in innovating Islamic theology and their eligibility to assume leadership roles. For various cultural and economic reasons, Arab women still face significant challenges, especially in their countries' poorer regions. There are, however, interesting innovations in religious thinking and practice led by Muslim women in the US, Indonesia and South Africa. These indicate that, freed from certain cultural influences, Islamic thinking could make quick strides in areas where it has been held back for decades, often centuries.

Crucially, Islamism has so far failed to confront the reality that Salafist jihadist ideas have captured significantly large areas of the Islamic world. In 2014, one group, ISIS, controlled an area larger than several European countries. Damascus and Baghdad, two of the Arab and Islamic worlds' most important cultural centres, have repeatedly faced the threat of falling to jihadist brigades. Jihadist Salafist groups have become by far the most powerful Islamist actors in eastern Libya, the western parts of the Sahara and large areas of West Africa. This will likely prove to be a short-lived state of affairs, but, irrespective of the fate of these specific groups, the exceedingly conservative and violent ideas that underpin their thinking have become entrenched in these lands. With the increasing availability of modern communication and social media, those ideas have and will spread across certain Islamic communities. (They will, for instance, find some sympathizers among the millions of refugees scattered across the eastern Mediterranean.) That the largest Islamist groups have not considered this to be a strategic threat to their ideology and their future – one that merits a huge mobilization of efforts and resources, rather than simply feeble denunciations – betrays a calamitous failure of judgement.

Yet, opportunities could arise from these challenges. The Islamists cannot offer immediate solutions to the questions triggered by their thinking and Islamism itself. But by confronting them, they could lead the way in areas that matter not only to their ideology and project but, more importantly, to their societies. In his book *Church and State*, the Sicilian priest Luigi Sturzo argued that after spending centuries stifling social and political liberties, the Catholic Church underwent a period of strife, a confrontation with the powers that opposed its ecclesiastical understandings of how Christian societies should function. But when it became clear to its leaders that the Church was losing that confrontation, they not only accepted the introduction of social and political liberties, they even demanded them. The backgrounds, intellectual journeys and modern circumstances of Western Christian institutions and large Arab Islamist groups bear no resemblance to each other. But still, there is a lesson for the Arab Islamists. Narrowing their experience (as they have been doing since their fall from power) to confrontation with secularist forces helps many of their leaders to deflect blame for the mistakes they committed in the brief moment they ruled their countries. Framing their project as a struggle to change their societies gives it a messianic appeal, enlivens hardcore adherents and helps with raising resources. But this strategy could prove disastrous: a historical struggle that ultimately pits them against large sections of their societies would be the worst outcome in terms of the path they have been traversing since the mid-nineteenth century.

The Islamists might yield to victimization; they might embrace antagonism; they could choose to demonize the 'liberals' who sacrificed liberalism to ensure the crushing of Islamism in their societies. But the

Islamists cannot ignore the major social groups that fear them deeply and which saw in the Islamists' rise a threat to the way in which they define their countries and live their lives. The Islamists also cannot ignore the swathes of well-educated and increasingly secular youths, who might not constitute the majority of the 180 million Arabs under the age of thirty-five, but who are certainly the most affluent and influential in that colossal social segment. By facing up to the deficiencies in their thinking and the grave mistakes they committed while in power, the Islamists could assume the role that their best thinkers have always wanted: that of social luminaries, confronting the most difficult questions that their societies face. By continuing to embrace their ideological and political evolution (and seeing the bigger picture of what is happening within Islam itself), the Islamists would not only maintain their place as important political players in their countries, but might even win new constituencies in groups that have viewed them with acute suspicion. This could be the Islamists' route out of the identity problem, political predicament and social polarization that their project has triggered across the region.

Conclusion

Islam has always been politicized. The notion that it is *deen wa dawla* (a faith and a state) has been challenging, and challenged, for over 150 years now, ever since the Arab and Islamic worlds' mass exposure to Western modernity. All modern Islamization projects have been manifestations of that idea. Various Islamists, from different schools of thought, have tried to find a balance. On the one hand, they have attemped to retain their societies' Islamic identity and their religion's traditionally decisive role as the pillar of political legitimacy, legislation and the main social frame of reference. On the other, they have sought to not obstruct their societies' attempts to 'catch up with the West' and escape the lethargy that had undermined the Islamic civilization and extinguished its old grandeur.

None of these attempts have worked. A few luminaries put forward theoretical ideas that seemed to find a modus vivendi between the two, but the ideas were hardly ever put into practice on a grand scale, in a large society with a Muslim majority. The Arab liberal age offered large parts of the Arab world the opportunity to experiment with different amalgamations of ideas: the secular with the religious, the Salafist with the modern, the Arab with the European, the agrarian with the maritime. That promise was lost as the largest and most culturally and politically influential countries in the Arab and Islamic worlds fell for militarized forms of secular nationalism. The projects of the most prominent Islamist groups in the region clashed with those of the secularists. Throughout the period from the 1950s to the 1990s, the clash of ideas became a political struggle between Islamist groups and authoritarian regimes that were slowly losing the consent of the people.

As the Arab uprisings shook many of these regimes, prospects arose for establishing plurality in open, liberal political systems. The Islamists' accession to power was supposed to put the notion of 'a faith and a state' to the test. Few expected it to work quickly or smoothly. Because of the experiences of the previous 150 years, this experiment was expected to be protracted and fraught and composed of many trials, most of which would have turned out to be errors. But the most important factor in that transition was to end the 'struggle' between Arab secularism and Islamism. The Islamists' accession through democratic means to the top of the political systems of large and politically and culturally influential Arab countries ignited a new promise: that the Arab world could advance fresh and peaceful solutions to the relationship between Islamism and modernity. This promise was buttressed by the fact that the force that had made the transition possible, and that had challenged the old powerful entrenched regimes, represented tens of millions of Arab youths, whose exposure to the world has been far greater and more significant than that of any previous Arab generation. That the largest Arab Islamist groups (as well as some non-Arab Islamist ones, such as the Turkish AKP) had, in the previous decade, put forward new ideas and rhetoric that merged Islamism with acceptance of the secular nation state and equal citizenry boosted that hope.

That promise has now expired. The relationship between Arab Islamism and secularism has reverted to a severe, bloody and vindictive struggle. The situation is even starker than it was a few decades ago. Whereas the struggle was traditionally between the secular elite and a selection of Islamist groups, now it is between large sections of many Arab societies with opposing, and often inimical, views of their identities, ways of living and desired futures. For decades these differences lurked beneath authoritarian ruling systems. The Arab world's experience after the 2011 uprisings, however, has brought these acute differences to the fore and imbued them with at best, antipathy and at worst, animosity and hate. This was hardly ever in evidence before, but it is now glaringly conspicuous.

Arab Islamists are now not only mired in very fraught relationships with significant proportions of their societies, they are also entangled in multi-sided struggles. Arab Islamism has been drawn to the heart of the war between Sunnism and Shiism across the entire Middle East; it lies at the heart of the conflicting endeavours to reshape the eastern Mediterranean; and it is an active player in the rapidly shifting geostrategic scene.

It will soon have to fight to save the soul of Islamism. As Salafist jihadist groups grow, augment their resources, build their brands and widen their footprint across parts of the Arab and Islamic worlds, the large Islamist groups and the serious Islamist thinkers will have to defend the idea of Islamism against the charge of being fundamentally equated with violence and terror. The large Islamist groups and their leading thinkers will have to battle the militant jihadists over what it means to be an Islamist.

Some of the largest and most influential Islamist groups (most notably the Egyptian Muslim Brotherhood, but also Annahda and other Islamist movements) have suffered internal schisms concerning how they respond to the strong and passionate rejections (as well as bloody ejections) they have received – not only from their countries' powerful and entrenched power centres, but more importantly from wide segments of their societies. The divisions map out the unique circumstances that each group finds itself in, the various options available to them, the rupture between the thinking of different generations, and the disparate answers to dilemmas that various Islamists have put forward. The struggle over the soul of Islamism will not only be against the Salafist jihadists, but will also rage within these large Islamist groups over the rival paths they could take. Arab Islamism will find itself torn between Mohammed Abdou and Sayyed Qutb. The choice will be either to look back to the 'tenets of the rational religion' and try to merge them with modernity, openness to change and highly flexible understandings of what an Islamic frame of reference means; or to look back in anger, reject modernity, see secularism as a threat destroying Islamic heritage, and insist on a combative Islamism that repudiates the 'other'.

This latter path will confirm and strengthen the struggle mind-set. Here, many Islamists will embrace and espouse 'jihad' in its broader definition: self-exertion for a higher cause. Some will hold the idea that Islamism is fighting the 'enemies of Islam' – be they 'infidel Westerners', corrupt elites or secular Muslims. The fight could manifest itself in acts of terror, such as the different attacks that Egypt and Tunisia suffered in 2014 and 2015. In March 2015, over twenty people were killed in an attack on Tunis's Bardo Museum. Though most of the dead were Western tourists, the perpetrators described it as the price that should be paid by 'the sinful groups that plague Islamic Tunisia', a reference to secular Tunisians. But the struggle need not involve acts of violence committed by militant jihadists; it could be political, social and cultural. What lies beneath it is a perspective that disengages the 'believers', the 'true Muslims', from the 'others'. Even in its most peaceful manifestation – when it ceases to be a 'fight' and Islamists 'pray' for others to 'return to righteousness' – there is a separation, a detachment. What is at issue is not necessarily that the jihadists' thinking dominates that of the political Islamists; and it is not that Islamism becomes violent. It is that the ideas of equal citizenry irrespective of faith, of genuine loyalty to the nation states and of respect for the rich multi-faceted Arab heritage all crumble. This threatens to roll back Islamism's evolution over the last two decades. It could regress Arab Islamism to much earlier points on its historical path. The result would be the loss of accumulated experience. Not only will the promise of peaceful solutions to the Islamism–secularism dilemma be lost, but young Islamists (and secularists) will repeat many of the mistakes and sins that the Arab and Islamic worlds have suffered and continue to suffer.

Other Islamists might reject the Sayyed Qutb view; eschew the temptation of self-victimization; restrict their struggles to those who are hijacking their Islamism and defining it as acts of violence to coerce and terrorize their societies; and insist that their relationships with all major sections of society will be based on tolerance and acceptance of plurality. They could insist that their future lies in resuscitating the approach of Gamal al-Din al-Afghani and Mohammed Abdou. The question here will be whether the Arab secularists (especially within the economically powerful upper-middle classes in the large and culturally influential Arab countries) accept the Islamists, demand their inclusion in their countries' political systems, and realize that exclusion and demonization exacerbate the social polarization. If they do, then a new promise will be born.

But this is far from certain. The leading powers in Arab secularism, and especially those that have led the fight against Islamism in the last few years, could preserve their antagonism. Large sections of the Arab middle classes could remain indifferent to the persecution and marginalization of the Islamists; influential media outlets and state institutions could refuse to acknowledge their major social presence. But that would not miraculously solve the Islamism–secularism dilemma: Islamism will neither be crushed nor bankrupted any time soon, in any society with a Muslim majority.

Arab Islamism has always tried to design the future in the image of the past. The Islamists have repeatedly tried to impose their own interpretations of certain episodes in Islamic history upon how their societies should live in the present. The approach might have had some merit when the Arabs and the Muslims first encountered modernity, in the mid-to-late nineteenth century. They might have had some excuse to adopt it when they needed to base their thinking and messages to the people in solid examples to which major sections of society could relate. It was arguably acceptable when the Islamists wanted to contrast their ideology with secular Arab liberalism and nationalism. But now, this approach has been exhausted. Neither the early Islamic community in Medina, nor Islamic civilization under the Abbasids in the ninth century, nor Islamic Andalusia can offer a realistically workable social, political, economic or cultural frame of reference for today's half a billion Muslims under the age of thirty-five. These and other episodes in Islamic history will always be integral parts of Islamic heritage; they will always be important anchors for the cultures of societies with Muslim majorities; they will continue to enrich the identity of anyone who associates him or herself with Islam (as a faith and/or a cultural background). But they will not guide political-economy systems in today's world.

As science (especially physics), technology and our understanding of the universe advance, all historical faith systems – particularly the monotheistic religions that appeared in the axial age: Judaism, Christianity and Islam – will confront unprecedented challenges that will prove hugely significant to the thinking that has dominated the Islamic world for the last few centuries. Because it has not been subject to much public scrutiny for at least the last 200 years this thinking has been shaped in opposition to the most remarkable breakthroughs in Islamic philosophy, rather than benefiting from them; and because it has been guarded by institutions that have not developed for over a century, this thinking will slowly but surely fail to resonate with future generations of Muslims. Already, large groups of young Muslims are exploring new, non-mainstream and often esoteric understandings of Islam. Sufism is flourishing across the Islamic world, and new forms are being created in which the classic and conventional is merged with imports from different heritages (especially from Asian traditions). Significant numbers of young Muslims are rejecting the canonical tenets of the faith. Even with the most tolerant and open-minded interpretations of the brightest and most inspiring episodes in Islamic history, the Islamists' insistence on looking backwards will be detrimental to their ideology and to their ability to put forward meaningful ideas in today's world. It could exacerbate the disconnect between the most dominant understandings of Islam in the last few centuries and generations of young Muslims. The Islamists have no choice but to look to the future and creatively reinvent their ideology.

The question of how Islam could form the basis of political legiti-macy and the primary frame of reference for modern societies with Muslim majorities has not been settled – and will not be any time soon. The hope, however, is that these societies will learn not only from their agonizing experiences in the last few years, but from their journey over the last century. The future of Islamism will ultimately rest on how the Islamists redefine it and try to present it again to their societies. And in this, the Islamists' bitterest enemies are not the region's secularists, but themselves. As Imam Ali Ibn Abi-Taleb said: 'The most helpless person is the one who is helpless in reforming himself.'

Notes

Introduction

1. One of the primary messages of the Prophet Mohammed in seventh-century Mecca, in the western part of the Arabian Peninsula. Reza Aslan's *No God But God: The origins, evolution, and future of Islam* (Random House, 2005) presents the social and economic environment in which Islam appeared. Karen Armstrong's *A History of God: The 4000-year quest of Judaism, Christianity, and Islam* (Knopf, 1993) situates Islam's early messages in the larger monotheistic tradition. Abbas Mahmoud al-Akkad, *Allah* (in Arabic) (Supreme Council for Islamic Affairs, 1999) offers theological, historical and social views of the 'Islamic message' in the religion's early years.
2. Especially in the period from the tenth to the twelfth century. See Jonathan Lyon's *The House of Wisdom: How the Arabs transformed western civilisation* (Bloomsbury Press, 2010) and Steven Weinberg's discussion of 'Arab Science' in *To Explain the World* (Allen Lane, 2015).
3. Under the Muwahhids, whose dynasty ruled Morocco and parts of Andalusia from 1120 to 1269.
4. The time of the first Saudi state, which was established after an alliance of Najd's Saudi family and the Islamic reformist Mohammed Ibn Abdel-Wahhab and his followers managed to subjugate the tribes of that part of Arabia and establish a small political entity in the region surrounding Diriyah. We explore that alliance in chapter 7.
5. In his book *World Order*, former US Secretary of State Henry Kissinger chose that specific perspective as his point of departure in presenting and analysing the 'Islamic world order'. I discuss his analysis in my review of his book, published in the spring 2015 issue of the *Cairo Review* (the journal of the School of Global Affairs and Public Policy at the American University in Cairo): www.aucegypt.edu/GAPP/CairoReview /Pages/articleDetails.aspx?aid=801
6. Many scholars in the twentieth and twenty-first centuries have investigated the sources on which the Islamic faith has been based, especially the Koran and the sayings of the Prophet Mohammed, and have put forward interpretations of these tenets that significantly deviate from the most widely accepted ones, especially with regard to Muslims' perceptions of the divine nature, the 'message' of the Prophet Mohammed, Islam's relationship to Judaism and Christianity, and the Koran. The most prominent of those

scholars in the last hundred years was the Egyptian scholar, novelist and critic Taha Hussein ('the Dean of Arabic Literature'). His book *On Jahili Literature* (Cairo, 1926) and the reflections on the Koran that he presented in it are a solid starting point on this issue. More recent introductory work would include the research by the late Nasr Hamid Abu-Zeid (especially during his time at Leiden University in the Netherlands), the Syrian mathematician Mohammed Shahrour, and Mohammed Mabrouk (at Cairo University's Faculty of Philosophy). They, and many others, follow the tradition of the rationalist school of Islamic thinking, al-Mutazila, in the eighth and ninth centuries, as well as the work of Islamic philosophers such as al-Farrabi and Ibn-Sina (Avicenna).

7. The most notable in the past two decades has been the case to separate the Egyptian Koranic and Islamic philosophy scholar Nasr Hamid Abu-Zeid from his wife, a fellow academic, on the grounds that some of his writings showed him to have 'gone beyond the boundaries of Islamic faith', and as such to render their marriage (between an 'infidel' and a Muslim wife) null and void.

8. John Esposito and Dalia Mogahed addressed that issue, though with a particular focus on militant Islamist groups, in their book *Who Speaks for Islam?* (Gallup Press, 2008).

9. Some scholars limit the 'Arab liberal age' to the period from the 1920s to the 1940s, when nascent forms of parliamentary democracies began to appear in the Arab world. I adopt a wider definition that covers the period in which the region witnessed major advancements in translation, education, art, culture, religious discourse and the mechanisms of political representation, in addition to the beginnings of constitutional ruling systems. We explore that period in detail in chapter 5.

10. See the author's essay 'A struggle for the soul of Islam' for the *Cairo Review*, April 2015: www.aucegypt.edu/gapp/cairoreview/Pages/articleDetails.aspx?aid=810

Chapter 1: The Islamists' Coming to Power

1. He was not the only one, though. The sultans of Morocco adopted the titles 'caliph' and 'commander of the faithful'. Several leaders of religious movements in Sudan in the mid- and late nineteenth century used the title 'caliph'. The head of the religious sect that ruled Yemen in the nineteenth century also adopted the title. Caroline Fenkel's *Osman's Dream* (John Murray, 2006) is a major account of the Ottoman 'caliphs'; Peter Holt's *The Mahdist State in Sudan: 1881–1898* (Clarendon Press, 1970) recounts the story of the Sudanese 'caliphs'; and Jamil Abou-Nasr's *A History of the Maghrib in the Islamic Period* (Cambridge University Press, 1987) is a source of the Moroccan counterparts.

2. See Joshua Teitelbaum's *The Rise and Fall of the Hashemite Kingdom of the Hijaz* (Hurst, 2001). Eugene Rogan's *The Fall of the Ottomans: The Great War in the Middle East 1914–1920* (Allen Lane, 2015) situates the Hashemites' claim in the context of the key changes that surrounded the fall of the Ottoman caliphate.

3. Stephen Sheehi's *Foundation of Modern Arab Identity* (University Press of Florida, 2004) focuses on the various intellectual movements that had appeared in the Arab world in the late nineteenth and early twentieth century. His discussion, however, details the thought that inspired the means by which a change might be brought about in Islamic thinking, as opposed to Islam itself. The book sheds light on why these intellectual changes, and the social developments that gave rise to them, remained confined to social and national rather than religious thought. Another valuable source is the writings of Mustafa Lutfi al-Manfalouti (1876–1924). Al-Manfalouti hardly wrote about Islamic theology, but his highly successful novels, short stories, literary critiques and poems popularized the notion of re-energizing the 'Muslim person' and 'the Islamic community'. In chapter 3, we discuss the thinking, rhetoric and legacy of Jamal al-Din

al-Afghani and Mohammed Abdou, two of the most prominent thinkers who espoused that notion.

4. In 1978–79 the University of California's Near Eastern Studies Centre published a selection from the collection of Hassan al-Banna's messages under the title *Five Tracts of Hasan Al-Banna (1906–1949): A selection from the Majmuat rasail al-Imam al-shahid Hasan al-Banna*. Though the commentary does not provide the context in which the *rasail*s were written, the volume is a valuable source for tracing changes in al-Banna's thinking and language. Kamal Helbawy's 'The Muslim Brotherhood in Egypt: Historical evolution and future prospects' in Khaled Hroub (ed.), *Political Islam: Context versus ideology* (SOAS, 2011) offers an inside view of how al-Banna's thinking was perceived at the time, and later on, by successive generations of the group's members. Khalil al-Anani's 'The role of Hassan al-Banna in constructing the Muslim Brotherhood's collective identity' in *Sociology of Islam* (Brill, 2013), traces that same trajectory. I did not interview any member of the Brotherhood who had seen Hassan al-Banna or witnessed the group's first two decades. But the words quoted here were used by various Brotherhood members in the 2000s in their accounts of the organization's history and 'early mission'.

5. The book *Hassan al-Banna, Whom No One Knows* (in Arabic), by the Egyptian publisher Hassan al-Nimnim (Madbouli, 2013) is a recent study that focuses on al-Banna's ideas and life, much more than his political views. It covers ground that most books on the Brotherhood's early years do not delve into. Drawing on his chairmanship of one of Egypt's oldest publishing houses, al-Nimnim managed to access scores of al-Banna's personal letters.

6. Said Aburish's *Nasser: The last Arab* (Gerald Duckworth, 2004) presents Nasser's thinking about and long interaction with the Muslim Brotherhood. The memoirs of Khaled Moheiddin, one of Nasser's 'Free Officers' who planned and executed the 1952 coup/revolution, give an insider's view of the events that led to Nasser's confrontation with the Brotherhood. Moheiddin's memoirs were published in English as *Memoirs of a Revolution: Egypt 1952* (American University in Cairo Press, 1995).

7. Nathan Brown's work is arguably the most comprehensive in tracing the history and development of the Jordanian branch of the Muslim Brotherhood and that of its political arm, the Islamic Action Front. His book *When Victory is Not an Option* (Cornell University Press, 2012) provides a succinct and insightful view of the group's relationship with the Jordanian monarchy. Adli Selim Hawwari's research at Westminster University, and especially his PhD thesis 'Challenging the Incompatibility Paradigm', is a detailed study of that relationship. Though it focuses on King's Hussein's thinking about, and relationship with, the Islamists in his kingdom, Avi Shlaim's *Lion of Jordan: The life of King Hussein in war and peace* (Allen Lane, 2007) situates that relationship in the social and political circumstances that shaped the king's thinking and often dictated his modus vivendi and operandi. My understanding of the Jordanian Brotherhood also owes a great deal to many discussions with the country's politicians from various backgrounds who played primary roles in shaping the group's relationship to the palace, especially during King Hussein's reign.

8. There are several interpretations for that. Morocco has always been a unique Arab country. At least 20 per cent of its population is non-Arab, belonging primarily to the Berber Amazighs. Morocco has absorbed the cultural heritage of Andalusia (the middle and southern parts of Spain under Islamic rule from the ninth to the fifteenth century). And unlike the majority of Arab countries, it was never part of the Ottoman Empire. Morocco's geographical location (at the far western end of the Arab world) has also always lent it some detachment from the prevailing trends. The country is arguably the most prolific base of Islamic Sufism, a rich and varied movement within Islam that focuses on spirituality, much more than laws and rituals. Also unlike most Arab countries, Morocco has always been ruled, at least since the eleventh century, under a clear

Islamic system in which the king is proclaimed *Amir al-Mumenein* (commander of the faithful). All these factors produced in Moroccan society a set of features distinct from all other Arab societies.

9. The French Protectorate in Morocco was officially established by the Treaty of Fez in 1912, (paradoxically) signed in a palace in the historic city that was created by a descendant of the founder of the Mourabitoun (the Muravids), a dynasty that had successfully fought the Iberian Christians in the eleventh century. France's decisive influence over the country, however, began earlier, especially in 1908–09.

10. Nasser's socialist programme was vastly different from other socialist experiments implemented in the Arab world, let alone in other parts of what was, in the 1960s and 1970s, called the 'Third World'. It did not adhere to the strict ideological frames of reference that guided other experiments, but nor was it flexible enough to merit being described as detached from socialism altogether. To a large extent, it was a socioeconomic programme that reflected Nasser's own understanding of social justice, as well as the special economic circumstances of the country from the late 1950s to the late 1960s. Rami Ginat's *Egypt's Incomplete Revolution* (Cummings Centre Series, 1997) focuses on the thinking of specific socioeconomic theorists who influenced Nasser. The scope of the book and the myriad examples it provides make it a valuable reference on the topic. Alan Richards and John Waterbury's *A Political Economy of the Middle East* (Westview Press, 2007) situates the Nasserite socialist period in the region's overall developmental experience in the second half of the twentieth century. Khalid Ikram's *The Egyptian Economy, 1952–2000: Performance policies and issues* (Routledge, 2005) is a detailed analysis of the Egyptian economy in that half-century, and places Nasser's policies in a longer historical context.

11. Since the 1948 Arab–Israeli war, the dominant view in official Arab rhetoric concerning Palestine has been to lead, support and sustain a 'struggle to liberate that Arab land'. For several Arab nationalist strategists, the 'struggle' transcends Palestine. In this view, Israel is seen as a 'strategic challenge' and often 'threat' to the 'Arab nation' or the 'collective Arab national security'. Mohamed Hassanein Heikal's 'The Thirty Years War' series of books is the most rigorous presentation of that view.

12. Marc Lynch's paper 'The Brotherhood's dilemma', in volume 25 of the *Middle East Brief*, published by the Crown Centre for Middle East Studies at Brandeis University, analyzes the changes in the Brotherhood's rhetoric in the early and mid-2000s. Though Soumia Bardhan's essay 'Egypt, Islamists, and the internet: the case of the Muslim Brotherhood and its rhetoric of dialectics in Ikhwanweb', *Digest of Middle East Studies*, 23:2 (2014) focuses on one of the Brotherhood's main websites, it takes a longer view that incorporates the years following the 2011 uprising.

13. During his years in power (1957–87), Bourghuiba repeatedly talked about his views, often on TV. However, his earlier writings in the 1940s and early 1950s provide a more thorough understanding of how he perceived the role of Islam in society. His 1950s' letters to his friend Ali el-Taher are especially valuable here. See *Rasael Bourghuiba ila Sadiqahou Ali el-Taher* [*Bourghuiba's Messages to his Friend Ali el-Taher*] (Beirut, 1966).

14. Rached Ghannouchi expounded on his ideas in several books and essays. See *al-Hurreyat al-Amma fi al-Dawla al-Islameya* [*General Freedoms in the Islamic State*] and *al-Elmaneya wa al-Mumanaa al-Islameya* [*Secularism and Rejectionism in the Rhetoric of Arab Unity*]. The first was published by Markaz Derasat al-Wehda al-Arabeya in Beirut in 1993, the second by Saqi Books in London in 1999. Azzam Tamimi's *A Democrat within Islamism* (Oxford University Press, 2001) is a rigorous analysis of Ghannouchi's thinking. I have listened to Ghannouchi on several occasions, including during a long one-to-one interview with him.

15. Asef Bayat's *Life as Politics: How ordinary people change the Middle East* (Stanford University Press, 2009) presents the observations and insights of a scholar with a long

and intimate knowledge of several large societies in the Middle East. The book offers a rich and compelling analysis of how organized and unorganized social constituencies in different Middle Eastern countries have exploited some political openings in that period to drive change in areas that matter to wide social segments. Laith Kubba's 'The awakening of civil society', *Journal of Democracy*, 11 (2000) covers the same phenomenon, but from a political scientist's perspective. Mohamed el-Sayed Said's 'Global civil society: an Arab perspective' (in *Global Civil Society 2004–2005*, published by Sage for the International Development Institute at the London School of Economics) provides a pre-2011 assessment of Arab civil society and relates it to experiences in other parts of the world. The Tunisian scholar and former World Bank professional Hedi Larbi has conducted a long study at Harvard University's Kennedy School of Government, focusing on interactions between Arab civil society and state institutions.

16. In the 2000s, Abdel-Moneim Abul-Fottouh was the most visible Brotherhood leader engaging in such discussions, especially with international stakeholders. Abul-Fottouh built his standing within the organization in the late 1970s and early 1980s, when he led a major part of the group's expansion of its social infrastructure, as well as its presence in key Egyptian universities and professional syndicates. Some see him as not particularly representative of the Brotherhood's views. In 2011, he resigned from the organization and later established an independent political party in Egypt. However, in the period from the early to the mid-2000s, he was not just a key leader within the organization, but also one of the architects of its social and political views.

17. Ahmed Selim al-Awwa, Tarek al-Bishri, Ahmed Kamal Abul-Magd and Fahmi Huweidi were arguably the most prominent of this group. All of them came from legal and journalistic backgrounds. In dozens of articles and a number of books, most notably *Fi al-Nizam al-Seyasi lil Dawla al-Islameya* (*On the Political System of the Islamic State*), Al-Awwa provided a rigorous, detailed and innovative analysis of how Islam can be a framework for a modern society and how many of the concepts considered to be some of its main tenets can relate to modern liberal democracy. Al-Bishri's work focused on how Islam could be (and in his view was) the governing system of tolerant, multi-faith societies. In several books, most notably *Studies in Egyptian Democracy* and *The Political Movement in Egypt: 1945–1952*, he studied the influence that Islamic thinking had had on the key political movements in the Arab liberal age in the first half of the twentieth century. Abul-Magd is the author of many essays on Islamism. His paper 'Crossing the divide: dialogue among civilizations', commissioned by the United Nations and presented to the General Assembly in November 2001, relates many concepts of Islamic Sharia to several international human rights charters. Fahmi Huweidi, one of the most prominent Arab columnists of the last two decades, has developed a major constituency of readers and followers. Unlike the productions of the other three scholars mentioned here, most of Huweidi's writings are commentaries on current affairs across the Middle East, from a perspective that adheres to an Islamic frame of reference.

18. See the 2012 WikiLeaks record of various reports made by US diplomats to Washington. The following report comments on corruption in Tunisia in the mid-to-late 2000s: https://wikileaks.org/cable/2008/06/08TUNIS679.html

19. Estimates put Libya's population at circa 6 million people. Independent experts estimate that the country has the potential to produce over 4.5 million barrels of oil per day.

Chapter 2: Halal Money, Halal Regimes

1. Sadat's economic opening-up came to be referred to as the *infitah* (the opening). In time, the term came to signify more than just economic opening-up: it became associated with an abundance of opportunity, as well as the gradual loss of the cultural elegance that, many believed, had characterized Egypt in the preceding decades. *Infitah* effected

a gradual but decisive change in the composition of the Egyptian middle class. Henry Bruton's 'Egypt's development in the seventies', *Economic Development and Cultural Change*, 31:4 (1983) presents the specific policies that Sadat had initiated and the main social implications that followed. Joseph Licari's *Economic Reform in Egypt in a Changing Global Economy* (OECD, 1997) presents a detailed analysis of how the *infitah* brought about major changes in key economic metrics. The work of Ahmed Galal, at Egypt's Economic Research Forum, has traced the achievements, pitfalls and missed opportunities of Egypt's economic reform over the period from the 1970s to the late 2000s. I discussed *infitah*'s political and social implications in my book *Egypt on the Brink* (Yale University Press, 2010).

2. See Naim Qassem's *Hezbollah: The story from within* (Saqi Books, 2010). Qassem, one of the central leaders of the group in the 2000s, presents Hezbollah's official narrative of its inception, growth and emergence as a 'resistance movement against Israel'. Nicholas Blanford's *Warriors of God: Inside Hezbollah's thirty year struggle against Israel* (Random House, 2011) offers a more nuanced account of the group by an informed observer with intimate knowledge of Lebanon. Matthew Levitt's *Hezbollah: The global footprint of Lebanon's party of god* (Georgetown University Press, 2013) spans the group's global presence and operations, focusing specifically on its alleged links to underground groups in different countries. Farid al-Khazen's *The Breakdown of the State in Lebanon* (Harvard University Press, 2000) provides a macro view of the circumstances in which Hezbollah developed its social and economic presence. Matthew Levitt's *Hezbollah's Finances* (Washington Institute, 2000) details several examples of how Hezbollah expanded into several services sectors in Lebanon.

3. For a rigorous and detailed analysis of the existence of such a social divide, despite the relatively high economic growth rates, see *Daring to Care*, published by the Cairo office of the International Labour Organization in 2011. The report's essays were aggregated into a book published in the same year by the American University in Cairo Press. Mohamed Salih's *Economic Development and Political Action in the Arab World* (Routledge, 2014) links this social divide to a succession of economic policies and socioeconomic circumstances from preceding decades.

4. Gamal al-Banna wrote extensively on a myriad of theological issues in Islam. For a general view of his thinking, see *Tatweer al-Koran [Developing the Koran]* (Dar al-Fikr al-Islami, Cairo, 2000) and *al-Islam Deen w'Ummah, lais Deen w'Dawla [Islam: Religion and nation, not religion and state]* (Dar al-Shorouk, Cairo, 2008).

Chapter 3: The Salafists, from Cultural Salons to Jihadists' Battlefields

1. Yacoub Artine was a prolific writer on history, social customs and eighteenth- and nineteenth-century eastern Mediterranean geopolitics. But he is best remembered for his varied efforts to advance modern education in Egypt. In addition to his efforts to stem religion-based education, Artine played a significant role in convincing several rulers of Egypt (from the Mohammed Ali dynasty) to increase exponentially the financing they allocated to 'civil education'. He led efforts to Egyptianize French and Italian educational curricula. And he was a major force behind the expansion of the Alsun College, the Middle East's first graduate school focusing on learning and teaching European languages.

2. For different perspectives on al-Afghani's and Abdou's intellectual journey, see Sharifah al-Attas (ed.), *Islam and the Challenge of Modernity* (International Institute of Islamic Thought and Civilization, 1994); Othman Amin, *Mohammed Abdou* (Dar al-Maaref, 1953); Mark Sedgwick, *Muhammad Abduh* (Oneworld, 2010); Nikki Keddie, *Sayyid Jamal ad-Din 'al-Afghani': A political biography* (University of California Press, 1972); and Hisham Sharabi, *Arab Intellectuals and the West: The formative years, 1875–1914*

(Johns Hopkins University Press, 1970). John Esposito's *Islam and Politics* (Syracuse University Press, 1984) situates the two thinkers' ideas in the context of Islamic political philosophy. William Montgomery Watt's *Islamic Philosophy and Theology* (Edinburgh University Press, 1985) widens the discussion; his presentation combines Islamic philosophy with Islamic theology. Albert Hourani's *Arabic Thought in the Liberal Age* (Oxford University Press, 1962) is a macro introduction to the period in which al-Afghani and Abdou appeared and the circumstances in which this movement developed.

3. There are several translations of al-Tahtawi's book. In 2011, London's Saqi Books published a translation by Daniel Newman under the title *An Imam in Paris: Al-Tahtawi's visit to France, 1826–1831*. In 2001 Mansoor Moaddel of Eastern Michigan University wrote an interesting study that linked and compared al-Tahtawi's experience and thinking with those of some of his contemporaries in other Islamic communities which were witnessing waves of modernization at the same time: see 'Conditions for ideological production: the origins of Islamic modernism in India, Egypt, and Iran', *Theory and Society*, 30:5 (2001).

4. The Egyptian legal theorist Ahmed Hassan al-Zayat, founder of the 1930s' cultural weekly *Al-Risala*, wrote a series of articles in the 1940s in which he reflected on al-Tahtawi's thinking, perception of the West and his 'criteria for what he considered gold' in mid-nineteenth-century Paris. Four decades later, al-Zayat returned to the same topic through a long correspondence with Taha Hussein, the 'dean of Arabic literature', who himself had studied in France in the early twentieth century. The Egyptian newspaper *Al-Kotob: Weghat Nathat* published parts of that correspondence in 2002.

5. There is debate over whether al-Afghani and Abdou could be categorized as Salafists. For some, their activism, especially in leading a transformative wave of change in teaching theology, and later their journalistic endeavours, disqualify them from Salafism's traditional quietism. Some also argue that Abdou's insistence on 'rational readings of the Koran' took him away from the Salafists' traditional reverence for the 'predecessors', and so rendered him outside – some even say an intellectual opponent to – Salafism. These arguments use a late-twentieth-century understanding of Salafism as the yardstick by which al-Afghani's and Abdou's adherence to Salafism is assessed. As this chapter argues, Salafism has changed significantly in the last hundred years. A close reading of the output of al-Afghani and Abdou confirms that their point of departure was always their understanding of the 'Islamic message'; their borrowing from different cultures and their attempts at 'reforming Islamic understandings' were consistently undertaken with the objective of sustaining Islam as the primary – and for al-Afghani almost certainly the sole – frame of reference for 'Islamic societies'.

6. Al-Akkad was a prolific writer. Apart from his novel *Sara*, poems and countless informed essays on and critiques of Islamic and Western schools of philosophy, he penned two series: one on 'Genius in Islamic History', in which he reflected on the character of leading Muslims, from the Prophet Mohammed to several of his key companions; and the second on the tenets of the Islamic faith, in which he analyzed the notion of God and scripture in Islam. To the best of my knowledge, there are only limited sources on al-Akkad in English. The reflections of the Egyptian writer Anis Mansour in *Fi Salon al-Akkad* [*al-Akkad's Cultural Salon*] published by Dar al-Maaref in Cairo in different editions throughout the 1980s, offer an overview (and often simple analysis) of al-Akkad's intellectual interests and how he approached different topics. As the book was written by one of al-Akkad's closest disciples, it has intimacy and a thorough understanding of the man that other Arabic sources lack.

7. His most famous books comprise the series *The Dawn of Islam*, *The Rise of Islam* and *The Noon of Islam*, which appeared in the late 1940s. The Lebanese Dar al-Kitab al-Arabi published several editions of the series.

8. Qutb's most important books are *Maalim ala al-Tareeq* (*Milestone on the Road*) and *Fi Thelal al-Koran* (*In the Shadows of the Koran*). For an analysis of Qutb's writings and thinking, see Albert Bergesen (ed.), *The Sayyid Qutb Reader* (Routledge, 2008) and John Calvert, *Sayyid Qutb and the Origins of Radical Islam* (Hurst, 2010). Roxanne Euben and Mohammed Zaman (eds), *Princeton's Readings in Islamic Thought: Texts and contexts from al-Banna to Bin-Laden* (Princeton University Press, 2009) situates Qutb's thinking in a stream of Islamist views that condoned the use of violence. This book not only presents different studies on the thinking of key Islamist figures, but also subtly traces the historical development and geographical shifts of radical Islamism, especially in the last 80 years. Gilles Kepel's masterly studies *Jihad: The trail of political Islam* (Harvard University Press, 2003) and *The Roots of Radical Islam* (Saqi Books, 2005) are authoritative analyses of militant Islamism that combine the theological with the historical, social and political. William Montgomery Watt's *Islamic Fundamentalism and Modernity* (Routledge, 1988) draws on the author's extensive work on Islamic history and philosophy in analysing militant Islamism. Jonathan Brown's *Misquoting Muhammad: The challenge and choices of interpreting the Prophet's legacy* (Oneworld, 2014) provides interesting accompanying material to widen the reader's view of the complexity of the heritage of Islamic philosophy, especially when it comes to interpreting the meaning of the sayings and actions of the Prophet Mohammed.

9. This is a rich story of intrigue, political subversion and decades-long preparation for a theological revolution aimed at overthrowing one ruling dynasty and installing another. The story is also full of complex characters, convoluted plots and unexpected twists and turns. Mohamed Shaban's *The Abbasid Revolution* (Cambridge University Press, 1979) is a detailed account of the historical, political and social sides of that story.

10. There are scores of books about Islamic philosophy in the ninth and tenth centuries. See Henry Corban's *History of Islamic Philosophy* (republished Routledge, 2014); Oliver Leaman's *Introduction to Classical Islamic Philosophy* (Cambridge University Press, 2002); and Harry Austryn Wolfson's *The Philosophy of the Kalam* (Harvard University Press, 1976).

11. William Montgomery Watt's *Islamic Political Thought* (Edinburgh University Press, 1968) and Jeffry Halverson's *Theology and Creed in Sunni Islam* (Palgrave Macmillan, 2010) are major studies on Islamic political and socio-political thinking that situate Ibn Taimiyyah's work in the long march of Islamic philosophy. Jon Hoover's *Ibn Taimiyyah's Theodicy of Perpetual Optimism* (Brill, 2007) contrasts his thinking on specific theological and philosophical questions with that of major Islamic schools in the period from the ninth to the thirteenth centuries, especially those of al-Mutazila. Yossef Rapoport and Shahab Ahmed (eds), *Ibn Taimiyyah and His Times* (Oxford University Press, 2010) combines different perspectives of the scholar's writings and relates them to the key political trends that, in the writers' view, influenced him. Ahmad Ahmad's *Structural Interrelations of Theory and Practice in Islamic Law: A study in six works of Islamic jurisprudence* (Brill, 2006) relates Ibn Taimiyyah's oeuvre to that of other pillars of Islamic thought in the period from the tenth to the fourteenth centuries, most notably Imam al-Ghazali. For further and ongoing analysis of Ibn Taimiyyah's contributions to Islamic theology and for the myriad views regarding how close or far he was from militant radicalism, see the published essays of Cairo University's Faculty of Literature, Islamic Philosophy Section, and those in the *Journal of Arabic and Islamic Studies* at Khalifa University of Science, Technology and Research in the United Arab Emirates.

12. In 2015, Yale University Press published Sherman Jackson's translation of the treatise written by the leaders of al-Jamaa al-Islamiya, one of the Arab world's most violent Islamist groups in the period from the late 1970s to the 1990s, in which they explain the reasons that drove them to adopt violence and the rationale by which they came to denounce it. The Egyptian journalist Makram Mohamed Ahmed conducted dozens of interviews with the most prominent of those leaders in the late 1990s, which offer

valuable insights into their thinking. The Egyptian magazine *Akher-Saaa* published these interviews in 2002–03.

13. Ahmed Rashid's *Taliban: Militant Islam, oil, and fundamentalism in Central Asia* (Yale University Press, 2000) tells the story 'on the ground', as it unfolded in Afghanistan and Pakistan. *Defence of Islamic Lands: The first obligation after believing* (Maktabah Publications, 2002) was written by Abdullah Azzam, who for a decade or so in the 1980s was the chief architect of the Arabs' move into Afghanistan. Azzam supplemented his logistical work by presenting a theological framework that motivated tens of thousands of young Muslims (primarily but not solely Arabs) to leave their countries to fight the 'atheist Soviets'. Those Arabs, who later came to be known as 'the Arab Afghans', formed the basis for international militant Islamist organizations such as al-Qaeda. Azzam's writings depict the intellectual links and justifications that laid the basis for the phenomenon that evolved into multiple global terror organizations. Lawrence Wright's *Looming Tower: al-Qaeda and the road to 9/11* (Knopf, 2006) tells that story in detail. David Commins' *The Wahhabi Mission and Saudi Arabia* (I.B. Tauris, 2006) focuses on the hugely important Saudi angle in the Arab Afghan phenomenon. Marc Segman's *Understanding Terror Networks* (University of Pennsylvania Press, 2004) delves into al-Qaeda's operations, which at least until the mid-2000s were based on the experiences of the Arab Afghans in the 1980s and 1990s. Olivier Roy's *Globalized Islam: The search for a new Ummah* (Columbia University Press, 2002) offers a wider perspective that is less focused on pure militant Islamism, and which takes into account how that militancy interacted with other attempts in the 1980s and early 1990s to invoke Islamism in various regional struggles, including social ones in western Europe.

14. Gilles Kepel's *Muslim Extremism in Egypt: The prophet and pharaoh* (University of California Press, 2003, second edition) is a detailed study of Egypt's experience with Islamic radicalism up until the early 2000s, including the tumultuous 1990s. The memoirs of Montasser al-Zayat, the most prominent lawyer of the leading figures of militant Islamist groups, who represented many of them in Egyptian courts, shed light on that experience from the inside. The most important part is al-Zayat's reflections on Ayman al-Zawahiri, one of the leading architects of al-Qaeda, and its head after the killing of Osama Bin Laden in 2011. In 2003, the University of Chicago Press published an English version of that section under the title *The Road to al-Qaeda: The story of Bin-Laden's right-hand man*.

15. For an understanding of the Algerian civil war, see Luis Martinez and John Entelis, *The Algerian Civil War* (Columbia University Press, 2000) and Hugh Roberts, 'The battlefield: Algeria, 1988–2002', *International Journal of African Historical Studies*, 38 (2005). For a wider understanding of Algeria's experience in the last half-century, see Martin Evans and John Phillips, *Algeria: Anger of the dispossessed* (Yale University Press, 2008).

16. See the 1994 British Broadcasting Corporation (BBC) documentary on Taher Djaout: *Shooting the Writer* (available on YouTube).

17. See footnote 12 above.

18. He was studying physics at a leading university in London.

Chapter 4: The Islamists' Fall from Power

1. Most of al-Aswany's articles in that period were collected in his book *Democracy is the Solution* (Ginkgo Library, 2015).

2. The largest aggregation of which was the National Salvation Front, which comprised various political forces.

3. The Salafist group Jabhat al-Islah (Reform Front) was a key bloc in the Tunisian Labour and Reform Front; others fielded their candidates as independents.

4. Some of which traced their ancestry to royal dynasties in Islamic Iberia before the Muslims were expelled in the twelfth and thirteenth centuries.

5. Many Moroccans describe these power centres as the *Maghzen*. This term – the literal translation of which is 'the reservoir' or 'the store' – is loaded. Many observers see it as 'the establishment' of the Moroccan society. It is much more than that. The *Maghzen* is the store of political power, as well as the basis for granting or withholding legitimacy. It controls the country's economy, but it also administers the country's informal charitable and social support structures. It is the store of the country's multiethnic identity. For some, the term *Maghzen* synthesizes the blur between power and wealth, the extreme concentration of power and the convoluted decision-making processes that have afflicted Morocco for centuries. For others, it is the reservoir of Morocco's strength: its unique identity that distinguishes that country from all its Arab and African neighbours, its cherished view of itself, and its rich traditions – from a creative cuisine and dress code to a vibrant cultural life. In 2013 and 2014, Morocco's historical and cultural publication *Zamane* ran a long series tracing how the concept of the *Maghzen* came to develop, expand and entrench itself in the country's politics and culture. The memoirs of King Hassan II, published in 1993 under the title *Memory of a King*, reveal how Hassan, arguably the most powerful and influential Moroccan monarch of the last two centuries, saw the legitimacy basis, power structure and social customs that formed and enabled the existence and growth of the *Maghzen*.

6. Tunisia has been witnessing a growing terror campaign, similar to the one that Egypt confronted in the 1990s. Over fifty people were killed in the first half of 2015 in two attacks on one of Tunis's main museums and a resort near the tourist town of Sousse.

Chapter 5: The Secularists' Predicament

1. Al-Dostour, the Popular Alliance, the Free Egyptians, and al-Wafd.
2. In this case, Ahmed Najeeb al-Shabi and Maya Jribi.
3. The UGTT's experience in the last century reveals the intellectual cycle that many large Arab civil society organizations have undergone over that period, as well as their convoluted relationships with the regimes of their countries, especially in the decade of liberation from European colonialism in the 1960s. Eva Bellin traces that story, with a special focus on the UGTT, in *Stalled Democracy: Capital, labor, and the paradox of state-sponsored development* (Cornell University Press, 2002). Also see Christopher Alexander 'State, labour, and the new global economy in Tunisia', in Dirk Vandewalle (ed.), *North Africa: Development and reform in a changing global economy* (St Martin's, 1996).
4. In the first half of the twentieth century, secular political figures such as Egypt's Saad Zaghloul and Mustafa Kamel, and the Levant's Riad al-Solh had become iconic figures across the region. Afaf Lutfi al-Sayyid's *Egypt and Cromer: A study in Anglo-Egyptian relations* (John Murray, 1968) situates Zaghloul's role in the prevailing political and cultural circumstances of his time. There are various books and essays on Riad al-Solh. Patrick Seale's *The Struggle for Arab Independence: Riad el-Solh and the makers of the modern Middle East* (Cambridge University Press, 2010) is a detailed account of the man's public life, the regional circumstances in which he operated, and his legacy.
5. Aflaq and Habash were among a large group of Levantine (and generally Francophone) writers and activists who played leading roles in organizing the Arab secular nationalist movement, and later party, al-Baath (The Resurrection). Aflaq, in particular, emerged as the decisive theorist behind al-Baath's revolutionary, and often militant, ideology. His most famous book is *The Battle for One Destiny* (Dar al-Hureya, 1958).
6. Said Aburish's *Nasser: The last Arab* (Gerald Duckworth, 2004) is a detailed account of Nasser's reign. Mohamed Hassanein Heikal's series of books 'The Thirty Years War'

presents the major political events that shaped Middle Eastern politics in the period from the mid-1950s to the mid-1970s, from the perspective of Nasser's closest advisor. The series is a rare window into Nasser's thinking and worldview, though written from a highly sympathetic stance.

7. There are various sources that have discussed media and power in the Arab world in the last fifty years. Adeed Dawisha's *Arab Nationalism in the Twentieth Century: From triumph to despair* (Princeton University Press, 2003) discusses that relationship in detail. Bernard Lewis's *The Multiple Identities of the Middle East* (Schocken, 2001) situates that relationship in a historical context. For a study of Nasser's case in Egypt, see Hussein Amin and James Napoli, 'Media and power in Egypt', in James Curran and Myung-Jin Park (eds), *De-Westernizing Media Studies* (Routledge, 2000).

8. Before his descent in the 2000s into utter megalomania (among other things, calling himself 'the King of African Kings'), Gaddafi had, in the 1980s and 1990s, written several essays on governance in the Arab world in addition to his famous *Green Book*, which purportedly put forward a 'new way of social interaction and governing'. Irrespective of the quality and originality of his arguments, his point of departure at that time was always rooted in a secular worldview, heavily influenced by the writings of leading scholars of the Arab liberal age.

9. In terms of his economic outlook, Gamal Mubarak was indeed a liberal. But, as I argued in my book *Egypt on the Brink* (Yale University Press, 2010), the political project of which he was part was completely divorced from the political heritage of the Arab liberal age.

10. For a detailed account of Mohammed Ali's reign and the key ideas, developments and figures that made his project a reality, see Khaled Fahmy, *All the Pasha's Men: Mehmed Ali, his army, and the making of modern Egypt* (Cambridge University Press, 1998) and Henry Dodwell, *The Founder of Modern Egypt: A study of Muhammad Ali* (Cambridge University Press, 1931). It is interesting to compare how two rigorous scholars analyze the same events. Dodwell's book follows a classic historical approach to the pasha's story. Fahmy's, however, provides a panoramic view of early nineteenth-century Egypt, paying special attention to how personalities (and the interactions between them) affected many political decisions of consequence at the time.

11. Especially Hussein Bey, the most prominent member of the Husseinid dynasty that ruled the country from 1705 to 1956.

12. There are different views as to whether the Tunisian political elite at the time actually wrote and owned the 1881 charter. By the late 1860s, Tunisia's finances were almost totally controlled by France and Italy, which a few years later established a considerable presence within the Tunisian Diwan al-Muhasaba (the equivalent then of the finance ministry). In 1878, the Congress of Berlin recognized Tunisia as being under 'France's sovereign protection'. Yet the 1881 charter was not entirely a European diktat: leading Tunisian activists, including from the court of Mohammed Bey (the key Tunisian ruler in the mid-nineteenth century), were actively involved in the discussions and drafting that led to the emergence of the constitution. See Kenneth Perkins, *A History of Modern Tunisia* (Cambridge University Press, 2004). For a wider discussion of the evolution of social forces in the country, see Lisa Anderson's *The State and Social Transformation in Tunisia and Libya* (Princeton University Press, 1986).

13. See Bruce Maddy-Weitzman, *The Crystallization of the Arab State System: 1945–1954* (Syracuse University Press, 1992).

14. I am not aware of many books that have studied the growth of the Arab middle classes in the first half of the twentieth century. Keith Watenpaugh's *Being Modern in the Middle East: Revolution, nationalism, colonialism, and the Arab middle class* (Princeton University Press, 2006) focuses on the political and social dynamics that helped give rise to a middle class in a number of regions, and especially the eastern Mediterranean.

Tarik Youssef's 'Development, growth, and policy reform in the Middle East and North Africa Since 1950', *Journal of Economic Perspectives*, 18:3 (2004), focuses on a later period, but provides valuable insights into trends that began in the first half of the twentieth century.

15. See Michael Oren, *Six Days of War: June 1967 and the making of the modern Middle East* (Presidio Press, 2003).

16. See Jean-Pierre Chauffour (ed.), *From Political to Economic Awakening in the Arab World: The path of economic integration* (World Bank, 2013) for an overarching introduction to the political-economy dynamics that have led to persistent weaknesses in Arab public institutions.

17. Robert Fisk, *Pity the Nation* (Andre Deutsch, 1990).

Chapter 6: The Minorities' Fears

1. Takla, along with his brother and a group of Levantine intellectuals, founded *al-Ahram*, which since the late 1940s has been the Arab world's largest newspaper in terms of offices, circulation and revenue.

2. Youssef Cattaui was a particularly important figure in modern Arab banking. In addition to serving twice as Egypt's finance minister in the 1920s, he was a founding member of the Arab world's first modern credit institution, Banque Misr. Joel Beinin, an authority on the history of Egypt's Jewish community, recounted Cattaui's role in developing Arab banking and industry in his essay 'Egyptian Jewish identities', in *Contested Identities*, 5:1 (1996).

3. His lengthy memoir, published in Arabic by Cairo's Dar al-Shorouk, offers many insights into the political, economic and social changes that Egypt, the eastern Mediterranean, and to some extent Turkey, underwent in the second half of the nineteenth century.

4. I am aware of no books in English or Arabic that present the rich history of Morocco's Jewish community. Taha Za'Noun's *Tareekh al-Maghreb al-Arabi* [*The History of the Arab Maghreb*] (Beirut, 2004) recounts how a relatively large Jewish community came to settle in Morocco during and after the European Reconquista of Islamic Spain in the fifteenth century. Mark Cohen's *Under Crescent and Cross: The Jews in the Middle Ages* (Princeton University Press, 1995) is another source on that migration from Spain to Morocco.

5. Published by Dar al-Maaref in Cairo in 1938.

6. There was a tripling in the price of oil between 1974 and 1978. These price increases began in the midst of the Arab–Israeli Yom Kippur War in October/November 1973, after key Arab oil producers cut their oil shipments to those Western countries that they deemed supportive of Israel against Arab interests. Many books address the Arab 'oil embargo' from the geopolitical, geoeconomic and oil-economics perspectives. Daniel Yergin's *The Prize: The epic quest for oil, money, and power* (Simon and Schuster, 2008) covers the three perspectives. Jeffery Robinson's *Yamani: The inside story* (Fontana Press, 1989) tells the story by focusing on the role played by Saudi's highly influential 1970s' oil minister, Zaki al-Yamani.

7. Myriad books have analyzed these social changes. Politics, economics and sociology aside, Alaa al-Deeb's *Waqfa Qabl al-Munhadar* [*A Pause before the Plunge*] (Dar al-Shorouk, 1995) is a poignant personal reflection on these changes and their impact on Arab societies' ways of living, values and worldviews in the 1970s and 1980s.

8. Gerard Russell's *Heirs to Forgotten Kingdoms* (Basic Books, 2014) is an on-the-ground account of changes that took place in several communities of religious minorities in the Middle East.

9. This assessment is derived from the author's interviews with two ministers in two Iraqi governments in the last decade and the work of the Chaldaean Patriarchate of Babylon Pontifical Babel College.

10. Nicholas Blanford, *Killing Mr Lebanon: The assassination of Rafik Hariri and its impact on the Middle East* (I.B. Tauris, 2006).
11. From two lectures given by the late Lebanese journalist Samir Qaseer, who was assassinated in Beirut in June 2005.
12. Samir Qaseer's *Being Arab* (Verso Books, 2013) explains his view of why these values were suppressed in the Arab world throughout the twentieth century. Kassir links key political trends in modern Arab history with how large segments of Arabs came to support policies that ended up diluting their own political, civil and human rights.
13. And for a substantial percentage of them, against the presence of Syrian troops and security apparatuses in their country – a relic of the multifaceted and complicated Lebanese civil war. See Robert Fisk, *Pity the Nation* (Andre Deutsch, 1990).
14. The 'Cedar Revolution' gave rise to a nationalist movement which, in 2005, compelled the Syrian Assad regime to withdraw its armed forces from Lebanon, after two decades of semi-occupying the country. But soon after, Lebanon returned to its classic sectarianism, factionalism and obsession with personality cults, all of which continue to plague and paralyse the country's politics. By mid-2015, Lebanon had spent eighteen months trying to formulate a compromise by which it could elect a president – to no avail.
15. Partly a result of having two different but hugely popular leaders: Kamal Jumblatt in the 1960s and 1970s, and his son Walid since Kamal's assassination in 1977. To the best of my knowledge, there are virtually no reliable sources about the Druze written by scholars who have done primary research into this relatively mysterious community. This makes Nejla Izzedin's *The Druzes: A new study of their history, faith, and society* (Brill, 1993) a valuable source. Mordechai Nisan's *Minorities in the Middle East: A history of struggle and self-expression* (MacFarland, 1991) focuses on how the theological and political thinking of various religious minorities in the Middle East, and especially in the eastern Mediterranean, including the Druze, has evolved in the last century. Unlike Gerard Russell's *Heirs to Forgotten Kingdoms*, which is based primarily on personal observations of these minorities' social and cultural lives, Nisan's book delves into how the complicated history of these communities has formed their understanding and interpretation of their region's social and political events.

Chapter 7: The Gulf's View of Islamism

1. For the first time since Kuwait's independence from the UK in 1961, there was a deficit in the national budget.
2. Accounting for over 80 per cent of the region's total sovereign income streams.
3. Especially the descendants of Sheikh Mohammed Ibn Abdel-Wahhab, who latterly became known as 'al al-Sheikh' (the family of the Sheikh).
4. Robert Lacey's *Inside the Kingdom* (Hutchinson, 2009) tells the story of the Kingdom of Saudi Arabia throughout the twentieth century, and links it to the history of the House of Saud's earlier kingdoms in Najd. Steve Coll's *The Bin Ladens: Oil, money, terrorism, and the secret Saudi world* (Penguin, 2009) focuses on the Bin Laden family, which, irrespective of the story of its most famous member Osama, has been one of the richest and most influential merchant families in Saudi Arabia in the last half century. Coll's telling of the Bin Laden story sheds light on the fabric of Saudi society and on the bargain that was struck between the ruling family and the Wahhabi establishment. I presented the history of that Saudi–Wahhabi alliance, and several views of what it meant and its consequences, in my 2015 BBC documentary *Sands of Time: The story of Saudi Arabia*.
5. For example, Abu Dhabi's ruling family, the al-Nahayans, the leading branch of the Bani Yas tribe that has dominated Abu Dhabi, al-Ain and the surrounding area for the past

two centuries, came to prominence as a result of its leading role in fending off attacks on the region from several Wahhabi groups, including the Saudis. The current ruling families of the UAE, Kuwait, Qatar and Bahrain came to power during the eighteenth and nineteenth centuries through guerrilla fights in which they subjugated the other extended families and tribes that had inhabited these areas. In all of these states, the ruling families had sought the approval of the most revered religious authorities in the area. Often, such as in the case of the al-Thani, Qatar's ruling family, and al-Qassimis of Ras al-Khaimah in the UAE, both ideologically close to the Wahhabis, these religious authorities resided at the heart of the Arabian Peninsula, in what is today Saudi Arabia.

6. In the early nineteenth century, Britain's highly influential East India Company, which controlled a significant percentage of the trade between the eastern Mediterranean and India, suffered pirate attacks on its ships that were mounted by the tribes that ruled the lower Gulf. At the instigation of the Company, the British government responded with limited military campaigns, as well as by offering 'truce agreements' to the leading tribes of the region. By the 1850s, several 'truces' had been aggregated into the Perpetual Maritime Truce, by which the key families within these tribes promised to cease all pirate activity against British interests, in return for British protection and acknowledgement of their rights as the legitimate rulers of the different sheikhdoms. The relationship became much more important with the discovery of oil, initially in the early 1930s in Bahrain, and then later across the entire Gulf. Petroleum Concessions Limited, a majority-owned British oil extractor and trader, was given exclusive rights over oil discoveries in these 'protectorates'. Direct British influence continued until 1968, when Britain, reeling from its strategic defeat in the Suez Crisis of 1956 and in an effort to cut 'imperial costs', decided to withdraw gradually from all its possessions 'east of Eden' – and most crucially the Gulf. Kuwait became an independent state in 1961, Qatar in 1970, and the UAE, combining most of the smaller sheikhdoms, came into being in 1971. The work of Christopher Davidson – and especially *Power and Politics in the Persian Gulf Monarchies* (Hurst, 2012) – provides detailed histories and analyses of this topic.

7. Gulf capitals and cities are awash with banners and billboards carrying digitally enhanced pictures of kings, emirs and senior princes depicted wearing traditional Arabic clothes against backgrounds evocative of Umayyad and Andalusian palaces. The local media devote hours of airtime to the religious and charitable activities of the kings and emirs. And there is an emphasis on traditional arts and sports, such as composing Arabic poetry, horse riding, falcon domestication, classical fencing and shooting. In an effort to build regal grandeur, 'His Royal Highness' has become a title that is *de rigueur* for almost all senior princes across the Gulf. Christopher Davidson elaborates on these phenomena in *Power and Politics in the Persian Gulf Monarchies*.

8. And especially at the peak of their state power during the reign of caliph Abdel-Malik Ibn Marwan (646–705).

9. In terms of the percentage that the private sector contributes to the nation's gross domestic product.

10. On the one hand, dispersing gatherings and rounding up many demonstrators; on the other, launching a national dialogue to which the young, American-educated crown prince invited dozens of activists, including from the most prominent Shii political groups.

11. Stephane Lacroix's *Awakening Islam: The politics of religious dissent in contemporary Saudi Arabia* (Harvard University Press, 2011) situates the history of the Saudi–Brotherhood relationship in the context of Islamic activism in the kingdom. Carrie Rosefsky Wickham's *The Muslim Brotherhood: Evolution of an Islamist movement* (Princeton University Press, 2013) looks at the relationship from the Brotherhood's own perspective.

12. See Nathan Brown's many essays and papers on Islamist movements in Kuwait, and especially the Constitutional Front. Many of these papers were published in the Middle East Series of the Carnegie Endowment for International Peace. For a historical account of the development of these groups, see Sami Nasser al-Khalidi's *al-Ahzab al-Seyaseyah al-Islameyah fi al-Kuwait* [*Islamist Political Parties in Kuwait*] (1999).

13. See Nathan Brown's *When Victory is Not an Option* (Cornell University Press, 2012), and Carrie Rosefsky Wickham's *The Muslim Brotherhood*.

14. After his ascent to the throne, Saudi King Salman sought to improve the kingdom's relationship with Qatar. Several meetings between leading figures in the two regimes took place in the first half of 2015. The prevailing logic behind the potential rapprochement was that both countries need to come together in a unified Sunni bloc to oppose the Iran-sponsored Shii expansion.

Chapter 8: Turkish Islamism as a Model for the Arab World

1. Parts of these *Tanzimat* were inspired by reforms that had taken place earlier in the century in the Arab world, most notably in Mohammed Ali's Egypt. But whereas the Arab reformists proceeded cautiously, the Turks were much more ambitious and assertive in dealing with their society and the religious institutions. Rasheed Pasha, arguably the leading figure in shaping the *Tanzimat*, was adamant about implementing the reforms not just in Turkey's urban areas, but across the Ottoman Empire. Unlike most of their counterparts in the Arab world, Turkish reformers deliberately excluded the Ottoman Islamic authorities (for example, the office of Sheikh-ul-Islam) from the seriously important decisions relating to social and educational reform. See Caroline Fenkel, *Osman's Dream* (John Murray, 2006).

2. Andrew Mango's *Atatürk: The biography of the founder of Modern Turkey* (Overlook Press, 2000) is a detailed source on the man's life, achievements and limitations.

3. Not a single political leader in the Arab world had detached his modernizing project from religion. In Egypt, Mohammed Ali and his grandson Khedive Ismail had marginalized al-Azhar through co-option and the subtle weakening of its influence (especially in education), but they repeatedly and strenuously avoided any confrontation with its sheikhs and leading scholars. In Morocco, Sultan Abdel-Majeed, who ruled in the second decade of the twentieth century, after France began its effective occupation of the country, and under whose reign the country witnessed a major modernization programme, empowered the religious authorities by increasing their endowments. In Iraq of the 1920s and 1930s, and in Jordan of the 1940s, the Hashemites secured their rule through religious pedigree (descent from the Prophet Mohammed), and placed themselves atop their countries' religious establishments, while at the same time implementing a major westernization programme. Even Nasser, who had brought Egypt's al-Azhar under state control, tried to find a rhetoric that placated the country's – and the Arab world's – largest religious institutions, and linked Arab nationalism to its 'overarching', vaguely defined, Islamic civilization. Only Ataturk severed national identity from religion, and truly separated the state from Islam.

4. This success would have been unthinkable without the republic's concentration of power, top-down governance style and strict monitoring mechanisms. In the absence of these, it is highly likely that Turkey's transformation from being the core of the Islamic Ottoman Empire into a new independent and highly secular state would have been messy, and potentially quite violent. Hugh Pope's and Nicola Pope's *Turkey Unveiled: A history of modern Turkey* (Overlook Press, 2011) presents the tensions that this political and social transformation unleashed.

5. Metin Heper and Sabri Sayari (eds), *Political Leaders and Democracy in Turkey* (Lexington Books, 2002) situates the Menderes experience in the country's modern

political trajectory. Mango's biography of Ataturk reflects on how various segments in Turkey's power structures viewed Menderes and his power base.

6. What complicated the problem was that the militarization of the Ataturk state and the position that the armed forces had assumed (above all other institutions) were not congruent with Turkey's experience in the century prior to Ataturk's founding of the republic. The *Tanzimat* reforms were the product of the efforts of visionary civil servants, who, almost without exception, lacked any military experience. It was actually not possible to usher in the *Tanzimat* reforms before the elimination of the janissaries, who were correctly seen by the civilian reformers and the palace as representative of an Ottoman military force that had grown too influential and self-serving for the state's good. The Ottoman military's record in the second half of the nineteenth century (even after getting rid of the janissaries) was hardly inspiring. It lost successive battles against Russia, and this in turn led to the secession of various territories from the empire. The Ottoman navy had never recovered from its total surrender to Mohammed Ali's Egypt in the 1840s. This record, prior to Mustafa Kemal Ataturk's saving of Turkey, meant that the armed forces did not have the social cache and reverence to emerge as the sole institution entrusted with overseeing the entire political structure and having the right to interfere in government, oust elected representatives of the people and 'guide the nation to its founding principles'. The establishment was aware of that. This was a key reason behind the consistent and adamant insistence that the Turkish Republic was an entirely new political entity, based on a modern concept, and not in any way a continuation, or a legacy, of the Ottoman Empire. Such severance from history was a necessity, to give the republic's guardians the legitimacy they needed to play the role that its founder had reserved for them.

7. Marvine Howe's *Turkey: A nation divided over Islam's revival* (Westview Press, 2004) reflects on the changing attitudes to various 'features of Islamic revival', most notably the veil. Merve Kavaci (ed.), *Headscarf Politics in Turkey* (Palgrave Macmillan, 2014) analyzes 'the politicisation of religion in modern Turkey' with a special focus on the social implications of the major limitations on the headscarf in Turkey. Also see Deniz Kandiyoti and Ayse Saktanber (eds), *Fragments of Culture: The everyday of modern Turkey* (Rutgers University Press, 2002).

8. Industrialization was also, correctly, seen as a way to significantly improve the country's current account and balance of payments, as it resulted, in the short term, in local products replacing imports, and in the long term, in higher exports – and so in new revenue streams for the country.

9. In the last 200 years of the Ottoman Empire, Sufi orders were at the heart of the state's power structure. Several Ottoman prime ministers in the second half of the eighteenth century belonged to the Naqshbandi order, historically one of the largest across the Caucasus, Iraq, Kurdistan and Turkey. Almost all leaders of the janissaries, the sultan's special forces who played major roles in the expansion of the Ottoman Empire in the Balkans and central and eastern Europe, belonged to the Bektashi order. In the second half of the nineteenth century, the Khalidi order, an offshoot of the Naqshbandi, became so close to the imperial palace that rumours circulated that Sultan Abdelhamid II was himself a follower. Sufism is a versatile and loose school of thought in Sunni Islam that has always focused on the spiritual aspects of religion, much more than on jurisprudence, disputations, law and practices. The founders of the major Sufi schools, most notably the legendary Mawlana (our guardian) Rumi, sought paths to understanding the nature of the divine, the connection between what is sacred and what is material, and how to elevate the soul to transcend the hustle and bustle of life, to relate to God. Sufi orders that had originated in Persia, Kurdistan and Turkey (such as the Khalidi order) were enriched by the traditions of Persia and the west Asian steppes. Relative to the Sufi orders that had emerged out of the Arab world, these Persian and

Turkish orders tended to be more creative and daring, borrowing from various cultures; and so they were more detached from the scriptural schools that rooted themselves in interpretations of the Koran. In Turkey, these Sufi orders had schools that taught children basic Islamic rules. But their main focus was on developing their shrines and 'sanctuaries', where the order's devoted members gathered to meditate, reflect on the thinking of the order's leaders, and 'lose' themselves through procedural rumination and contemplation. In the late nineteenth century, some of these procedures became known across the Islamic world, and later in the West, as *dervishi dkhir* (the dervishes' remembrance), in reference to the order members' practice of whirling while they thought about God's grace. Ottoman Turkey was a fertile ground for Sufism. Unlike all previous caliphates, the Ottomans saw Islam as the primary, but far from sole, basis for entrenching their legitimacy as the rulers of most of the Islamic world. For over 150 years, the house of Osman had ruled parts of the steppes of western Asia under a dynastic suzerainty. Gradually, they encroached on Anatolia, crushed other ruling families and established their realm through sheer force and their reputation as fearsome warriors. For decades, the Ottoman sultan, despite being Muslim, was a secular king, without any claim to divine connection, or to the political inheritance of the Prophet Mohammed. The Ottoman sultans assumed the title of the caliph only after Selim the Conqueror took possession of Egypt in 1517, which at the time had effective control over the Hijaz (the region in which Islam's two holy cities of Mecca and Medina are). Even after that, the Ottoman sultans' legitimacy continued to be based on the empire's ability to expand and acquire more territories, maintain stability, secure the important trading routes in the territories under its control, and protect the populations from the violence and avarice of the minor Mamluks (the warrior class that ruled Egypt, parts of the Hijaz, and the eastern Mediterranean from the mid-1300s to the early 1500s). After entering Cairo and surveying its palaces and souks, Selim the Conqueror decided to take thousands of artisans, labourers and artists back with him to Istanbul. He was not interested, however, in any of al-Azhar's scholars.

10. In his four years in the job, Erdogan brought about major improvements to the city's administration, finances, traffic and the hitherto chronic garbage collection problem. His council was a savvy and prudent investor in the city's infrastructure. Most neutral Turkish observers praise his ability to confront and significantly reduce municipal corruption. Erdogan was, arguably, the best mayor this huge metropolis has ever had. See Hootan Shambayati's 'A tale of two mayors: courts and politics in Iran and Turkey', *International Journal of Middle East Studies*, 36:2 (2004).

11. For a political-economy perspective and assessment of these reforms, see Sadik Unay, *Neoliberal Globalization and Institutional Reform: The political economy of planning and development in Turkey* (Nova Publishers, 2006), and the work of Sinan Ulgen at Turkey's Centre for Economic and Foreign Policy Studies.

12. In a decade, Turkey grew from an unstable developing economy with acute debt problems into the world's fifteenth-largest economy, a trading hub connecting Europe with the eastern Mediterranean and the Gulf, a significant player in traditional heavy industries, a major tourism destination, and a country with an enviable fiscal situation, especially as neighbouring countries (including traditional foes such as Greece) were unravelling into an economic mess.

13. Arda Kumbaracibasi, *Turkish Politics and the Rise of the AKP: Dilemmas of institutionalisation and leadership strategy* (Taylor and Francis, 2009).

14. There were also attempts to weaken the AKP within Turkey itself. The secular parties' main candidate to oppose Erdogan in the 2014 presidential election was Ekmeleddin Ihsanoglu, an academic who had completed most of his studies at Egyptian universities, and who for the previous decade had been secretary general of the Saudi-backed Organisation of Islamic Cooperation. For many observers, it was strange that a man

with such a background was chosen as the candidate to unite the secular parties against the Islamist AKP. His strong connections to some Arab regimes, however, and his perceived ability to mobilize a lot of capital behind his campaign, explained some of the momentum that his candidacy generated.

15. See Helen-Rose Ebaugh, *The Gulen Movement: A sociological analysis of a civic movement rooted in moderate Islam* (Springer, 2009) and Joshua Hendrick, *Gulen: The ambiguous politics of market Islam in Turkey and the world* (New York University Press, 2013).

Chapter 9: Iranian Islamism as a Model for Arab Islamists

1. Since Yemen's civil war of the 1960s, which ended with the abolition of the country's 900-year-old 'imamate', one of the various forms of theological state that appeared in the Islamic world after the fall of the Abbasid dynasty in Baghdad in 1258.

2. The Houthis' military advances were reversed after Saudi Arabia undertook, in the first quarter of 2015, a major aerial campaign against their forces and allies in Yemen.

3. The Baath hardly favoured the Sunnis out of a sense of ideology. Historically, it was hostile to all forms of excessive religiosity; and in its ranks there were Sunnis, Shiis and Iraqi Christians. The Baath's increasing hostility to the Shiis, from the mid-1970s to the early 2000s, stemmed from the significant influence that leading Iraqi Shii 'references' had on its followers – an influence that the Baath leaders, and especially Saddam Hussein, deemed perilous to the regime. The war with Iran's Islamic Republic exacerbated the Baath's suspicion of Shiis, especially the communities in the country's south which had exhibited sectarian sympathy towards Iran. Most of the American strategists and administrators who implemented the de-Baathification thought of it as a mechanism to cleanse the country of people who served a corrupt and oppressive political regime. As a result, however, almost everyone who had had any prominent role in Iraq in the previous three decades, the vast majority of whom hailed from Iraqi Sunni tribes, were thrust aside. Scores of senior bureaucrats, administrators and diplomats, as well as thousands of officers, quietly left the country (to settle in Jordan, Egypt and, for the comfortably well-off, London or Dubai). Donald Rumsfeld's memoir *Known and Unknown* (Sentinel, 2011) elaborates on the reasons that led the Bush administration to adopt the de-Baathification strategy. Emma Sky's *The Unravelling: High hopes and missed opportunities in Iraq* (Public Affairs, 2015) argues why this strategy was a colossal mistake.

4. Khomeini's choice of the word 'oppressor' was anchored in the old Shii tradition of viewing a succession of Islamic regimes as 'oppressors of the faithful'. This was a key reason why the usage of that word was quickly adopted by Shii communities in Iraq, Yemen, Bahrain and Lebanon. Abdelaziz Sachedina's *The Just Ruler in Shiite Islam* (Oxford University Press, 1988) provides a historical and theological analysis of how this concept has evolved in Shii Islam.

5. He had spent the last of his fourteen years in exile in a village less than thirty kilometres outside Paris, and yet he had adamantly refused to visit the city of light and love, seeing it as a milieu of sin and corruption.

6. In his view, most notably, al-Azhar's Grand Sheikh Mahmoud Shaltout, whom we introduced in chapter 3.

7. Khomeini was not the only or the first Shii leader to challenge the shah's rule. Before the rise of Khomeini, several leading Shii theologians played active roles in stirring up discontent with the shah, his family, the political-economy structure he presided over, and his foreign policy and international alliances, especially with the US. Ali Shariati was among the most notable of those leaders. See his book *The Islamic View of Man* (Free Islamic Literatures, 1979, in English).

8. No one described the bitterness surrounding the decision to end the war more than Khomeini himself, when he confided that 'it was like drinking a chalice of poison'.

9. John Murphy's *Ali Khamenei* (Chelsea House, 2007) – one of the Modern World Leaders series – is among the few books available in English on the man's background, experience during Khomeini's era and rise to power.

10. He learnt from Bill Clinton's focus on economics and especially job creation as a decisive way of retaining popular approval, as well as from his personal fondness for the German economic model, which pays special attention to small and medium-sized companies. He put forward several economic initiatives aimed at creating jobs, most of which focused on vocational skills targeted at the lower-middle-class and young Iranians without college education. His first budget, for which he fought ferociously in parliament and the Guardian Council, entailed a growth rate of 6 per cent, which his economic advisors estimated was the minimum threshold for the jobs he aspired to create. He advanced gradual measures to reduce subsidies on key food staples and on fuels and electricity. He and his reformist economic and finance ministers held several meetings with local and international investors, including the CEOs of European corporations, in which he promised regulations that would guarantee profit repatriation and full investor protection.

11. See Mohammed Khatami's elaboration on this thinking in *Islam, Dialogue, and Civil Society* (CreateSpace Publishing Platform, 2014).

12. Khomeini expounded upon his thinking in several books, especially *Islamic Government: Governance of the jurist* and *A Clarification of Questions* (both published in Boulder, Colorado, in 1984), and *Marajae al-Salekeen* [*The References of Those on the Road*], an Arabic edition of which was published in Beirut in 1982. Ahmad Ferhi wrote two books, also published in Beirut (and often distributed for free), in which he explained some of Khomeini's theological stances and how they related to the lives of ordinary Shiis. Also see Vanessa Martin, *Creating an Islamic State and the Making of a New Iran* (I.B. Tauris, 2003). Hamid Mavani's *Religious Authority and Political Thought in Twelver Shiism: From Ali to post-Khomeini* (Routledge, 2013) situates Khomeini's thinking in the long historical flow that influenced him, and emphasizes how he interpreted that long tradition. Often some of Khomeini's media interviews were more revelatory of his thought than his dense writings. See his interview with Mohamed Hassanein Heikal, incorporated in the latter's *The Return of the Ayatollah* (Andre Deutsch, 1982) and with Richard Falk, incorporated in many of the latter's books. Hamed Algar's interview with Khomeini's son, Ahmad, in 1982, published in Beirut in 1982 under the title 'Majmaa Athar al-Imam' (The collection of the imam's heritage), is another source on Khomeini's thinking from one of the people closest to him. For an opposing view of how political representation and 'Islamic government' is envisioned in Shii Islamism, see Sayyed Hossein Nasr, *The Heart of Islam: Enduring values of humanity* (HarperOne, 2002).

13. In a way, the reformers were inspired by one of Iran's formative historical episodes, the Safavid state. The sixteenth- and seventeenth-century Safavid monarchs were responsible for entrenching Shiism as the dominant and official state sect in Iran (to a large extent to differentiate their kingdom from the Sunni Ottoman Empire). The Safavids encouraged the spread of the Qom religious establishment's influence across the country. They included leading Shii scholars in their courts; and gradually the approval of the leading Shii references of the age became a principal factor in legitimizing Safavid rule. But the Safavids were not aiming for a religious state: their vibrant courts welcomed and encouraged various representations of Iranian culture, from arts such as music, poetry and painting, to crafts such as carpet weaving and ceramics. And crucially, the Safavid worldview transcended Iranian Shiism. It was founded on seeing Persianness – the culture, the civilization – as the pillar upon which their state stood. Their worldview regarded Iran as the centre of human enlightenment. And whereas Arabs had almost consistently perceived the Safavid state as an enemy, partly as a result of its many confrontations with the Ottoman Empire, and so equated it with adversity and often

heresy, Iranians regarded the Safavid era as a golden age. The Iranian reformers of the 1990s and 2000s sought to borrow from that long experience and worldview. See Homa Katouzian's *The Persians: Ancient, medieval, and modern Iran* (Yale University Press, 2010) and Michael Axworthy's *A History of Iran* (Basic Books, 2008).

14. In 2006 and 2007, most large urban centres in Iran underwent a sea-change in their administrative structures. In some cases, municipal managers who had been in their positions for two decades were promptly replaced by younger, more energetic ones, often drawn from young people who had served in entities controlled by the Republican Guard and the Basij. Ahmadinejad paid considerable attention to improving security and cracking down on gangs that had appeared in some cities, especially Tehran, in the early to mid-2000s. And though inflation rose in his first term, by double digits in the case of several important food staples, the period from 2005 to 2009 was one of significant economic expansion. Internal and external trade, including with Arab neighbours across the Gulf, flourished. The period witnessed a real estate boom, even in hitherto small towns in the eastern and northern parts of the country. The performance of capital markets fluctuated, but for the first time in history, large sections of middle-class Iranians had their first foray into acquiring relatively sophisticated financial products, whether in Iran or through proxies in the nascent equity markets of Dubai, Kuwait and Bahrain.

15. Mir Hussein Mousavi, his main reformist challenger in that election, described Ahmadinejad's win – 63 per cent of a turnout of 85 per cent – as a 'charade'. Scores of reform-leaning non-governmental organizations questioned various aspects of the election, including the official ballot counting.

16. Energy subsidies have pushed the fiscal deficit to dangerous levels, especially given the country's dependence on oil, the price of which declined in 2013 and 2014. The sanctions forced Iran to increase its dependence on peripheral distribution networks for its oil, often dumping huge quantities at rock-bottom prices to raise cash in the short term. Despite the reduced trade with key markets, as a result of the sanctions inflation on basic goods rose, often to double digits in 2013 and 2014.

17. Because of its deep involvement in the Syrian war, Hezbollah needed quickly to make good the losses it incurred in its fight with Sunni jihadists in the country. The substantial subsidies offered to Hezbollah became a hefty item in the Iranian budget. Iran also significantly increased support for its clients in Iraq, primarily to secure its influence after Saudi Arabia began to up its financial and logistical assistance to several large Sunni tribes. The real worry, however, especially among circles close to the Supreme Leader, was that the Revolutionary Guard, the Basij and several outspoken 'references' were carried away by the successes that Iran had secured in the years since the beginning of the Arab uprisings. 'It was getting personal', as one Lebanese Shii scholar put it to me, referring to some of the Revolutionary Guard's senior officers who were deployed in Syria.

18. Sufism is a versatile and loose school of thought in Sunni Islam that has always focused on the spiritual aspects of religion, much more than on jurisprudence, disputations, law and practices.

Chapter 10: Islamism and the West

1. See Kanan Makiya's *Cruelty and Silence* (Jonathan Cape, 1993) and Fouad Ajami's *The Arab Predicament: Arab political thought and practice since 1967* (Cambridge University Press, 1992).

2. See the collection of essays entitled 'What have we learned?', *Foreign Affairs*, 93:6 (2014).

3. To a large extent, this was a modification of the 'Modernization Theory' advanced by various schools of political economy, especially in the early 1990s.

4. For a view of the development of this thinking over the past five years, and especially how it was affected by the experience of the Iraq war and then by the rise of political Islam following the Arab uprisings, see Larry Diamond, 'Why are there no Arab democracies', *Journal of Democracy*, 21:1 (2010), and Olivier Roy, 'The transformation of the Arab world', *Journal of Democracy*, 23:3 (2012).

5. See Ichiro Iwasaki and Taku Suzuki, *Radicalism versus Gradualism: A systematic review of the transition strategy debate* (Russian Research Centre at Hitotsubashi University's Institute of Economic Research, 2014). This focuses on the transition experiences of several eastern and central European countries after communist rule. Though the backgrounds and circumstances are vastly different from the situations in most Islamic countries, and though the context is different from what we discuss here, that kind of economic and political-economy research helps demonstrate the 'transition thinking' we allude to here.

6. There are several important studies on this topic. See Bernard Lewis, *What Went Wrong? The clash between Islam and modernity in the Middle East* (Orion, 2002); Olivier Roy, *Globalised Islam: The search for a new Ummah* (Hurst, 2004); Fazlur Rahman, *Islam and Modernity: Transformation of an intellectual tradition* (University of Chicago Press, 1982); Mustafa Akyol, *Islam without Extremes: A Muslim case for liberty* (W.W. Norton & Co., 2011); and Abdelwahab Meddeb, *Islam and its Discontents* (William Heinemann, 2003).

Chapter 11: The Dilemmas of Islamist Thinking Now

1. As highlighted in the introduction, see Jonathan Lyons, *The House of Wisdom: How the Arabs transformed western civilization* (Bloomsbury Press, 2010) and Steven Weinberg's discussion of 'Arab science' in his *To Explain the World* (Allen Lane, 2015).

2. Maria Rosa Menocal, *The Ornament of the World: How Muslims, Jews, and Christians created a culture of tolerance in medieval Spain* (Back Bay Books, 2003).

Bibliography

Abdelaziz, Mohsen, *Al-istibdad min Al-khilafa ila al-Reeasa* [*Tyranny from Caliphate to Presidency*] (Al-Dar Lil-Tibaa W'Al-Nashr, Cairo, 2007)

Abdel-Fattah, Nabil (ed.), *Taqrir al-Halah al-Diniyah fi Misr* [*Report on the State of Religion in Egypt*] (Markaz al-Derasat al-Siasiya w'al-Istratijia, Ahram, 1996)

Abdelrahman, Maha, *Civil Society Exposed: The politics of NGOs in Egypt* (American University in Cairo Press, 2004)

Abdelrazek, Ali, *Al-Islam w'Osoul Al-Hokm* [*Islam and the Principles of Governance*] (Dar Al-Maaref, Cairo, 1925)

Abou-Nasr, Jamil, *A History of the Maghrib in the Islamic Period* (Cambridge University Press, 1987)

Abrahamian, Ervand, *Khomeinism: Essays on the Islamic Republic* (I.B. Tauris, 1993)

Aburabia, Ibrahim, *Intellectual Origins of Islamic Resurgence in the Modern Arab World* (State University of New York Press, 1996)

Aburish, Said, *Nasser: The last Arab* (Gerald Duckworth, 2004)

Abuzaid, Nasr Hamid, *al-Tafkeer fi Asr al-Takfeer* [*Thinking in the Age of the Accusation of Heresy*] (Madbouli, 1995)

Adib-Moghaddam, Arshin, *A Critical Introduction to Khomeini* (Cambridge University Press, 2014)

Aflaq, Michel, *The Battle for One Destiny* (Dar al-Hureya, Beirut, 1958)

Ahmad, Ahmad, *Structural Interrelations of Theory and Practice in Islamic Law: A study in six works of Islamic jurisprudence* (Brill, 2006)

Ahmad, Feroz, *The Making of Modern Turkey* (Routledge, 1993)

Ahmad, Makram Mohamed, *Muamara am Murajaa: Hiwar qadat al-tataruf fi sijn al-Aqrab* [*Conspiracy or Reconsideration: Dialogues with the leaders of radicalism in the Aqrab prison*] (Dar al-Shorouq, 2002)

Ahmed, Leila, *Women and Gender in Islam: Historical roots of a modern debate* (Yale University Press, 1992)

Ajami, Fouad, *The Arab Predicament: Arab political thought and practice since 1967* (Cambridge University Press, 1992)

Akhavi, Shahrough, *Religion and Politics in Contemporary Iran* (State University of New York Press, 1980) al-Akkad, Abbas Mahmoud, *Allah* (in Arabic) (Supreme Council for Islamic Affairs, 1999)

Akyol, Mustafa, *Islam without Extremes: A Muslim case for liberty* (W.W. Norton & Co., 2011)

Alexander, Catherine, *Personal States: Making connections between people and bureaucracy in Turkey* (Oxford University Press, 2002)

Algar, Hamed, 'Majmaa Athar al-Imam' in *The Collection of the Imam's Heritage* (Beirut, 1982)

Amin, Hussein and James Napoli, 'Media and power in Egypt' in James Curran and Myung-Jin Park (eds), *De-Westernizing Media Studies* (Routledge, 2000)

al-Anani, Khalil, 'The role of Hassan al-Banna in constructing the Muslim Brotherhood's collective identity' in *Sociology of Islam* (Brill, 2013)

Anderson, Benedict, *Imagined Communities: Reflections on the origin and spread of nationalism* (Verso, 1991)

Anderson, Lisa, *The State and Social Transformation in Tunisia and Libya* (Princeton University Press, 1986)

Anscombe, Frederick, *The Ottoman Gulf: The creation of Kuwait, Saudi Arabia, and Qatar* (Columbia University Press, 1997)

Arat, Yesim, *Rethinking Islam and Liberal Democracy* (State University of New York Press, 2005)

Arkoun, Mohammed, *Rethinking Islam* (Boulder, Colorado, 1994)

Arkoun, Mohammed and Gaber Al-Ansari, *Al-Arab w'Al-Seyasa: Eina Al-Khalal [Arabs and Politics: Where the fault lies]* (Dar Al-Saki, London, 2000)

Armstrong, Karen, *A History of God: The 4000-year quest of Judaism, Christianity, and Islam* (Knopf, 1993)

Asad, Talal, *Formations of the Secular: Christianity, Islam, modernity* (Stanford University Press, 2003)

Ashmawi, Mohammed Saeed, *al-Islam al-Siyasi [Political Islam]* (Sinaa Publishing, 1989)

——, *al-Khilafa al-Islameya [Islamic Caliphate]* (Sinaa Publishing, 1990)

Aslan, Reza, *No God But God: The origins, evolution, and future of Islam* (Random House, 2005)

al-Aswany, Alaa, *Democracy is the Solution* (Ginkgo Library, London, 2015)

al-Attas, Sharifah (ed.), *Islam and the Challenge of Modernity* (International Institute of Islamic Thought and Civilization, Kuala Lumpur, 1994)

Axworthy, Michael, *A History of Iran* (Basic Books, 2008)

——, *Revolutionary Iran: A history of the Islamic Republic* (Allen Lane, 2013)

Ayubi, Nazih, *Political Islam: Religion and politics in the Arab world* (Routledge, 1993)

Azzam, Abdullah, *Defence of Islamic Lands: The first obligation after believing* (Maktabah Publications, 2002)

Baker, Raymond William, *Islam Without Fear* (Harvard University Press, 2004)

al-Banna, Gamal, *Tatweer al-Koran [Developing the Koran]* (Dar al-Fikr al-Islami, Cairo, 2000)

——, *al-Islam Deen w'Ummah, lais Deen w'Dawla [Islam: Religion and nation, not religion and state]* (Dar al-Shorouk, Cairo, 2008)

Baran, Zeyno, *Torn Country: Turkey between secularism and Islamism* (Hoover Institution Press, 2010)

Bayat, Asef, *Making Islam Democratic: Social movements and the post-Islamist turn* (Stanford University Press, 2007)

——, *Life as Politics: How ordinary people change the Middle East* (Stanford University Press, 2009)

——, *Post-Islamism: The Many Faces of Political Islam* (Oxford University Press, 2013)

Bayoumi, Moustafa, *How Does it Feel to Be a Problem? Being young and Arab in America* (Penguin Press, 2008)

Beinin, Joel, 'Egyptian Jewish identities', *Contested Identities*, 5:1 (1996)

Beinin, Joel and Joe Stork (ed.), *Political Islam: Essays from Middle East Report* (I.B. Tauris, 1997)

Bellin, Eva, *Stalled Democracy: Capital, labor, and the paradox of state-sponsored development* (Cornell University Press, 2002)

____, 'Reconsidering the robustness of authoritarianism in the Middle East', *Comparative Politics*, 44:2 (2012)

Ben-Baz, Sheikh Abdelaziz, *Bayaan wa' Tawdeeh* (Message of Islam, 1998)

Benhenda, Mostapha, 'Liberal democracy and political Islam: the search for common ground', *Politics, Philosophy, and Economics*, 10:1 (2011)

Bergesen, Albert (ed.), *The Sayyid Qutb Reader* (Routledge, 2008)

Betts, Richard, 'Is strategy an illusion?', *International Security*, 25:2 (2000)

Binder, Leonard, *Islamic Liberalism: A critique of development ideologies* (Chicago University Press, 1988)

Blanford, Nicholas, *Killing Mr Lebanon: The assassination of Rafik Hariri and its impact on the Middle East* (I.B. Tauris, 2006)

____, *Warriors of God: Inside Hezbollah's thirty-year struggle against Israel* (Random House, 2011)

Boubekeur, Amel, *Salafism and Radical Politics in Postconflict Algeria* (Carnegie Middle East Centre, 2008)

Boubekeur, Amel and Olivier Roy, *Whatever Happened to the Islamists? Salafis, heavy metal Muslims and the lure of consumerist Islam* (Hurst, 2012)

Boukhars, Anouar, *Politics in Morocco: Executive monarchy and enlightened authoritarianism* (Routledge, 2010)

Bowker, Robert, *Egypt and the Politics of Change in the Arab Middle East* (Edward Elgar Publishing, 2010)

Brown, Carl, *International Politics and the Middle East: Old rules, dangerous games* (Princeton University Press, 1984)

____, *Religion and State: The Muslim approach to politics* (Columbia University Press, 2000)

Brown, Jonathan, *Hadith: Muhammad's legacy in the medieval and modern world* (Oneworld, 2009)

____, *Misquoting Muhammad: The challenge and choices of interpreting the Prophet's legacy* (Oneworld, 2014)

Brown, Nathan J., *When Victory is Not an Option: Islamist movements in Arab politics* (Cornell University Press, 2012)

Bruton, Henry, 'Egypt's development in the seventies', *Economic Development and Cultural Change*, 31:4 (1983)

Bunt, Gary, *Islam in the Digital Age: E-jihad, online fatwas, and cyber Islamic environments* (Pluto Press, 2003)

Buruma, Ian and Avishai Margalit, *Occidentalism: The west in the eyes of its enemies* (Penguin Press, 2004)

Calvert, John, *Sayyid Qutb and the Origins of Radical Islam* (Hurst, 2010)

Campante, Philipe and Davin Chor, 'Why was the Arab world poised for revolution? Schooling, economic opportunities, and the Arab Spring', *Journal of Economic Perspectives*, 26:2 (2012)

Carkoglu, Ali, 'Ideology or economic pragmatism? Profiling Turkish voters in 2007', *Turkish Studies*, 9:2 (2008)

Carr, Matthew, *The Infernal Machine: An alternative history of terrorism* (Hurst, 2011)

Chauffour, Jean-Pierre (ed.), *From Political to Economic Awakening in the Arab World: The path of economic integration* (World Bank Group, 2013)

Cinar, Alev, *Modernity, Islam, and Secularism in Turkey: Bodies, places, and time* (University of Minnesota Press, 2005)

Cochran, Judith, *Democracy in the Middle East: The impact of religion and education* (Lexington Books, 2011)

Cohen, Mark, *Under Crescent and Cross: The Jews in the Middle Ages* (Princeton University Press, 1995)

Coll, Steve, *The Bin Ladens: Oil, money, terrorism, and the secret Saudi world* (Penguin, 2009)

Commins, David, *The Wahhabi Mission and Saudi Arabia* (I.B. Tauris, 2006)

Cook, Michael, *Commanding Right and Forbidding Wrong in Islamic Thought* (Cambridge University Press, 2001)

Corban, Henry, *History of Islamic Philosophy* (Routledge, 2014)

Daadaoui, Mohamed, *Moroccan Monarchy and the Islamist Challenge: Maintaining Makhzen power* (Palgrave Macmillan, 2011)

Davidson, Christopher, *Power and Politics in the Persian Gulf Monarchies* (Hurst, 2012)

Davies, James, 'Toward a theory of revolution', *American Sociological Review*, 27:1 (1962)

Davies, Merryl Wyn, *Beyond Frontiers: Islam and contemporary needs* (Continuum International Publishing, 1989)

Davis, John, *Libyan Politics: Tribe and revolution* (University of California Press, 1988)

Dawisha, Adeed, *Arab Nationalism in the Twentieth Century: From triumph to despair* (Princeton University Press, 2003)

al-Deeb, Alaa, *Waqfa Qabl al-Munhadar [A Pause before the Plunge]* (Dar al-Shorouk, 1995)

De Jang, Frederick and Bernd Redtke (eds), *Islamic Mysticism Contested: Thirteen centuries of controversies and polemics* (Brill, 1999)

Dekmejian, Hrair, 'The rise of political Islamism in Saudi Arabia', *Middle East Journal*, 48 (1994)

___, *Islam in Revolution* (Syracuse University Press, 1995)

Dhareef, Mohammed (ed.), *al-Islam al-Siyasi fi al-Watan al-Arabi [Political Islam in the Arab Nation]* (Maktabat al-Ummah, Casablanca, 1992)

Diamond, Larry, 'Why are there no Arab democracies', *Journal of Democracy*, 21:1 (2010)

Dodwell, Henry, *The Founder of Modern Egypt: A study of Muhammad Ali* (Cambridge University Press, 1931)

Ebaugh, Helen-Rose, *The Gulen Movement: A sociological analysis of a civic movement rooted in moderate Islam* (Springer, 2009)

Eickelman, Dale and James Piscatori, *Muslim Politics* (Princeton University Press, 1996)

El-Ashwal, Nagwan, *Egyptian Salafism Between Religious Movement and Realpolitik* (German Institute for International and Security Affairs, 2013)

Eligur, Banu, 'Turkey's March 2009 local elections', *Turkish Studies*, 10:3 (2009)

Enayat, Hamid, *Modern Islamic Political Thought* (I.B. Tauris, 2005)

Esposito, John, *Voices of Resurgent Islam* (Oxford University Press, 1983)

___, *Islam and Politics* (Syracuse University Press, 1984)

___. (ed.), *Turkish Islam and the Secular State* (Syracuse University Press, 2003)

Esposito, John and Dalia Mogahed, *Who Speaks for Islam?* (Gallup Press, 2008)

Euben, Roxanne and Mohammed Zaman (eds), *Princeton's Readings in Islamic Thought: Texts and contexts from al-Banna to Bin-Laden* (Princeton University Press, 2009)

Evans, Martin and John Phillips, *Algeria: Anger of the dispossessed* (Yale University Press, 2008)

Fahmy, Khaled, *All the Pasha's Men: Mehmed Ali, his army, and the making of modern Egypt* (Cambridge University Press, 1998)

Fakhry, Majid, *A History of Islamic Philosophy* (Columbia University Press, 2004)

Fayoumi, Mohammed Ibrahim, *Al-Shafei: Al-Imam w'Al-Adeeb [Al-Shafei: The theologian and the writer]* (Al-Dar Al-Mesreya Al-Lubnaneya, Cairo, 2003)

Feldman, Noah, *The Rise and Fall of the Islamic State* (Princeton University Press, 2008)

Fenkel, Caroline, *Osman's Dream* (John Murray, 2006)

Filiu, Jean-Pierre, *Arab Revolution: Ten lessons from the democratic uprising* (Hurst, 2011)

Findley, Carter Vaughn, *Turkey, Islam, Nationalism, and Modernity* (Yale University Press, 2010)

Firro, Kais, *Inventing Lebanon: Nationalism and the state under the Mandate* (I.B. Tauris, 2003)

Fisk, Robert, *Pity the Nation: Lebanon at war* (Andre Deutsch, 1990)

Galioun, Burhan and Mohammed Selim Al-Awwa, *Al-nizam Al-Seyasi fi Al-Islam* [*Political System in Islam*] (Dar Al-Fikr, Damascus, 2004)

Gates, Caroline, *The Merchant Republic of Lebanon: Rise of an open economy* (London, 1998)

Gellner, Ernest, *Nations and Nationalism* (Oxford University Press, 1983)

Gelvin, James, *The Modern Middle East: A History* (Oxford University Press, 2008)

Gerber, Haim, *The Social Origin of the Modern Middle East* (Lynne Rienner, 1987)

Ghannouchi, Rached, *al-Hurreyat al-Amma fi al-Dawla al-Islameya* [*General Freedoms in the Islamic State*] (Markaz Derasat al-Wehda al-Arabeya, Beirut, 1993)

———, *al-Elmaneya wa al-Mumanaa al-Islameya* [*Secularism and Rejectionism in the Rhetoric of Arab Unity*] (Saqi Books, 1999)

Gholz, Eugene and Daryl Press, *Energy Alarmism: The myths that make America worry about oil* (Cato Institute, 2007)

Ginat, Rami, *Egypt's Incomplete Revolution* (Cummings Centre, London, 1997)

Goldstone, Jack, 'Toward a fourth generation of revolutionary theory', *Annual Review of Political Science*, 4 (2001)

Gole, Nilufer, 'Islam in public: new visibilities and new imaginaries', *Public Culture*, 14:1 (2002)

Goodman, Len, *Islamic Humanism* (Oxford University Press, 2003)

Guazzone, Laura and Daniela Pioppi, *The Arab State and Neo-Liberal Globalization: The restructuring of state power in the Middle East* (Ithaca Press, 2012)

Habib, Kamal al-Said, *Al-Haraka al-Islamiyya min al-Muwajaha ila al-Murajaa* [*The Islamic Movement from Confrontation to Reconsideration*] (Maktabat Madbouli, 2002)

Hadad, Mohammed, *Mohammed Abdou: Qeraa Gadida fi Khitab Al-Islah Al-Deeni* [*Mohammed Abdou: A new reading in the rhetoric of religious reformation*] (Dar Al-Taliaa, Beirut, 2003)

Hale, William, *Turkish Politics and the Military* (Routledge, 1994)

Halpern, Manfred, *The Politics of Social Change in the Middle East and North Africa* (Princeton University Press, 1963)

Halverson, Jeffry, *Theology and Creed in Sunni Islam* (Palgrave Macmillan, 2010)

Hamid, Shadi, *Temptations of Powers: Islamists and illiberal democracy in a new Middle East* (Oxford University Press, 2014)

Hanafi, Hassan, *Al-Osoleya al-Islameya* [*Islamic Fundamentalism*] (Madbouli, 1989)

Hansen, Karen Tranberg, *Master and Disciple: The cultural foundations of Moroccan authoritarianism* (University of Chicago Press, 2007)

Harris, Lee, *The Suicide of Reason: Radical Islam's threat to the Enlightenment* (Basic Books, 2007)

Hasseb, Kheir Eldin, *Mustaqbal Al-Iraq: Al-Ihtilal, al-muqawama, al-tahrir, w'al-dimoqrateya* [*The Future of Iraq: Occupation, resistance, liberation, and democracy*] (Centre for Arab Unity Studies, Beirut, 2004)

Hefner, R.W. (ed.), *Remaking Muslim Politics: Pluralism, contestation, democratization* (Princeton University Press, 2005)

Heikal, Mohamed Hassanein, *The Return of the Ayatollah* (Andre Deutsch, 1982)

Helbawy, Kamal, 'The Muslim Brotherhood in Egypt: Historical evolution and future prospects' in Khaled Hroub (ed.), *Political Islam: Context versus ideology* (SOAS, 2011)

Hendrick, Joshua, *Gulen: The ambiguous politics of market Islam in Turkey and the world* (New York University Press, 2013)

Heper, Metin and Sabri Sayari (eds), *Political Leaders and Democracy in Turkey* (Lexington Books, 2002)

Herrera, Linda, 'Youth and generational renewal in the Middle East', *International Journal of Middle East Studies*, 41:3 (2009)

Hill, Charles, *Grand Strategies: Literature, statecraft, and world order* (Yale University Press, 2011)

Hodgson, Marshall, *The Venture of Islam* (University of Chicago Press, 1977)

Hoexter, Miriam, Shmuel Eisenstadt and Nehemia Levtzion (eds), *The Public Sphere in Muslim Societies* (State University of New York Press, 2002)

Holt, Peter, *The Mahdist State in Sudan: 1881–1898* (Clarendon Press, 1970)

Hoover, Jon, *Ibn Taimiyyah's Theodicy of Perpetual Optimism* (Brill, 2007)

Horoub, Khaled, 'Turkia: Islamayea, elmaneya' [Turkey: Islamic, secular], *Weghat Nazar*, 10:117 (2008)

Hourani, Albert, *Arabic Thought in the Liberal Age* (Oxford University Press, 1962)

Howe, Marvine, *Turkey: A nation divided over Islam's revival* (Westview Press, 2004)

Huntington, Samuel, *Political Order in Changing Societies* (Yale University Press, 1968)

Hussein, Taha, *On Jahili Literature* (Cairo, 1926)

Ikram, Khalid, *The Egyptian Economy, 1952–2000: Performance policies and issues* (Routledge, 2005)

Imara, Mohammed, *Maarakat al-Islam wa Osoul al-Hokm* [*The Battle of Islam and the Tents of Governing*] (Dar al-Shorouq, 1989)

Ismail, Salwa, 'Confronting the Other: Identity, culture, politics, and conservative Islamism in Egypt', *International Journal of Middle East Studies*, 30 (1998)

——, *Rethinking Islamist Politics: Culture, the state, and Islamism* (I.B. Tauris, 2003)

——, *Political Life in Cairo's New Quarters* (University of Minneapolis Press, 2006)

Iwasaki, Ichiro and Taku Suzuki, *Radicalism versus Gradualism: A systematic review of the transition strategy debate* (Russian Research Centre at Hitotsubashi University's Institute of Economic Research, Tokyo, 2014)

Izzedin, Nejla, *The Druzes: A new study of their history, faith, and society* (Brill, 1993)

Jervis, Robert, *American Foreign Policy in a New Era* (Routledge, 2005)

Joffe, George (ed.), *Islamist Radicalisation in North Africa: Politics and process* (Routledge, 2011)

Kandil, Amani, *Moassassat Al-Mogtama Al-Madani* [*Civil Society Institutions*] (Al-Ahram Centre for Political and Strategic Studies, Cairo, 2005)

Kandiyoti, Deniz and Ayse Saktanber (eds), *Fragments of Culture: The everyday of modern Turkey* (Rutgers University Press, 2002)

Kaotharani, Wagih, *Al-Dawla w'Al-Khilafa fi Al-Khitab Al-Arabi iban Al-Thawra Al-kamaleya* [*State and Caliphate in Arabic Rhetoric During the Turkish Kamalist Revolution*] (Dar Al-Taleea, Beirut, 1996)

Katouzian, Homa, *The Persians: Ancient, medieval, and modern Iran* (Yale University Press, 2010)

Kavaci, Merve (ed.), *Headscarf Politics in Turkey* (Palgrave Macmillan, 2014)

Kazemi, Farhad, *Poverty and Revolution in Iran* (New York University Press, 1981)

Keaton, Trica Danielle, *Muslim Girls and the Other France: Race, identity, politics, and social exclusion* (Indiana University Press, 2006)

Keddie, Nikki, *Sayyid Jamal ad-Din 'al-Afghani': A political biography* (University of California Press, 1972)

Kennedy, Paul (ed.), *Grand Strategies in War and Peace* (Yale University Press, 1992)

Kepel, Gilles, *Jihad: The trail of political Islam* (Harvard University Press, 2003)

——, *Muslim Extremism in Egypt: The prophet and pharaoh* (University of California Press, 2003)

Kerr, Malcolm, *Islamic Reform: The political and legal theories of Mohammed Abdou and Rachid Reda* (University of California Press, 1966)

Kersten, Carool, *Cosmopolitans and Heretics: New Muslim intellectuals and the study of Islam* (Hurst, 2011)

al-Khalidi, Sami Nasser, *al-Ahzab al-Seyaseyah al-Islameyah fi al-Kuwait* [*Islamist Political Parties in Kuwait*] (1999)

Khatami, Mohammed, *Islam, Dialogue, and Civil Society* (CreateSpace Publishing Platform, 2014)

al-Khazen, Farid, *The Breakdown of the State in Lebanon* (Harvard University Press, 2000)

Khomeini, Ayatollah Ruhollah, *A Clarification of Questions* (Westview, 1984)

——, *Islamic Government: Governance of the jurist* (Al-Hoda, 2002)

Kirmani, Nida, 'The relationships between social movements and religion in the processes of social change: a preliminary literature review', Working Paper 23, Religious and Development Research Programme (University of Birmingham, 2008)

Kubba, Laith, 'The awakening of civil society', *Journal of Democracy*, 11 (2000)

Kumbaracibasi, Arda, *Turkish Politics and the Rise of the AKP: Dilemmas of institutionalisation and leadership strategy* (Taylor and Francis, 2009)

Lacey, Robert, *Inside the Kingdom* (Hutchinson, 2009)

Lacroix, Stephane, *Awakening Islam: The politics of religious dissent in contemporary Saudi Arabia* (Harvard University Press, 2011)

Lawrence, Bruce, *The Defenders of God: The fundamentalist revolt against the modern age* (University of Southern Carolina Press, 1995)

Leaman, Oliver, *Introduction to Classical Islamic Philosophy* (Cambridge University Press, 2002)

Lee, Robert, *Overcoming Tradition and Modernity: The search for Islamic authenticity* (Westview, 1997)

Leiken, Robert, *Europe's Angry Muslims: The revolt of the second generation* (Oxford University Press, 2011)

Levitt, Matthew, *Hezbollah's Finances* (Washington Institute, 2000)

——, *Hezbollah: The global footprint of Lebanon's party of god* (Georgetown University Press, 2013)

Lewis, Bernard, *The Political Language of Islam* (University of Chicago Press, 1991)

——, *The Multiple Identities of the Middle East* (Schocken, 2001)

——, *What Went Wrong? The clash between Islam and modernity in the Middle East* (Orion, 2002)

Licari, Joseph, *Economic Reform in Egypt in a Changing Global Economy* (OECD, 1997)

Lipset, Seymour, *Political Man: The social basis of modern politics* (Doubleday, 1960)

Luttwak, Edward, *Strategy: The logic of war and peace* (Harvard University Press, 1987)

Lyons, Jonathan, *The House of Wisdom: How the Arabs transformed western civilization* (Bloomsbury Press, 2010)

Maddy-Weitzman, Bruce, *The Berber Identity Movement and the Challenge to North African States* (University of Texas Press, 2011)

——, *The Crystallization of the Arab State System: 1945–1954* (Syracuse University Press, 1992)

Mahmoud, Manee Abdelhalim, *Manaheg Al-Mufasereen* [*The Interpreters' Approaches*] (Al-Iman Library, Cairo, 2003)

Makdisi, Ilham, *The Eastern Mediterranean and the Making of Global Radicalism: 1860–1914* (University of California Press, 2010)

Makiya, Kanan, *Cruelty and Silence* (Jonathan Cape, 1993)

Mamood, Saba, *Politics of Piety: The Islamic revival and the feminist subject* (Princeton University Press, 2005)

Mango, Andrew, *Atatürk: The biography of the founder of modern Turkey* (Overlook Press, 2000)

March, Andrew, 'Political Islam: theory', *Annual Review of Political Science*, 18 (2015)

Martin, Vanessa, *Creating an Islamic State and the Making of a New Iran* (I.B. Tauris, 2003)

Martinez, Luis, 'The distinctive development of Islamic violence in Algeria' in Amelie Blom, Laetitia Bucaille and Luis Martinez (eds), *The Enigma of Islamic Violence* (Hurst & Co., 2007)

Martinez, Luis and John Entelis, *The Algerian Civil War* (Columbia University Press, 2000)

Mavani, Hamid, *Religious Authority and Political Thought in Twelver Shiism: From Ali to post-Khomeini* (Routledge, 2013)

Meddeb, Abdelwahab, *Islam and its Discontents* (William Heinemann, 2003)

Menocal, Maria Rosa, *The Ornament of the World: How Muslims, Jews, and Christians created a culture of tolerance in medieval Spain* (Back Bay Books, 2003)

Meyer, Birgit and Annelies Moors, *Religion, Media, and the Public Sphere* (Indiana University Press, 2006)

Migdal, Joel, *Strong Societies and Weak States* (Princeton University Press, 1988)

Moaddel, Mansoor, 'Conditions for ideological production: the origins of Islamic modernism in India, Egypt, and Iran', *Theory and Society*, 30:5 (2001)

Mogahed, Dalia, 'Tracking the revolutionary mood', *Foreign Policy* (24 January 2012)

Moheiddin, Khaled, *Memoirs of a Revolution: Egypt 1952* (American University in Cairo Press, 1995).

Montgomery Watt, William, *Islamic Political Thought* (Edinburgh University Press, 1968)

———, *Islamic Philosophy and Theology* (Edinburgh University Press, 1985)

———, *Islamic Fundamentalism and Modernity* (Routledge, 1988)

Mortimer, Edward, *Faith and Power: The politics of Islam* (Vintage Books, 1982)

Munson, Henry, *Islam and Revolution in the Middle East* (Yale University Press, 1988)

———, 'Lifting the veil: understanding the roots of Islamic militancy', *Harvard International Review*, 4 (2004)

Murphy, Caryle, *A Kingdom's Future: Saudi Arabia through the eyes of its twentysomethings* (Woodrow Wilson International Center for Scholars, 2013)

Murphy, John, *Ali Khamenei* (Chelsea House, 2007)

Murray, Williamson, Richard Hart Sinnreich and James Lacey (eds), *The Shaping of Grand Strategy: Policy, diplomacy, and war* (Cambridge University Press, 2011)

Nabulsi, Shaker, *Al-Arab bina Al-Libraleya w'Al-Asoleya Al-Diniya* [*The Arabs Between Liberalism and Religious Frames of Reference*] (Al-Mouassasah Al-Arabeya Lel-drasat w'Al-Nashr, Amman, 2010)

Narizny, Kevin, *The Political Economy of Grand Strategy* (Cornell University Press, 2007)

Nasr, Sayyed Hossein, *The Heart of Islam: Enduring values of humanity* (HarperOne, 2002)

Nasr, Vali, 'The rise of Muslim democracy', *Journal of Democracy*, 16:2 (2005)

———, *The Shia Revival: How conflict within Islam will shape the future* (W.W. Norton, 2007)

Nisan, Mordechai, *Minorities in the Middle East: A history of struggle and self-expression* (MacFarland, 1991)

Olidort, Jacob, *The Politics of Quietist Salafism* (Brookings Center for Middle East Policy, 2015)

Oren, Michael, *Six Days of War: June 1967 and the making of the modern Middle East* (Presidio Press, 2003)

Osman, Tarek, *Egypt on the Brink* (Yale University Press, 2010)

Ottoway, Marina and Amr Hamzawy, *Getting to Pluralism: Political actors in the Arab world* (Carnegie Endowment for International Peace, 2009)

Ottoway, Marina and Thomas Carothers, 'Think again: Middle East democracy', *Foreign Policy* (November/December 2004)

Owen, Roger, *State, Power and Politics in the Making of the Modern Middle East* (Routledge, 2004)

Ozbudun, Ergun, 'From political Islam to conservative democracy: the case of the Justice and Development Party in Turkey', *South Europe Society and Politics*, 11:3–4 (2006)

Perkins, Kenneth, *A History of Modern Tunisia* (Cambridge University Press, 2004)

Pettersen, Donald, *Inside Sudan: Political Islam, conflict, and catastrophe* (Basic Books, 2003)

Piven, Frances Fox and Richard Cloward, *Poor People's Movements: Why they succeed, how they fail* (Vintage Books, 1979)

Pope, Hugh and Nicola Pope, *Turkey Unveiled: A history of modern Turkey* (Overlook Press, 2011)

Qahawi, Hameed, *Al-Muwaten Al-Arabi w'Al Waii Al-Qawmi* [*The Arab Citizen and National Awareness*] (Centre for Arab Unity Studies, Beirut, 2004)

Qaradawi, Yousef, *Hatmeyat al-Hall al-Islami* [*The Inevitability of the Islamic Solution*], vols 1, 2 and 3 (Matbaat Wahba, 1986–87)

——, *Al-Deen W'al-Seyasa* [*Religion and Politics*] (Dar Al-Shorouk, Cairo, 2007)

Qassem, Naim, *Hezbollah: The story from within* (Saqi Books, 2010)

Rabeero, Ali, *Al-Harakat Al-Islameya min Manzour Al-Khitab Al-Arabi Al-Moaser* [*Islamic Movements from the Perspective of Modern Arabic Rhetoric*] (Arab Cultural Centre, Casablanca, 2007)

Rahman, Fazlur, *Islam and Modernity: Transformation of an intellectual tradition* (University of Chicago Press, 1982)

Rapoport, Yossef and Shahab Ahmed, *Ibn Taimiyyah and His Times* (Oxford University Press, 2010)

Rasheed, Abdelwahab, *Al-Iraq Al-muaaser* [*Contemporary Iraq*] (Dar Al-Madaa Lil-Nashr w'Al-Tawzee, Damascus, 2003)

Rasheed, Masawi, Carool Kersten and Marat Shterin, *Demystifying the Caliphate* (Hurst, 2012)

Rashid, Ahmed, *Taliban: Militant Islam, oil, and fundamentalism in Central Asia* (Yale University Press, 2000)

Richards, Alan and John Waterbury, *A Political Economy of the Middle East* (Westview Press, 2007)

Roberts, Hugh, 'The battlefield: Algeria, 1988–2002', *International Journal of African Historical Studies*, 38 (2005)

Robinson, Jeffery, *Yamani: The inside story* (Fontana Press, 1989)

Rogan, Eugene, *The Fall of the Ottomans: The Great War in the Middle East 1914–1920* (Allen Lane, 2015)

Roy, Olivier, *The Failure of Political Islam* (I.B. Tauris, 1999)

——, *Globalised Islam: The search for a new Ummah* (Hurst, 2004)

——, 'The transformation of the Arab world', *Journal of Democracy*, 23:3 (2012)

Rubin, Barry (ed.), *Revolutionaries and Reforms: Contemporary Islamic movements in the Middle East* (State University of New York Press, 2003)

Rumsfeld, Donald, *Known and Unknown* (Sentinel, 2011)

Russell, Gerard, *Heirs to Forgotten Kingdoms* (Basic Books, 2014)

Sachedina, Abdelaziz, *The Just Ruler in Shiite Islam* (Oxford University Press, 1988)

Sageman, Marc, *Understanding Terror Networks* (University of Pennsylvania Press, 2004)

Saktanber, Ayse, *Living Islam: Women, religion, and the politicization of culture in Turkey* (I.B. Tauris, 2002)

Salih, Mohamed, *Economic Development and Political Action in the Arab World* (Routledge, 2014)

Salvatore, Armando (ed.), *Muslim Traditions and Modern Techniques of Power: Yearbook of the sociology of Islam*, vol. 3 (Transaction Publishing, 2001)

Salvatore, Armando and Mark Levine (eds), *Religion, Social Practice, and Contested Hegemonies: Reconstructing the public sphere in Muslim majority societies* (Palgrave Macmillan, 2005)

Sater, James, *Civil Society and Political Change in Morocco* (Routledge, 2007)

el-Sayed Said, Mohamed, 'Global civil society: an Arab perspective' in *Global Civil Society 2004–2005* (Sage, 2004)

al-Sayyid, Afaf Lutfi, *Egypt and Cromer: A study in Anglo-Egyptian relations* (John Murray, 1968)

Schlumberger, Oliver (ed.), *Debating Authoritarianism: Dynamics and durability in non-democratic regimes* (Stanford University Press, 2007)

Seale, Patrick, *The Struggle for Arab Independence: Riad el-Solh and the makers of the modern Middle East* (Cambridge University Press, 2010)

Segman, Marc, *Understanding Terror Networks* (University of Pennsylvania Press, 2004)

Shaban, Mohamed, *The Abbasid Revolution* (Cambridge University Press, 1979)

Shambayati, Hootan, 'A tale of two mayors: courts and politics in Iran and Turkey', *International Journal of Middle East Studies*, 36:2 (2004)

Sharabi, Hisham, *Arab Intellectuals and the West: The formative years, 1875–1914* (Johns Hopkins University Press, 1970)

Shariati, Ali, *The Islamic View of Man* (Free Islamic Literatures, 1979)

Sheehi, Stephen, *Foundation of Modern Arab Identity* (University Press of Florida, 2004)

Shenawi, Mohammed, *Al-Fikr Al-Seyasi Al-Islami [Islamic Political Thought]* (Makaz Al-Kitab, Cairo, 2005)

Shlaim, Avi, *Lion of Jordan: The life of King Hussein in war and peace* (Allen Lane, 2007)

Silvia Colombo, 'The Southern Mediterranean: Between changes and challenges to its sustainability', *MedPro Technical Papers*, 1 (2010)

Sky, Emma, *The Unravelling: High hopes and missed opportunities in Iraq* (Public Affairs, 2015)

Soroush, Abdolkarim, *Reason, Freedom, and Democracy in Islam: Essential writings of Abdolkarim Soroush* (Oxford University Press, 2000)

al-Tahtawi, Refaa, *An Imam in Paris: Al-Tahtawi's visit to France, 1826–1831* (trans. Daniel Newman) (Saqi Books, 2011)

Tamimi, Azzam, *A Democrat Within Islamism* (Oxford University Press, 2001)

Taylor, Charles, *Modern Social Imaginaries* (Duke University Press, 2004)

Teitelbaum, Joshua, *The Rise and Fall of the Hashemite Kingdom of the Hijaz* (Hurst, 2001)

Tepe, Sultan, 'Turkey's AKP: a model Muslim democratic party?', *Journal of Democracy*, 16:3 (2005)

Tessler, Mark (ed.), *Public Opinion in the Middle East: Survey research and the political orientation of ordinary citizens* (Indiana University Press, 2011)

Tibi, Bassam, *The Crisis of Modern Islam: A preindustrial culture in the scientific-technological age* (University of Utah Press, 1988)

——, *Arab Nationalism: Between Islam and the nation state* (St Martin's, 1997)

——, 'The politicization of Islam into Islamism in the context of global religious fundamentalism', *Journal of the Middle East and Africa*, 1:2 (2010)

——, *Islamism and Islam* (Yale University Press, 2012)

Trabulsi, Fawwaz, *A History of Modern Lebanon* (Pluto, 2007)

Tugal, Cihan, 'The appeal of Islamic politics: ritual and dialogue in a poor district of Turkey', *Sociological Quarterly*, 47 (2006)

Ulrichsen, Kristian Coates, 'Gulf security: Changing internal and external dynamics', London School of Economics SE Kuwait Programme Research Papers (2009)

Unay, Sadik, *Neoliberal Globalization and Institutional Reform: The political economy of planning and development in Turkey* (Nova Publishers, 2006)

UNDP, *The Arab Human Development Report 2005: Towards the rise of women in the Arab world* (United Nations Development Programme, 2006)

Vandewalle, Dirk (ed.), *North Africa: Development and reform in a changing global economy* (St Martin's, 1996)

Von Grunebaum, Gustave, *Modern Islam: The search for cultural identity* (Vintage, 1964)

Watenpaugh, Keith, *Being Modern in the Middle East: Revolution, nationalism, colonialism, and the Arab middle class* (Princeton University Press, 2006)

Weinberg, Steven, *To Explain the World* (Allen Lane, 2015)

White, Benjamin, *The Emergence of Minorities in the Middle East: The politics of community in French Mandate Syria* (Edinburgh University Press, 2011)

Wickham, Carrie Rosefsky, *Mobilizing Islam: Religion, activism, and political change in Egypt* (Columbia University Press, 2003)

——, *The Muslim Brotherhood: Evolution of an Islamist movement* (Princeton University Press, 2013)

Wolfson, Harry Austryn, *The Philosophy of the Kalam* (Harvard University Press, 1976)

Wright, Lawrence, *Looming Tower: al-Qaeda and the road to 9/11* (Knopf, 2006)

Yaghmaian, Behzad, *Social Change in Iran: An eyewitness account of dissent, defiance, and new movements for rights* (State University of New York Press, 2002)

Yergin, Daniel, *The Prize: The epic quest for oil, money, and power* (Simon and Schuster, 2008)

Yilmaz, Hakan, 'Islam, sovereignty, and democracy: a Turkish view', *Middle East Journal*, 61:3 (2007)

Youssef, Tarik, 'Development, growth, and policy reform in the Middle East and North Africa since 1950', *Journal of Economic Perspectives*, 18:3 (2004)

Zamir, Meir, *Lebanon's Quest: The road to statehood, 1926–1939* (I.B. Tauris, 1997)

Za'Noun, Taha, *Tareekh al-Maghreb al-Arabi* [*The History of the Arab Maghreb*] (Beirut, 2004)

Zeidan, David, 'The Islamist fundamentalist view of life as a perennial battle', *Middle East Review of International Affairs*, 5 (2001)

Zubaida, Sami, *Islam, the People, and the State: Political ideas and movements in the Middle East* (I.B. Tauris, 2001)

——, *Law and Power in the Islamic World* (I.B. Tauris, 2003)

——, 'Culture, international politics and Islam: Debating continuity and change' in William Brown, Simon Bromley and Suma Athreye (eds), *Ordering the International: History, change and transformation* (Pluto Press, 2004)

Zucher, Erik, *Turkey: A modern history* (I.B. Tauris, 2004)

Illustrations

13 The Basij clash with students protesting the presidential elections outside Tehran University, June 2009. Fouman.

14 President Barack Obama speaking at Cairo University, June 2009. photo.sf.co.ua.

15 Aerial view of al-Zaatari refugee camp in northern Jordan.

Index